GREEK CIVILIZATION

BY A. LYTTON SELLS

The Italian Influence in English Poetry

ANDRÉ BONNARD

◎

GREEK CIVILIZATION

From the Iliad

to

the Parthenon

TRANSLATED BY A. LYTTON SELLS

LONDON: GEORGE ALLEN AND UNWIN LTD
NEW YORK: THE MACMILLAN COMPANY

FIRST PUBLISHED IN 1957
SECOND IMPRESSION 1958

Translated from the French
LA CIVILISATION GRECQUE
(*La Guilde du Livre, Lausanne*)

PRINTED IN GREAT BRITAIN
in 12 *point Fournier type*
BY ROBERT MACLEHOSE AND CO. LTD
THE UNIVERSITY PRESS, GLASGOW

TRANSLATOR'S NOTE

In the original edition of this work—*La Civilisation Grecque: de L'Iliade au Parthénon*, Lausanne, 1954—the quotations from Greek poets appear in French. For the purpose of the present version the same passages have been quoted from the following standard translations into English:

For Chapter I: *Aeschylus, the Prometheus Bound*, edited with Introduction, Commentary and Translation by George Thomson. Cambridge University Press, 1932.
    (For Alcaeus): *Lyra Graeca* . . . , edited and translated by J. M. Edmonds (The Loeb Classical Library). London and New York, 1922. Vol. I.
For Chapter II: *The Iliad of Homer*, translated by Sir William Marris. Oxford University Press, 1934.
For Chapter III: *The Odyssey of Homer*, translated by Sir William Marris. Oxford University Press, 1925.
For Chapter IV (Archilochus): *Elegy and Iambus* . . . , edited and translated by J. M. Edmonds (The Loeb Classical Library). London and New York, 1931. Vol. II.
For Chapter V (Sappho): *Lyra Graeca* . . . , edited and translated by J. M. Edmonds (The Loeb Classical Library). London and New York, 1922. Vol. I.
For Chapter VI (Solon): *Elegy and Iambus* . . . , edited and translated by J. M. Edmonds, Vol. I.
For Chapter VIII (Hesiod): *Hesiod*, etc. With an English translation by H. G. Evelyn-White. Cambridge, Mass. and London, 1943.
    (Theognis): *Elegy and Iambus*, Vol. I.
For Chapter IX (Aeschylus): *The Prometheus Bound*, edited with Introduction, Commentary and Translation by George Thomson. Cambridge University Press, 1932.
    The Oresteia of Aeschylus, edited with Introduction, Translation and a Commentary . . . , by George Thomson. Cambridge University Press, 1938.
For Chapter X (Plutarch): *Plutarch's Cimon and Pericles* . . . , newly translated, with Introduction and Notes, by Bernadotte Perrin. New York, 1910.

Finally, I have tried to render Professor Bonnard's thoughts faithfully and impartially, whether or not I have been in agreement with the views he expresses.

A. L. S.

October, 1955

ACKNOWLEDGEMENT

The Publishers acknowledge with thanks the permission granted by Messrs. William Heinemann Ltd., The Oxford University Press, and The Cambridge University Press to quote from the books listed on the previous page.

CONTENTS

ILLUSTRATIONS

CHAPTER ONE

THE GREEKS
IN THEIR COUNTRY

The Greeks were, in their time, a people like other peoples. For centuries they knew only that slow, plodding, primitive existence that emerges, or fails to emerge, into civilization.

More than that. Throughout the whole of their history and even during the brilliant and manifold flowering of their masterpieces in the age of Sophocles, Hippocrates and the Parthenon, the Greek people—including that vital burning heart of Greece that we call Athens, that 'Hellas of Hellas'—the Greek people did not cease to maintain and even to cultivate the strangest customs and superstitions—so strange, so 'Polynesian', so purely grotesque or atrociously cruel, that the historian might well think himself thousands of miles removed from any kind of civilization.

Ancient Greece is a living paradox which illustrates the astonishing complexity of the concept of civilization and the immense difficulty primitive man had in wrenching himself out of a blind animality in order to contemplate the world *as a man*.

Primitive men always fear that Spring will forget to replace Winter. So every year in Athens, to insure the return of Spring, the people solemnized the marriage of Dionysus, the goat-deity or bull-deity, with the 'queen' of Athens, that is, the wife of the king archon who was the first magistrate of the city. On this occasion they opened a country temple which was closed during the remainder of the year. Hither the people came in procession, headed by the authorities who had been democratically elected, to fetch an old wooden statue of the god and to carry it, amid the singing of canticles, into the house of the 'king'. Here it would spend the night in the 'queen's' bed. The princess had to be an Athenian citizen by birth and to have been wedded, as a virgin, by her husband the magistrate. The marriage of the god with the first lady of Athens—not a symbolic but a consummated marriage: the Greek word indicates this—insured that fields, orchards and vineyards should be fertile and herds and families fruitful.

The Feast of Flowers, or Anthesteria, was celebrated in Athens at the end of February. Every family would now taste the new wine which had been brought in from the vineyards. On the second day of the Festival there was a public drinking-competition; the victor being the man who, at a given signal, emptied his pot at one draught and most quickly. Very well: wine is a most civilized thing. But on the third day the dead woke up, wild with thirst and hunger, and demanded their share in the junketing. Invisible though they were, you could hear them running about the streets. Take care! Everyone barricaded his door after placing on the threshold, in an earthenware jar kept for the purpose, a 'battle' soup made from all kinds of seeds, which the living were careful not to touch. On that day, men protected the gods against the dead. Just as they lay snug in their own homes, so they had strapped the gods into their temples, great ropes being stretched round the sanctuary to preserve the immortality of the gods from the contagion of death. After which the dead, now replete with the soup which had not diminished in quantity—for the invisible take in nourishment invisibly—were dismissed until the following year.

There was also the practice of the scapegoat or 'pharmacos', pursued as a remedy for the great misfortunes which suddenly afflict cities. This was in vogue at Athens and in the great commercial ports of Ionia in the sixth and fifth centuries, in that springtime of civilization which seems to us so bright, so full of promises already fulfilled. First the towns were adorned with painted statues of pretty girls, rouged and smiling, with blue hair, many-coloured frocks and yellow necklaces. Now the Ionian 'sages' were already attempting a rational and materialistic explanation of the universe. And yet these cities, in many ways so modern, maintained a certain amount of flotsam and jetsam, cripples or imbeciles or condemned criminals, and, in the event of famine or pestilence, they stoned them as sacrifices to the gods. Or else, after placing in the scapegoat's hands some dried figs and cheese and a barley-loaf, they drove him out of the city: henceforth he was untouchable. Or else they flogged him seven times on the genital organs with branches of wild squill, then burned him and scattered the ashes in the sea. The use of the 'pharmacos' spread from Ionia to Marseilles.

On the very morning of Salamis, that battle in which the Athenians, 'sticking to liberty' as Herodotus puts it, saved Greek independence, Themistocles, the commander-in-chief, wishing to ensure victory for his side, offered three human victims as sacrifices to Dionysus, 'Eater of raw flesh'. These were three young prisoners of great beauty, magnificently attired, adorned with golden jewels, the nephews of the Great King himself. The general slew them with his own hand, on the flagship, in presence of the whole fleet. It was not an act of reprisal but a solemn consecration.

Democritus (repeated and perhaps improved on by Pliny and Columella), the great philosopher and famous founder of atomic materialism, required that at the time of their menstrual period, young girls should run three times round the fields that were ready for harvesting. He thought that menstrual blood contained a charge of fertile energy which was a perfect antidote against the insects that devour corn.

One could cite many other facts of the same kind, facts which are not simply survivals of an earlier primitive state. Some practices, which seem to us to be the queer aberrations of savages, were closely bound up with the essential structure of society. Their persistence through a period of two thousand years, their nature which is unquestionable, the good conscience with which they were followed and which derived from written or customary law, the manner in which the philosophers justified them—all this attests their importance. We shall revert to these practices because their obstinacy in not disappearing has something, at least partially, to do with the ultimate failure of Greek civilization.

To give a few examples: in all the Greek cities, except Thebes, the father had a right to get rid of his child at its birth, as he liked. Roadsides, and sometimes the steps of temples, were the scene of these daily abandonments. In all the cities of the Greek world, except Athens, the father could sell his children, even when no longer small, to the slave-dealers. Rich families made a wide use of these rights to preserve the inheritance intact. And for the poor folk, what a temptation to pay off a creditor by getting rid of one mouth to feed! Sparta devised better means. The sons of a noble family clubbed together by threes or fours to take a wife: one wife, with whom they associated in turn, and who would never give them too many children to keep or to liquidate. And what can one say of the status of woman, woman who by the beginning of the historical period, except in the Aeolian lands, had fallen into a state of semi-servitude? As a wife she was only good for looking after the household and for producing the children, preferably boys, that the master needed. As a courtesan, she played the flute at street-corners, danced at the philosophical and other banquets, and enlivened the pleasures of the bed. As for the slaves. . . .

But enough of that. In opening this book devoted to one of the finest of civilizations, it has been enough to show that the Greek people was none the less a people *like the others*, primitive in the manner of the most primitive. Its civilization sprang up and grew—not by a miracle but as a result of a few favourable circumstances and inventions due to the necessities of its work—in the same manure of superstitions and abominations as that in which all the peoples in the world have been rooted. It was this same primitive, credulous, cruel people who invented at the same time and as it were in the same movement . . . what? I sum it up in one word: 'civilization'—ours.

◎

What then is civilization? The word *civilized* is the same word in Greek that means *tamed, cultivated, grafted*. The civilized man is the grafted man, the one who grafts himself with a view to producing the most nourishing and savoury fruit. Civilization is the aggregate of inventions and discoveries which have been made to protect man's life and render it more independent of natural forces, to consolidate its existence in a physical universe whose laws, which in the stage of primitive ignorance can only hurt him, may, when better known, become the instruments of a counter-offensive. To protect human life, but also to embellish it, to augment the well-being of all men, to increase the enjoyment of life in a society in which more equitable relations between men are being slowly established. Lastly, to make it expand in the practice of arts which societies enjoy in common, to increase the essential humanity of man in this at once real and imaginary world which is the world of culture, a world refashioned and thought out anew by the arts and sciences, and so becoming in its turn an unfailing source of new creations.

Numberless discoveries, inventions, acquisitions. Here are a few which will serve as a rough table of contents for the present book.

When they arrived, in successive waves, in the Balkans, the Hellenic people were leading the life of nomads: they had tents, weapons of wood and later of bronze: they kept goats and lived on game. The horse, swiftest of all man's animals, was already domesticated. These savages subsisted principally by hunting; but when established in the peninsula which acquired the name of Hellas, they began to till the barren soil. They were always to be more of countrymen than town-dwellers: a peasant people in fact. Even Athens, in the time of its greatness, still remained, first of all, the market-town of Attica. Now, the Greeks cultivated cereals, the olive-tree, the fig and the vine. Soon they learned to exchange their oil and wine for the fabrics produced by their Asiatic neighbours; or they risked putting out to sea in order to barter these products, conveyed in fine painted jars, with the dwellers to the north of the Black Sea in return for the wheat and barley which were indispensable for the growing population of the new cities. By developing a specialized agriculture that replaced the primitive hunting and led them to discard their meat-eating habits for a more vegetarian diet suited to the climate of their new habitat, by developing commercial relationships soon to be very extensive, the Greeks acquired more material well-being and at the same time, still rude and unpolished as they were, they came in contact with peoples of older civilization.

But to do that they had to achieve another conquest, boldly, tremblingly and clumsily—the conquest of the sea. The Greeks reached their country by land-routes from the north. They had wandered for so long over the steppes of Asia and Russia, hunting or driving before them a few meagre flocks, that they had forgotten the name of those ocean wastes which were described by the same word by nearly all the Indo-European peoples to whom the Greeks were related. For the watery plain which Latin and the languages derived from it call *mare, mer* and so on, the Germanic languages *meer, see, sea,* etc. and the Slavonic languages, *more, morze,* etc., the Greeks had no name. They were reduced to borrowing a word from the populations they found on the soil which was to become their country: they called it *thalassa.* It was from these far more civilized peoples that they learned to build ships. Full of terror at first in face of the treacherous element, they took the risk, because they were harried by 'hard poverty ... bitter hunger ... and the necessity of the empty stomach', as the old poets put it, to face the kingdom of wave and wind, and to guide their boats laden with merchandise over the ocean depths. In this trade, though not without pain and loss, they became the most enterprising seafarers of antiquity, evicting even the Phoenicians themselves.

To make themselves peasants and seafarers—such were the first steps in Greek civilization.

Other achievements were soon to follow. The Greeks became masters of poetical expression; they explored and cleared those vast domains we now call the literary genres. At first the Greek language had no name for poetry: it simply flowered in masterpieces of unparalleled exuberance. It was a language as living as the meadow or the fountain, ready and able to express the subtlest shades of thought or reveal the most secret movements of the heart; a music now strong, now sweet, a powerful organ, a treble flute, a rustic reed-pipe.

All primitive peoples have songs and use a rhythmic language to accompany and lighten certain manual tasks. The Greek poets developed in the most fruitful manner rhythms of which the majority came to them from a dim folk-past. First they handled the great epic verse which served to celebrate, in noble yet changing cadences, the exploits of heroes of times gone by. Vast poems, half-improvised at the outset, were transmitted from generation to generation. They were recited to a very simple accompaniment of the lyre and, in the pleasure shared by the audience, they helped to educate social groups in the virtues of enterprise and courage. These somewhat variable poems became fixed in the course of time: they culminated in two major works which we still read, *The Iliad* and *The Odyssey,* which were the bibles of the Greek people.

Other poets connected verse more closely with music, singing and dancing; they drew inspiration from the daily life of the individual or the city; they mocked or exalted; they delighted or instructed; and these were the inventors of lyric poetry which was sometimes satirical, sometimes patriotic, or amorous.

Still others invented the play, tragedy and comedy, an imitation of life and also a re-creation of life. The dramatists were the educators of the Greek people.

And while, with the magic words of their tongue and out of the memory of their past, out of the sorrows and hopes of the present, out of the dreams and mirages of fantasy, they were inventing the three great poetical genres of all time: epic, lyric and drama—at the same time they were attacking with their chisels, not now wood, but the most splendid sculptural media that exist, hard limestone and marble; or they were running bronze into moulds; and producing by those means the representation of the human body, a body of incomparable beauty, which is also the body of the gods. For these gods, these mysterious and mischievous beings who people the world, had to be won over at all cost—they had to be tamed. To endow them with the fair, visible form of men and women was the best way of making them human and civilized. The Greeks built for these gods splendid temples in which they set up their images; though they honoured them in the open air. These glorious houses of the gods also bespoke the greatness of the cities that had built them. And if for ages, during the greatest ages, the sculpture and architecture of the Greeks were devoted to the dwellers in heaven, these arts, which the Greeks took over from their neighbours, none the less testified to man's power to make beauty out of metal or stone or by the assembling of stones.

And then—and still in the same age, in that great forward surge of the seventh and sixth centuries before our era, which brought the Greeks to an acquisition of all the good things of life—they attempted to disentangle the laws of science. They tried to understand the world they lived in, to say what it was made of and how it was made, to know its laws and to bend them to their own use. They invented mathematics and astronomy and laid the foundations of physics and medicine.

And for whom were all these inventions and discoveries made? For other men, for their interests and their pleasure; but not at present for all men. In the first instance, they were for the men of the 'city', by which one must understand the community of citizens dwelling in the same district (country and chief-town) of the Greek lands. Within this as yet narrow frame the Greeks tried at least to build up a society that desired to be free and that gave equality in political rights to those who formed part of it. In the most advanced of the Greek cities, this society was founded on the principle of popular sovereignty. The Greeks had therefore attained the first, though as yet still imperfect, form of democracy.

Such then were the most important achievements which in the aggregate make up Greek civilization.

They all tended to the same goal: to increase man's power over nature and to increase his own humanity. That is why Greek civilization is often called a human

1. *Landscape in the Pelopennese: circular threshing-floors on the plain*

ism; and rightly so. For it was man and man's life that the Greeks strove to make better.

As this purpose is still our purpose, the example of the Greeks who left it unfinished, and even their failure, deserve the reflection of the men of today.

Some of the stages in the long road that the Greek people followed, from the savage to the civilized stage, are enumerated by Aeschylus in the tragedy of *Prometheus Bound*. Of course, Aeschylus neither knows why nor how those wretched and untutored ancestors of his reached the first step in the knowledge that liberated them. He still shares many of their superstitions; he believes in oracles as a savage believes in witch-doctors. And he attributes to Prometheus, the god he calls the Philanthrope, all the inventions which man's labour had wrested from nature.

But in devoting the 'Benefactor of Men', *and men with him*, to the hatred of Zeus, 'tyrant' of heaven and earth, who was proposing without any reason to annihilate the proud human species and who would have done so had Prometheus not prevented him, he makes this thoughtful and active 'Friend of Man' the audacious witness to the energy of human reason in the struggle we have waged from time immemorial against the wretchedness and nakedness of our condition.

Prometheus is speaking:

> *. . . but hearken to the plight*
> *Of man, in whom, born witless as a babe,*
> *I planted mind and the gift of understanding . . .*
> *Who first, with eyes to see, did see in vain,*
> *With ears to hear, did hear not, but as shapes*
> *Figured in dreams throughout their mortal span*
> *Confounded all things, knew not how to raise*
> *Brick-woven walls sun-warmed, nor build in wood,*
> *But had their dwelling, like the restless ant,*
> *In sunless nooks of subterranean caves.*
> *No token sure they had of winter's cold,*
> *No herald of the flowery spring or season*
> *Of ripening fruit, but laboured without wit*
> *In all their works, till I revealed the obscure*
> *Risings and settings of the stars of heaven,*
> *Yea, and the art of number, arch-device,*
> *I founded, and the craft of written words,*

B

2. *Satyrs treading out grapes (Amphora attributed to Amasis. 6th Century B.C.)*

The world's recorder, mother of the Muse.
I first subdued the wild beasts of the field
To slave in pack and harness and relieve
The mortal labourer of his heaviest toil,
And yoked in chariots, quick to serve the rein,
The horse, prosperity's proud ornament;
And none but I devised the mariner's car
On hempen wing roaming the trackless ocean....
　　　Nay, hear the rest and thou wilt marvel more,
What cunning arts and artifices I planned.
　　　Of all the greatest, if a man fell sick,
There was no remedy, nor shredded herb
Nor draught to drink nor ointment, and in default
Of physic their flesh withered, until I
Revealed the blends of gentle medicines
Wherewith they arm themselves against disease....
Such help I gave, and more—beneath the earth,
The buried benefits of humanity,
Iron and bronze, silver and gold, who else
Can claim that he revealed to man but I? ...
Prometheus founded all the arts of man.[1]

◎

Let us now enter Greece with the Greek people.

They called themselves Hellenes, and, by their language (we will not risk speaking of race) they belonged to the great family of Indo-European peoples. In fact by its vocabulary, conjugations, declensions and syntax, Greek is closely related to the languages that were formerly and are still spoken in Italy, and to the majority of those which are today spoken in Europe—with the exception of Basque, Hungarian, Finnish and Turkish. The obvious relationship of a large number of words in all these languages sufficiently proves the point. Thus *father* is *pater* in Greek and Latin, *vater* in German, *père* in French. *Brother: frater* in Latin (and *phrater* is used in Greek for the members of an extensive family), *bruder* in German, *frère* in French, *brat* in Slavonic, *brâtâ* in Sanscrit, *bhrâtar* in Zend, the language of ancient Persia.

And so on. This kinship in language implies that the human groups which subsequently populated India, Persia and Europe began by living together and

---

[1] Aeschylus: *The Prometheus Bound*, edited with Introduction, Commentary and Translation by George Thomson. Cambridge University Press, 1932, pp. 81, 83, 85, 87.

speaking a common language. It is admitted that towards 3000 B.C. these peoples had not yet separated and that they were leading a nomadic existence between the Urals (or beyond) and the Carpathians.

Towards the year 2000 B.C. the Greeks, who were now detached from their original community and were occupying the Danubian plain, began to infiltrate the lands which are washed by the eastern Mediterranean, namely the Asiatic coast, the Aegean islands, and what later came to be called Greece proper. Hence from the outset the ancient Greek world includes the two shores of the Aegean and, in the way of civilization, Asiatic Greece was for many years ahead of European Greece. It was only recently, by the way—in 1922—that the Greeks of Asia were expelled by the Turks from that old and glorious Hellenic land which they had occupied for four thousand years.

When they began to settle in their new home, the Greek tribes learned the practice of agriculture from a people who occupied all these lands and who were much more advanced. We do not know their real name, but the Ancients sometimes called them Pelasgians. We call them Aegeans from the name of the sea they bordered on and the islands of which they occupied; or else Cretans, because Crete was the centre of their civilization. This Aegean people knew the art of writing, and in the sites that have been excavated a quantity of clay tablets covered with script have been found. It is only quite recently that archaeologists have begun to decipher this script. Now to the general astonishment of scholars, who had been teaching the opposite thing for fifty years, the language of the Aegean tablets has turned out to be Greek, transcribed in non-Greek syllabic letters. How this discovery should be interpreted, it is still too early to say.

In any event, if the Greek invaders transmitted their language to the Aegeans, they did not transmit writing, because they were ignorant of it. What is important is to determine the benefits that the primitive Greeks received from the Aegean peoples: these benefits were numerous and valuable.

For ages the Cretans had been practising the culture of the vine and olive, and of cereals. They raised flocks and herds. They knew of many metals such as gold, copper and tin. They made weapons of bronze. But they knew nothing of iron.

At the beginning of the twentieth century of our era, archaeologists brought to light, in Crete, the remains of vast palaces of the Aegean princes. These palaces contained a whole network of rooms and numerous halls, tangled together in the manner of a labyrinth around a wide courtyard. The palace of Cnossos covers a built-up space of 164 by 109 yards. There were at least two stories. On the walls of the reception rooms you can see frescoes of animals or flowers, processions of elegantly dressed women, and bull-coursing. Although the level of civilization is not primarily a question of bathrooms or toilets, it is interesting to observe that the palace of Cnossos was not lacking either in bath-tubs or water closets.

More deserving of note is the fact that in Cretan times woman enjoyed a liberty and respect far greater than Greek women in the fifth century. Cretan women seem to have practised a wide variety of trades; and, moreover, recent research has shown that there were in very ancient times on the shores of the Aegean several peoples among whom the status of woman was high. In some of them matriarchy prevailed; children took their mother's name and relationship was reckoned by the line of female descent. Women chose several husbands in succession and they dominated the community.

The Aegean peoples do not seem to have been warlike. No traces of fortifications have been found in the palaces or the remains of cities.

Thus, when the Greeks invaded these regions between the year 2000 B.C. and the year 1500, they encountered a people already civilized. At first they felt the prestige and accepted the domination of the Aegeans; then they revolted and towards 1400 B.C. they burned the palace of Cnossos.

From that time onwards the Greek peoples, while inheriting some of the gods and myths of the Aegeans and certain of their techniques, went their own way. The beautiful Cretan painting which drew its inspiration from nature, from flowers and foliage, birds, fishes and Crustaceans, seems to have left no trace in Greek art; nor does the Cretan language appear to have contributed anything but a few place names, the word *labyrinth* (with Minos, the bull-king who dwelt in it), the new name for the sea—*thalassa*—and a few others.

But the civilization of the Achaeans, who were the first Greek tribes, inherited from the earlier epoch something more definite than that. From the Cretans the Hellenic people received the two gifts which were to make it the peasant and seafaring people that it always remained, namely agriculture and navigation; the olive, the vine and the ship. These were to be Greek attributes for ages to come. Men lived by these means and poets sang of them.

But the Greek tribes were far more warlike than their unknown predecessors. After destroying and then half rebuilding the palace of Cnossos, they moved their political centre to the Peloponnese. There the kings built the formidable citadels of Mycenae and Tiryns whose cyclopean walls have not yet crumbled away. These Achaeans had been scarcely touched by Aegean civilization and were little more than bandits. Their tombs and palaces are crammed with the gold they had stolen.

The Greeks were at first much more timid as sailors than the Aegeans, who had pushed as far as Sicily. The boats of the Mycenaean Greeks scarcely ventured outside the Aegean; they followed the coasts or went from isle to isle. And their navigation was a matter of piracy rather than commerce. The lords of Mycenae and their soldiers undertook vast operations of pure brigandage, in the Delta and in Asia Minor; hence the quantities of gold that have been found in the royal tombs, the various jewels and goblets, the thin gold-leaf applied to the faces of the dead and especially the innumerable golden plaques very curiously chiselled.

The last of the warlike expeditions of the Achaean princes, followed by their vassals, was that of the Trojan war, which was no legendary event but historical. The city of Troy—Ilium—which was also an Hellenic city, located a short way from the Dardanelles, had grown rich by levying duties on the merchants who, to reach the Black Sea, took the land-route beside the Straits so as to avoid the currents, and carried their boats and merchandise on their backs. The Trojans mulcted them as they passed. These pillagers were pillaged in their turn. Ilium was taken and burned after a long siege at the beginning of the twelfth century (about 1180). Many very beautiful legends concealed the true reason for this rivalry between brigands, reasons that were economic and not heroic. The Iliad records a few of them. The archaeologists who excavated Troy in the last century found the remains of a city which showed traces of fire and which had been covered by the earth, on its hill, for more than three thousand years; and here they found objects of the same epoch as those discovered at Mycenae. Thieves do not evade the patient investigations of the archaeological sleuth.

Meanwhile, following the Achaeans, new Hellenic tribes—Aeolians, Ionians and finally Dorians—invaded the soil of Greece. The Dorian invasion, which was the last, took place about 1100 B.C.. Now, whereas the Achaeans had been half-civilized by their contact with the Cretans, the Dorians remained very primitive; but they possessed iron and from this they had forged various weapons. Among the Achaeans on the other hand iron was still so rare as to be considered nearly as precious as gold or silver.

It was with these new weapons, harder and especially longer (iron swords against bronze daggers) that the Dorians burst into Greece like a hurricane. Mycenae and then Tiryns were destroyed and plundered. The Achaean civilization, which had been inspired by the Aegean, sank into oblivion—or at least remained as a sort of legend. Torn up by the Dorian invasion, Greece now became a country occupied solely by Greek tribes. And now Greek history begins, in the night of the eleventh, tenth and ninth centuries. But the dawn is near.

◎

What was this country that was to become Hellas? What were the resources and obstacles that it offered to a primitive people over a long period of chaotic advance towards civilization? Here two important features are to be noted: the sea and the mountains.

Greece is a very mountainous country, although its peaks rarely reach the 10,000 foot level. But there are mountains everywhere, extending and rising in every direction, sometimes very steeply. The Ancients used to climb them by paths that went straight up, without troubling to zigzag. On the steepest slopes, steps were cut in the rock. These undisciplined mountains divided the country into a great number of small districts, most of which touched the sea. The result of this subdivision was to favour the form of state that the Greeks called a 'city'.

It was, so to speak, cantonal—a small territory easy to defend and which you naturally loved. You had no need of an ideology or even a map. You had only to climb to a hill-top and you saw the whole of your country at a glance. In the plain or near the foot of the slopes were a few villages. The capital was a little town built on an acropolis, serving as a fortress where the country-folk could shelter in times of invasion or as a market during the times—which were not of long duration— when peace reigned between cities. This fortified acropolis was the nucleus of the town when urban development began. The town was not built on the coast, owing to the danger of pirates, but near enough to have its own port.

Fields, villages, a fortified town on the way to becoming a city—such were the separate yet close-knit elements of a Greek state. The 'city' of Athens consisted of the country and its ploughed fields as much as of the town and its shops, the port and its shipping and it consisted of the whole Athenian people, with the mountain wall in the rear and its windows on the sea: it was the district called Attica.

There were dozens of other cities, in similar frames; and between these cities, countless rivalries, political and economic—with war as a conclusion. No peace treaties were signed between Greek cities, only truces, and truces only for a short term, five or ten years, or thirty years at most. But before the time was up, fighting would have been renewed. There were more wars of thirty years and longer in Greek history than periods of peace of thirty years.

But the eternal rivalry of the Greeks sometimes deserves a better name: that of emulation, in sport and culture. Competition was one of their favourite activities. The great sporting contests at Olympia and other places caused belligerents to lay down their arms; and at these times ambassadors, athletes and large crowds moved freely along all the roads. Within the cities, too, there were many kinds of competition. Athens held competitions in tragedy, comedy and lyric poetry. The prize for the poets was small enough: a crown of ivy or a basket of figs; but the glory was immense, and sometimes was even perpetuated by a monument. After he had produced the *Antigone*, Sophocles was elected a general! And he acquitted himself honourably of the operations he had to direct. At Delphi, under the patronage of Apollo or Dionysus, there were competitions in singing, to the lyre or flute, military airs, dirges or wedding-chants. Sparta, and all other places for that matter, held dancing-contests. Athens and some other cities held beauty-contests, between men or between women according to the place. The winner of the male beauty-contest at Athens received a shield.

The glory of a victory in the great national sporting contests did not belong merely to the nation, but to the city of the victorious athlete. The greatest poets— a Pindar or a Simonides—celebrated these victories in splendid lyrical compositions in which music, dance and poetry united to proclaim the greatness of the community of which the victor was but a delegate. Sometimes he was honoured with the highest reward which a public benefactor could receive, namely to be pensioned, and that is, lodged and fed in the Prytaneum, or city-hall.

During the national games, law courts as well as armies were idle and capital punishment was suspended. These truces usually only lasted a few days, though sometimes as long as a month.

Chronic warfare between cities was in the end to prove fatal to the Greeks. Their imagination hardly ever transcended the boundaries of the city-state. The mountain-horizon which limited and defended it seemed also to limit the vision or desire of each people to be Athenian, Theban or Spartan rather than Greek. The leagues, alliances and confederations of cities were precarious, and they more easily disintegrated from within than from any external attack. The strong city which headed a league was quick to treat as subjects the cities it continued, out of courtesy, to call allies; in fact, it turned the league into an empire the yoke of which weighed heavily in the form of tribute or military levies.

Yet there was no Greek city that was not keenly conscious of belonging to the Hellenic community. From Sicily to Asia, from the African coast to the lands beyond the Bosphorus, even as far as the Crimea and the Caucasus, 'the Hellenic corps', writes Herodotus, 'is of one blood, it speaks the same language, has the same gods, the same temples, the same sacrifices, the same customs, the same morals.' To ally oneself with the Barbarian against other Greeks was to be a traitor.

The 'Barbarian' (not a pejorative term) is simply the foreigner, the non-Greek, the man who speaks languages that sound like 'bar-bar-bar', so strange that they appear bird-languages. The swallow speaks barbarian. The Greek does not despise the Barbarians, he admires the civilization of the Egyptians, the Chaldeans and many other; but he feels different from them in having a passion for liberty, he does not wish to be 'the slave of any man'.

'The Barbarian is born for slavery and the Greek for freedom.' That is why Iphigeneia dies; but one notices that the saying contains a hint of racialism.

In face of barbarian aggression the Greeks would unite, but not all of them, and not for long. Salamis and Plataea showed Greece united for a year, but no more than a year. And even this was a text for orators rather than a reality. At the battle of Plataea, the Greek army fought not only against the Persians but against many contingents of Greek cities which had allowed themselves to be enrolled. This great war of national independence was still an internal war; and later the divisions between Greek cities opened the way for the Macedonians and the Romans.

◎

Mountains protect but separate, the sea frightens but unites. The Greeks were not confined by their mountain compartments: the sea enveloped the whole land and penetrated its recesses. There were few districts, even remote ones, which could not be reached by sea; a sea fearsome and yet attractive, more so than any other. Under the brilliant sky, through an atmosphere extraordinarily limpid, the mariner's eye could detect a mountainous island over ninety miles away: to him it appeared like 'a shield resting on the sea'.

The coasts provided many ports, sometimes gently sloping beaches where the first mariners could draw up their light boats for the night, sometimes deep-water basins, protected by rocky walls, where large trading vessels and war galleys could lie sheltered from the wind.

One of the names for the sea in Greek means road. To put to sea was to take the road. The Aegean was a road which from island to island led the sailor from Europe to Asia without his ever losing sight of land. These chains of islets were like the stones that boys throw into a stream so that they may cross it by jumping from stone to stone.

There is no Greek district where, by climbing to some hilltop, you cannot discern a sheet of water glittering on the horizon. There is no part of the Aegean more than forty-four miles from land. And there is no point in Greece more than fifty-six or fifty-seven miles from the sea.

Voyages were not costly: a few drachmas took you to the end of the known world. After the early centuries of piracy and distrust, Greek merchants or poets— they were sometimes both—entered into friendly contact with the old civilizations that had preceded them. The journeys of Racine and La Fontaine were to La Ferté-Milon or Château-Thierry. The journeys of Solon, Aeschylus, Herodotus and Plato took them to Egypt, Asia Minor and Babylon, or to Cyrenaica or Sicily. Not a Greek but was aware that the Barbarians had been civilized for thousands of years and had much to teach 'Us Greeks who are children'. The Greek sea was not simply a fishing ground for tunny and sardines; it led to the places where you exchanged goods, or saw great works of art, or amazing inventions, lands where corn grew thickly over vast plains or where gold lay hidden in the earth or in stream-beds—it took you to the land of marvels with the starry sky for your only compass. Beyond the sea lay many unknown lands to be discovered, cultivated and colonised. As early as the eighth century all the great cities planted colonies in the new countries. The seamen of Miletus founded no less than ninety on the shores of the Black Sea; and at the same time they founded astronomy.

In brief, the Mediterranean was a Greek lake with familiar sea-ways. The cities sat round its shores 'like frogs round a pond', as Plato says. Evohé! or Brekekekex! It was the sea that civilized the Greeks.

But the Greeks became a nation of seafarers only by necessity. It was the cry of the empty stomach that equipped the ships and launched them on the waves. For Greece was a poor country: 'Greece', says Herodotus, 'was reared in the school of poverty.' The soil is poor and barren; often very stony on the hillsides. The climate is too dry. After the early, ephemeral spring which brings a swift if magnificent flowering of trees and meadows, the weather turns 'set fair'. Summer burns up everything. Cicadas sing in the dust. For months there is not a cloud in the sky. Often in Athens not a drop of water falls from mid-May to the end of September. Autumn brings the rain and winter the storms. There are snow squalls which however scarcely last two days. But the rain comes down in torrents, even in water-spouts; there are places where an eighth or even a quarter of the annual precipitation falls in a single day. Then the half-dry rivulets turn into roaring and destructive torrents which eat away the thin layer of earth on the naked slopes and carry it down to the sea. The rain so long desired is now only a scourge. In certain confined valleys marshes are formed. And so, the peasant had to struggle both against drought which burned up his rye and against floods which drowned his meadows. He could only do it indifferently. He built terraced fields on the hillsides, carrying up in baskets from wall to wall the earth which had slipped down from his patch of ground. He tried to irrigate his fields, drain the marshes and clean out the funnels which should have led off the lake-water. But all this had to be done with primitive implements: it was very hard work and very inadequate. What was needed was to reafforest the bare mountains, but he did not know how. The mountains had originally been quite well wooded, clothed with tall forests of pine and plane, elm and oak, and swarming with game. But in primitive times the Greeks had felled the trees, to build their villages or to make charcoal. The forests lost ground. By the fifth century the hills and peaks showed the same naked ridges that they do today. And Greece in her ignorance was abandoned to the sun, to violent rainstorms and naked rocks. People fought 'to get into the shadow of a donkey'.

On this hard earth, under the capricious and pitiless heavens, the olive and vine were most successful; cereals, whose roots could not go deep enough to reach moisture, less so. It is not worth speaking of the ploughs, which were forked branches or rough wooden swing-ploughs which scarcely scratched the soil. Cereals being somewhat neglected, the Greeks went abroad for their corn to the more fortunate fields of Sicily or of what are now called Rumania and the Ukraine. The whole imperialist policy of Athens in the fifth century was in the first place a corn policy. To feed her population she had absolutely to remain mistress of the sea-routes and especially of the Straits which were the key to the Black Sea.

Oil and wine were the exchange-currency, as they were also the pride of the disinherited daughter of the ancient world. The precious fruit of the grey olive-tree, gift of Athena, supplied the elementary needs of everyday life. One cooked with oil, the house was lit with oil, for lack of water one washed in oil; with oil one rubbed and fed one's skin, which was always too dry. Wine, that marvellous present of Dionysus, was scarcely ever drunk except on feast days, and among friends after dinner and then always mixed with water:

Let us drink; why wait for the lamp-lighting? The day has but a finger's breadth to go. Take down the great cups, beloved friend, from the cupboard; for the Son of Semele and Zeus gave wine to make us forget our cares. Pour bumpers in a mixture of one and two, and let cup chase cup around hotfoot.[1]

'Plant no tree sooner than the vine'[2]—this is still old Alcaeus of Lesbos, centuries before Horace. Wine, mirror of truth, 'for wine is a spying-hole into man.'[3]

The vines, held up on poles, occupied the terraced slopes of the Greek country-side. In the plains they grew between the orchard-trees, festooned from tree to tree. Yet the Greek was sober. The climate, say the books, required it; no doubt—and poverty also required it. The Greek lived on barley and rye-bread, rolled out in flat cakes, on vegetables, fish, fruit, cheese and goat's milk. He ate plenty of garlic. Meat, whether game, poultry, lamb or pork, was like wine only taken on feast-days, except by the rich lords, the 'bigwigs' as they were called.

This poverty in diet and way of life was not merely a result of the barren soil or even the primitive agriculture; it was especially due to the uneven distribution of land.

The tribes who first occupied the country had treated the land as the collective property of the clan. Each village had its chief who was responsible for the tilling of the soil, for the work of each clan-member and for the distribution of the

---

[1] *Lyra Graeca*, edited and translated by J. M. Edmonds. London and New York, 1922, Vol I. Alcaeus, No. 163, p. 421.

[2] *Ibid.*, No. 167, p. 423.   [3] No. 169, p. 425.

produce. The clan grouped together a certain number of families—households in the broad sense of the term—each of which received a lot for cultivation. In these primitive times there was no private property. Land which fell vacant could not be bought or sold, nor could it be divided up on the death of the head of the family. It was inalienable. On the other hand, there could be a new allotment, the land could be redistributed to meet the needs of each family.

This land held in common was cultivated in common by the members of the household. The resulting produce was shared out under the guarantee of a deity known as *Moira*, which means share and lot, a deity who had also presided over the division, by lot, of the parcels of land. One portion of the domain, however, was always left fallow. They let the earth rest and did not yet practise the rotation of crops. The yield therefore was very poor.

But things did not remain like that. The old rural communism, a form of property peculiar to that stage of primitive life—as with the Bathongas of South Africa and certain peoples in Bengal—was beginning to disintegrate in the time of the Achaean brigands. The Mycenaean monarchy was military. War required a unified command. After a successful campaign the king of kings and the minor kings, his vassals, took the lion's share of the booty and also in the redistribution of land. Or certain chiefs simply appropriated lands which they were supposed merely to administer. The edifice of this corporative society, in which grave inequalities were appearing, was destroyed from the top. Private property was created to the advantage of the great.

It was also established in another way, which was progressive. Individuals might for various reasons be excluded from the clan; or they might leave it of their own free will. A spirit of adventure led many to take to the sea. Others occupied, outside the agricultural limits of the clan, lands which had been deemed too poor for cultivation; and in this way a class of small landholders was formed on the margin of the clan: here property ceased to be communal and became by stages individual. Now this class was very needy but also very active. It had broken its links with the clan, and sometimes it broke its link with the land. These men formed trade-guilds, and offered the clans the tools they manufactured or simply their labour as carpenters, blacksmiths and so on. Among such artisans we must not forget the doctors and poets. The physicians, who were grouped in corporations, had their own rules, their recipes, balms and other remedies which they offered from village to village; their recipes were their exclusive property. In the same way the fine verse-narratives, which were improvised and transmitted orally within the guilds of poets, were the property of these guilds.

All these new social groups came into being and grew within the framework of the city-state. So that now the 'cities' were divided into two halves of unequal strength: on the one side were the great rural landowners, on the other a class of little peasant proprietors very badly provided with land; a class of artisans, simple country-workmen; and a class of seafarers—all tradesmen of sorts, called 'demiurges'—a poverty-stricken crowd at the outset.

The whole drama and future greatness of Greek history are rooted in the appearance and progress of these new social groups. A new class was born, a class that would strive to wrest from the aristocracy the privileges whereby they were masters of the 'city'. For these nobles alone could be magistrates, priests, judges and generals. But the rabble were soon in a majority. Their desire was to re-establish the city-state on the basis of equal rights. They began the struggle which opened the way to popular sovereignty. Unarmed to all appearance, they advanced towards democracy; the powers and the gods might be against them, but they would none the less be victorious.

◎

Such in brief outline were some of the circumstances of which the combined action permitted and conditioned the birth of Greek civilization. Observe that it was not only natural conditions—the climate, the soil and the sea; nor merely the moment in history—the legacy of earlier civilizations; nor simply social conditions—the class-struggle, which has been called 'the motive-force of history'; but the convergence of all these elements that created a favourable conjuncture for the birth of this civilization.

And what do you make of the 'Greek miracle'? some scholars, or so-called scholars, will exclaim. There was no such thing. The notion of miracle is fundamentally unscientific, and also unhellenic. The word 'miracle' explains nothing; it replaces an explanation by exclamation marks.

What happened was that, in the conditions in which it found itself, with the means it had to hand and without its being necessary to appeal to any particular gifts that Heaven might have bestowed on it, the Greek people pursued an evolution which had begun before its time and which permitted the human species to live and to improve its way of life.

One example will suffice. The Greeks seem, as if by a miracle, to have invented science. They did in fact invent it, in the modern sense of the term; they invented scientific method. But the reason was that, long before them, the Chaldeans, the Egyptians and others had collected a quantity of observations about the stars and about geometrical figures, and that these enabled, for example, Greek sailors to find their way, and Greek peasants to measure their lands and fix the right dates for their labours.

The Greeks came at the moment when it was possible, by considering these observations on the property of figures and the regular course of the stars, to deduce laws and to formulate an explanation of phenomena. They did so, they were often in error, and they started afresh. There was nothing miraculous about this, it was merely a new step in the slow progress of mankind.

Other examples could be drawn in abundance from the other fields of human activity.

The whole of Greek civilization takes man as its point of departure and its object. It proceeds from his needs, it seeks what is useful to him and what will promote his progress. To this end, it explores man and the world, and each by means of the other. Man and the world are mirrors; they look each other in the face and read each other by this means. Thus Greek civilization may be said to articulate man and the world; and also to unite them, through struggle and combat, in a fruitful comradeship which is called Harmony.

CHAPTER TWO

THE *ILIAD* AND
HOMER'S HUMANISM

Homer's *Iliad* is the first great achievement of the Greeks—it represents the mastery of poetry. It is the poem of war, of men dedicated to war by their passions and by the gods. Here a great poet tells of man's nobility in face of this detestable scourge, of man a prey to Ares, that 'bloody scourge' whom Zeus execrates 'most of all the gods'. He tells of the courage of heroes who slay or who die, simply; of the willing sacrifice of those who defend their country; of the sorrow of the women; of the father's farewell to the son in whom he will in a sense survive; of the old men's supplications. He describes many other things: the ambitions and greed of the leaders, their quarrels and the insults they mete out to each other; he describes meanness, vanity and egoism side by side with bravery, friendship and tenderness; pity stronger than thirst for vengeance; the love of glory which raises man to the level of the gods. He describes these all-powerful gods and their serenity; and also their jealous passions, their capricious self-interest and their profound indifference to the poor rabble of mortals.

Above all else, this poem in which death seems to reign tells of the love of life, but also of man's honour which is higher than life and stronger than the gods. It is natural that this theme—man in the state of war—should occupy the first epic poem of the Greeks who were being constantly torn by war.

To develop his subject Homer chose a half legendary episode of the real, historical Trojan war which had taken place at the beginning of the twelfth century before our era. It is known that the cause of this war was the economic rivalry between the first Greek tribes established whether in Greece proper—the Achaeans of Mycenae—or on the Asiatic shores of the Aegean—the Aeolians of Troy. The episode on which the poet concentrates and which confers unity of action on the whole poem is the wrath of Achilles, his quarrel with Agamemnon, king of Mycenae and leader of the expedition against Troy; and then the disastrous consequences of the quarrel for the Achaeans who were besieging Troy.

Here is the plot: Agamemnon, the commander-in-chief, demands that Achilles, bravest of the Greeks, 'rampart of the army,' should yield up to him a fair captive named Briseis, who had fallen to his lot when the spoil of a captured city had been shared out. Achilles indignantly refuses to be defrauded of what belongs to him. At an armed assembly of the people, he gravely insults Agamemnon:

> *O shameless-mannered, selfish-minded man . . .*
> *Wine-sodden, dog in eye and doe at heart. . . .* [1]

He complains of having always to bear the burden of the heaviest fighting and of receiving in return a share inferior to Agamemnon's, cowardly soldier and greedy general, a 'folk-devouring king'. In presence of his companions he pronounces a solemn oath that he will withdraw from the fighting and remain in his tent until he has obtained reparation from Agamemnon for the affront to his bravery; and he does so.

Achilles, who is the first hero of the *Iliad*, is at the heart of the poem, he is the pivot on which the action turns. His withdrawal and that of his troops are followed by the gravest consequences for the Achaean army. On the plain under the walls of Troy, it suffers three defeats, each time more disastrous. Assailants hitherto, the Achaeans are now reduced to the defensive: and for the first time in ten years they see the Trojans bold enough to camp out on the plain. The Achaeans build an entrenched camp: and now it is they who are besieged. Even this camp is forced by the Trojans who are led by Hector, bravest of the sons of Priam. The enemy prepares to set fire to the Achaean ships and drive the army into the sea.

All through these hard-fought battles which fill a good part of the poem with deeds of valour and bloodshed, with desperate but obstinate courage, the absence of Achilles is, to the minds of his companions and to ours, nothing less than a brilliant witness to his strength and his power. Absence-presence—it commands every movement and moment of the struggle. The bravest of the Achaean chieftains—stout Ajax (Aias in Greek), the son of Telamon; swift Ajax, the son of Oïleus; fiery Diomed, and many others strive in vain to replace Achilles. But these valiant substitutes for his valour are merely, as it were, the small change of the hero who, in strength, swiftness, fire and courage, is the very incarnation of warlike virtue, without fault or weakness. Possessing everything and refusing his aid, he involves all the Achaeans in defeat.

One night—a tragic night between two disasters—while Achilles is gnawing

---

[1] Book I. This and the subsequent quotations from the *Iliad* are taken from Sir William Marris's version: *The Iliad of Homer*, translated by Sir William Marris. Oxford University Press, 1934, pp. 6, 9, etc.

his heart out in the idleness to which he has condemned himself, but which weighs upon him, he sees an embassy from the Achaeans approaching his tent. It consists of two great leaders; Ajax, first bulwark of the army, after Achilles, with a bravery as stubborn as that of an ass whom a band of children are trying to drag along; and the subtle Odysseus, who knows all the secrets of the heart and all the arts of speech. With these two warriors comes old Phoenix who had been his childhood's tutor and who speaks as it were with the accents and insistence of Achilles' father.

All three beg him to return to battle, not to fail in the loyalty a soldier owes to his fellow-soldiers, and to save the army. In the name of Agamemnon they promise splendid gifts and honours. But Achilles, who is less bound by his oath than by his self-esteem, responds to their tears and arguments and even to honour itself with a brutal no. He goes further; he declares that on the morrow he will put to sea and return home, as he prefers an old-age of obscurity to the undying glory he had decided to win by dying young before the walls of Troy.

This reversal of his first choice, this preference for life rather than glory, would debase him if he could maintain it.

But the morrow dawns and Achilles does not depart. That day the Trojans force the Achaean defences, and Hector, leaping on to the stern of a vessel which Ajax is defending, calls to his comrades to bring fire and set the whole fleet alight. At the other end of the camp, Achilles sees the flames rising from the first Achaean vessel, flames that proclaim the defeat of the Achaeans and his own dishonour. At this moment he cannot remain insensitive to the prayers of Patroclus, his dearest companion, whom he regards as the better half of himself. With tears in his eyes, Patroclus begs his leader to allow him to fight in his stead, clad in the splendid armour of the hero which cannot fail to terrify the Trojans. Achilles takes this opportunity of at least ordering his troops back into battle. He himself arms Patroclus, puts him at the head of the soldiers and urges him on. Patroclus drives the Trojans out of the camp and far away from the ships. But in the course of this brilliant offensive, he encounters Hector who faces him. Hector kills him in single combat, but not without Apollo's having a hand in his death which, as it is obtained by the intervention of a god, seems like a murder.

The sorrow of Achilles, when he learns of his friend's doom, is terrifying. Lying on the earth and refusing all food, tearing his hair, covering his face and clothes with ashes, he sobs and thinks only of death. Now in the eyes of the Greeks suicide was the shameful refuge of cowards. Keen as was the wound which Agamemnon had inflicted on his pride, the death of Patroclus now creates in Achilles' heart depths of suffering and rage which obliterate all other feelings. But this suffering restores him to life and action by unleashing in him a tempest of fury and rage for vengeance against Hector and Hector's people.

3. *Creto-Mycenaean Vase, discovered on Melos* (*Date:* 1450–1400 B.C.)
4. (Overleaf, left) *The blind Homer* (*Marble copy, early Imperial epoch, after a bronze original, c.* 450 B.C.)
5. (Overleaf, right) *Priam* (*Detail of Attic vase by Euthymides, subsequent to* 510 B.C.)

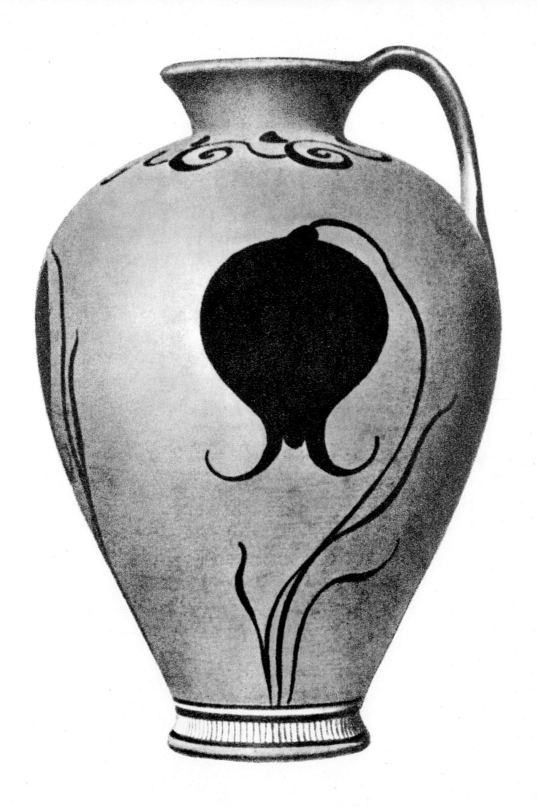

Thus in a moving *péripétie* produced simply out of the character of Achilles, the hero and motive-force of the *Iliad*, Homer operates a complete reversal of the dramatic situation which seemed to be immobilized for good through the inflexibility of this same hero, who yields to nothing except the violence of his own passions.

Achilles returns to the fight, and now begins the fourth battle of the *Iliad*. This is *his* battle, a frightful carnage of all the Trojans whom he encounters. When the Trojan army has been defeated, part of it annihilated, part drowned in the river into which Achilles has driven it, the demoralized survivors take refuge inside the city walls. Hector alone, despite his father's and mother's prayers, remains outside the gates in order to face the mortal enemy of his people.

The single combat between Hector and Achilles is the culminating point of the *Iliad*. Hector fights bravely, his heart full of the love he bears his wife and son and country. Achilles is the stronger. The gods who have protected Hector now turn away from him. Achilles strikes him down, and carries his body to the Achaean camp as a trophy, after outraging it. He ties his enemy's feet to the rear of the warchariot and lashes the horses,

> *And nothing loath the pair sped on: the dust*
> *Rose up as he was dragged, and his dark hair*
> *Flowed loose on either side, and all in dust*
> *His head lay, once so gracious. Zeus had now*
> *Abandoned him to foes to outrage him*
> *In his own native land.*[1]

The poem does not end with this scene. Achilles, whom Priam comes to supplicate in his tent, restores the body of his unfortunate son. Hector is buried by the Trojan people with funeral honours. The women's lamentations and the songs of mourning they improvise tell of the misfortune and the glory of the man who gave his life for his people.

◎

Such is the action of this vast poem. It is conducted in masterly fashion by a man of genius. Even if the Homer, to whom the ancients ascribed it, did not invent all of its many episodes, these episodes have been assembled and bound together in a magnificent unity.

During the four centuries which separate the Trojan War and the composition of the *Iliad*, which must be placed in the eighth century, many poets had no doubt

---

[1] Book XXII. Translation cited, p. 501.

c

6. The Stirrup-Cup (Detail of vase by Cleophrades, c. 500 B.C.)

composed many narratives about this war and even about the wrath of Achilles. These men improvised verses of which the rhythm was close to that of the spoken language but with cadences more noble and regular. Their verses were flowing and easy to remember. The *Iliad*, which stemmed from these improvised poems, is still a sort of continuous poetic stream that carries along in its course many strange forms of the now half-forgotten language spoken by the Aeolian ancestors. This language, with its splendid epithets, confers on the whole epic a kind of iridescent sonority and an incomparable brilliance.

The poems which had opened the way for Homer were no doubt transmitted by memory. Observers have noted that modern improvisers of epic poetry, such as the Serbs of the nineteenth century, can learn by heart and transmit without writing as many as 80,000 verses. The Greek improvisers who preceded Homer first recited their poems, in fragments, in the houses of nobles. These nobles were not the brigand chieftains of the Mycenaean age, they were mainly big rural land-owners who enjoyed listening to the warlike exploits of the past. Now there came a time when the first merchants appeared in the Greek world, in the cities of Ionia in Asia Minor, just south of the Aeolian country, in Miletus, Smyrna and other sea-ports. Homer lived in the eighth century in one of these cities on the Ionian coast —we do not know which. It was the era in which the class-war was to be unleashed with a violence more sudden perhaps than at any other moment in history. In this struggle the wretched masses, who had no land or only poor land, were led by the merchant class in an attempt to wrest from the noble landowners the almost ex-clusive privilege over the soil which they had arrogated to themselves. At the same time they wrested from the propertied class its culture, and appropriated it by fashioning the first masterpieces of Greek poetry.

Recent studies have suggested that the birth of the *Iliad* in eighth-century Ionia took place at the moment when the hitherto *improvised* and variable kind of poetry became fixed in a *written* and carefully wrought work of art. The appearance of the first and finest epic in our heritage is connected from the outset with the new mercantile middle-class. It was the merchants who suddenly began to spread the ancient but not widely known use of writing. An Ionian poet, whom tradition identifies with Homer, raised to the level of art a selected portion of the traditional epic cycle hitherto improvised. He composed and wrote down on papyrus our *Iliad*.

That is to say that the bourgeois class gave an artistic value and a form to a poetic culture hitherto formless. At the same time, by means of public recitations, it brought this poetic culture to the service of the city, of the whole people.

Such are the glimpses we have today into the origin of the *Iliad*. It was a great popular poem, due originally to many authors but finally to a single author: the patrimony of the Greek people, and our patrimony.

◎

If one wished to describe Homer's genius, one would say first of all that he is a prodigious creator of character. The *Iliad* is a world in itself, peopled with original beings as distinct from each other as are living beings. Homer would have the right to appropriate Balzac's claim: '*Je fais concurrence à l'état civil.*' This faculty for creating people in great numbers, distinct from one another, each with his individual condition, notation and behaviour—one might almost say, his finger-prints—this, Homer possesses in the highest degree like Balzac and Shakespeare, like the greatest creators of character of all time.

To make a character live without describing him—for one may say that Homer never describes—the poet sometimes only needs to endow him with a single word or gesture. Thus, hundreds of soldiers die in the battles; certain characters are introduced only to die. But always, or nearly always, a different feeling towards death is expressed in the gesture by which the poet confers life at the very moment when he is about to withdraw it.

> *Then was Diores...*
> *Caught in the toils of fate ... and backward in the dust*
> *He fell and stretched both hands out to his friends....*[1]

Have many poets created a being by such simple means and for so short a time? This one gesture goes to our hearts, by showing us Diores in his great love of life.

Here is another picture, hardly more elaborate—a picture of life and of death:

> *Then spear in hand Achilles went in chase*
> *Of godlike Polydorus, Priam's son.*
> *His father had forbidden him to fight,*
> *Because he was the youngest of his sons*
> *And dearest to him; and in speed of foot*
> *He outran all. Now like a foolish boy,*
> *Parading his fleet-footedness, he raced*
> *Along the forefront....*

At this moment Achilles strikes him:

> *And with a shriek he fell upon his knees;*
> *A cloud of darkness wrapped him, and he sank*
> *Clutching his bowels to him with his hands.*[2]

[1] Book IV, p. 89.   [2] Book XX, p. 461.

And here is the death of Harpalion; a brave man, who, however, cannot master an instinctive movement of fear:

> *. . . and he retired*
> *To cover among his friends avoiding fate,*
> *And glancing each way warily for fear*
> *A spear might find his flesh.*[1]

He is struck and his body, on the earth, still expresses his revolt by writhing 'like a worm'.

On the other hand the quiet attitude in which Cebriones is lying expresses the simplicity with which this hero of unspotted courage has encountered death. All around him the din of battle goes on: he only reposes in peace and forgetfulness:

> *So Trojans and Achaeans rushed together*
> *And slew, and neither thought of fatal flight.*
> *And round the dead man many sharp spears struck,*
> *And feathered arrows leaping from the string,*
> *And many heavy boulders smote on shields*
> *As men fought over him; but in the whirl*
> *Of dust he lay, so great and greatly fallen,*
> *Forgetful of his feats of horsemanship.*[2]

Thus Homer goes to the essential. However slight the person whom he is depicting, he brings out by means of a gesture or an attitude what is fundamental in each human being.

◎

Nearly all the characters in the *Iliad* are soldiers, and most of them brave; but it is a striking fact that no two of them are brave in the same way.

The bravery of Ajax, son of Telamon, is of the heavy kind, a bravery of resistance. He is a tall, broad-shouldered, in fact 'enormous' man. His courage is all of a piece and no one can shift it. A comparison, to which we have already alluded and which used to scandalize the classicists owing to its non-epic vulgarity, defines the obstinacy of Ajax:

[1] Book XIII, p. 298. [2] Book XVI, p. 379.

As when an ass
That passes by a cornfield overpowers
The boys who drive him, a phlegmatic ass
About whose ribs has many a stick been broken,
And in he goes and crops the standing corn,
And the boys hammer him with sticks, though all
Their strength is but of children; and at last
They beat him out when he has had his fill:
So on great Aias....[1]

He has the courage of obstinacy. He shows little dash in the offensive because his body, like a wild boar's, is unsuited for it. His mind is as heavy as his body, not stupid but limited. There are things he cannot understand. Thus when the Greek embassy waits on Achilles, he does not understand why the hero should hold out because of Briseis:

because
Of one mere girl and here we are offering
To give thee seven, and much the best there are
And more besides.[2]

The heaviness of Ajax serves him excellently, however, on the defensive. His order is to remain where he has been posted, and he remains. He is limited in the etymological sense, like the stone that limits a property and says that you must not pass. The poet calls him a *tower*, a *wall*. Bravery in concrete.

We see him on the vessel he is defending, moving 'with giant strides' about the deck, holding all the space he has been charged with and killing one assailant after another with methodical spear-thrusts or, if necessary, using an enormous sea-pike. His soldier eloquence can be expressed in four words: never yield an inch. 'Be men, my friends,' he cries:

Or do we think we have supports behind us,
Or yet a stronger wall...?
No, no! ... Therefore life lies
In our own hands and not in dainty fighting.[3]

Discouragement is another feeling he does not understand. He knows that a battle isn't a 'dance', as he says, but a place where

[1] Book XI, p. 246.   [2] Book IX, p. 202.   [3] Book XV, p. 351.

For us there is no better will nor way
Than to lay to our hands and all our might,
And close the fight up. Better once for all
To perish—or to win our lives—.[1]

Such are the simple thoughts which, in battle, bring 'a smile to the grim face of Aias'.

His bravery is that of the Spartan or Roman—of the Spartan whose military rule forbade retreat, or of Horatius on the bridge—the courage of all the good soldiers who get killed in order to hold on. Such is the heroism depicted by Homer centuries before Plutarch made it available for the use of any and every man of letters.

Quite different is the dashing bravery of Diomed. His is not Spartan courage, but *furia francese*. Diomed has the spirit, the fire and boldness of youth; he is in fact, after Achilles, the youngest of the heroes. He is bold in presence of his elders. In the scene of the night Council, he impetuously attacks Agamemnon's conduct; he asks that the king of kings make reparation to Achilles. Yet on the battlefield, he submits to discipline and accepts everything, even the most unjust reproaches, from the commander-in-chief.

Diomed's character is that of a volunteer, always ready to march. It is he who, after a hard day's fighting, offers to undertake a perilous night-reconnaissance of the Trojan camp. He likes to do more than his duty. A sort of intoxication leads him to the forefront of battle. When all the leaders flee before Hector, Diomed is still borne on by the courage that dwells in him. His very spear shares in his madness. 'My spear . . . is hot within my hand,' he declares. He draws old Nestor on to attack Hector; and Zeus, who desires Hector's victory, has to drive off the two warriors with his thunderbolts:

> *. . . He thundered terribly*
> *And shot his white flame out and hurled it down*
> *On earth in front of Diomedes' horses.*
> *There rose an awful flame of sulphur burning;*
> *And both the horses in a panic cowered*
> *Below the car. Then out of Nestor's hands*
> *Slipped the bright reins. . . .*[2]

But Diomed does not tremble.

Homer has given him the most brilliant courage of any of the heroes. He fights so far from his comrades that the poet says:

[1] *Ibid.*, p. 343   [2] Book VIII, p. 164.

> *But of Tydides no man could have told*
> *To which host he belonged, or whether he*
> *Had fellowship with Trojans or Achaeans.*[1]

The comparisons Homer uses to make us see him always have an impetuous quality. Diomed is the torrent that carries away the fences of orchards and the dykes by which the peasants try to prevent rivers from overflowing. To mark the brilliance of his courage, the poet kindles a symbolic fire on the crest of his helmet when he is fighting. And, lastly, this hero receives the unique privilege of fighting against the Gods. Neither Achilles nor any other warrior takes the risk of confronting the Immortals who mingle in this struggle between mortals: Diomed alone, in scenes of extraordinary grandeur, has the temerity to pursue and confront Aphrodite, Apollo and then Ares in person. He attacks the goddess of beauty when she is trying to rescue a Trojan adversary whom he has been engaged in striking down. He wounds her so that her blood flows:

> *. . . the spear*
> *Passed quickly through the ambrosial raiment which*
> *The very Graces wove her, and bored through*
> *The bone above the palm; and forth there flowed*
> *The goddess' blood immortal. . . .*[2]

In the same way he strikes Ares, and the god of war roars

> *As loud as nine, nay as ten thousand men.*[3]

But he has no arrogance, he utters no impious boasts. There is only that inner fire which drives him to every kind of audacity. An impassioned man: but what a difference there is between the sombre passions of Achilles and the bright passion of Diomed! This man is an *enthusiast*.

The etymology of the Greek word indicates a man in whom moves the spirit of a god. He is in fact befriended by a goddess, the warlike yet wise Athena who dwells in him and mixes her soul with his. She rides beside him on his chariot, urges him into the very thick of the mêlée, fills him with strength and courage. 'Hear me, Athena,' he cries. She points to Ares, 'this madman, this consummate pest'[4] as she calls him, for Diomed's attack—the god hated by gods and men because he unleashes hideous war, the god who had but few altars and temples among the Greeks.

The faith Diomed has in Athena's word is the deeper source of his courage.

---

[1] Book V, p. 94.   [2] *Ibid.*, p. 103.   [3] *Ibid.*, p. 121.   [4] *Ibid.*, pp. 95, 120.

There are moments when this faith makes the Achaean soldier seem akin to a knight of the Middle Ages. Diomed is the only hero in the *Iliad* who can be called knightly. One day before starting to fight a Trojan of whose name he is unaware, he learns when about to strike him that he is Glaucus, and that he is grandson of a guest of Diomed's father.

> *Then Diomedes, good at need, rejoiced:*
> *His spear he planted in the bounteous earth,*
> *And said to Glaucus very pleasantly:*
> *'Why then, thou art an old ancestral friend!*
> *   ... as to Tydeus*
> *I have no memories, for he left me still*
> *A little child when all the Achaeans were*
> *Destroyed at Thebes. In midmost Argos then*
> *I am thy friend and host, as thou art mine*
> *In Lycia when I go unto thy people:*
> *So let us, here or in the press alike,*
> *Avoid each other's spears: many there are,*
> *Trojans and famed allies for me to kill ...*
> *And many Achaeans too for thee to spoil ...*
> *   And now let us exchange*
> *Our armour, thou and I, that all who see us,*
> *May know we claim to be ancestral friends.*[1]

Thereupon the two warriors leap from their cars, clasp hands and conclude a pact of friendship.

The scene is radiant. To no other of the heroes save the enthusiast Diomed could Homer have attributed this generous movement. Yet it is an astonishing scene, for the end is still more surprising. This is how it concludes:

> *And then Zeus, son of Cronos, took away*
> *The wits of Glaucus, who exchanged his gear*
> *With Diomedes, gold for bronze, the worth*
> *Of five score oxen for the worth of nine.*[2]

The poet does not tell us that his favourite is delighted; but he gives us to understand it because Diomed does not point out his mistake to Glaucus. This element of rapacity in the chivalrous Diomed is the antidote to the conventional

---

[1] Book VI, pp. 131–32.   [2] *Ibid.*, p. 32.

idealism which always constitutes a mortal threat to poems about heroes. Here we see Homer's profound realism in the portrayal of the human heart.

◎

The *Iliad* does not merely contain soldiers; there are women and old men. And among the soldiers, all are not brave: there is Paris. The strange loves of Paris and Helen were, traditionally, at the origin of the war. They remain present and singularly active in the *Iliad*.

Paris had seduced and carried off Helen; he had been the first cause of the war, and he also caused the death of Achilles whom he slew with an arrow. There had been a time, one may suppose, in the epics of the Trojan cycle prior to the *Iliad*, when Paris figured as the hero of the war he had provoked, and as the champion of Troy and of Helen. It seems that it was Homer himself who replaced Paris in this noble role by his brother Hector, a more recent character in the Trojan cycle, and turned Paris into the coward of the story. In any event, Homer's dramatic instinct sets Paris at the opposite pole to Hector and maintains a permanent conflict between the brothers throughout the poem. Hector is the pure hero, the protector of Troy; Paris, the 'scourge of his country', is almost the pure coward.

Not that Paris does not, by fits and starts, feel the prestige of the ideal of his age. He would like to be brave; but when it comes to the point his heart and handsome body refuse to be actually brave. With groans and excuses in plenty he promises Hector that he will follow him to the fight which he has abandoned without adequate reasons. His explanations are wretched:

> *. . . Not so much*
> *From pique or grievance with the sons of Troy*
> *I sit here with the women, but I wanted*
> *To hug my gloom. . . .*[1]

His promises are vague:

> *Already has my wife*
> *Been working on me with persuasive words*
> *To go and fight.*

We have already listened to these persuasive words: they were a pack of insults and Paris had swallowed them almost without gulping. He continues:

[1] *Ibid.*, pp. 135–36.

> *And that is best, I know;*
> *For victory's but a fickle jade. See thou,*
> *Wait for me while I put on fighting gear,*
> *Or go and I will follow; I am sure*
> *To overtake thee.*[1]

The tone is rather off-hand for a soldier.

Certain material details give outline to Paris's cowardice. The bow is his favourite weapon: it enables him to avoid the hand-to-hand encounter which makes 'his knees tremble and his cheeks go pale'. When shooting he hides behind his comrades or behind the upright of a tomb; if he wounds an enemy:

> *Then up leapt Paris from his hiding-place*
> *With a light laugh. . . .*[2]

Yet Paris is not the absolute coward. If fear drives him from the fighting-line, vanity and vainglory bring him back; for Paris is vain of his beauty, vain of the leopard-skin he carries over his shoulder even when fighting, vain of the love-locks he wears like a woman. He is vain too of the weapons which he spends his time polishing in the women's quarters while the men are fighting. All these things, his beauty, his care of his person, his way of 'ogling the girls', his passion for women, his successes as a seducer, have ended by making Paris quite a personage in Troy, despised no doubt and yet important. To his various titles as a suborner—titles with which Hector overwhelms him—he would be glad to join the name of a brave warrior; provided he could obtain it cheaply, with his bow and quiver, those insignia of courage. Trapped in this struggle between fear and desire for glory, Paris escapes by means of offhand and yet half-sincere reticences which in fact reveal his own uncertainty about the feelings that will ultimately have the upper hand. Can this handsome, vain and cowardly fellow, into whose bed Aphrodite has thrown the rebellious Helen—can he be, in the last resort, despicable?

An analysis on the merely human plane offers no solution to this question, because it does not reach his essential character. His personality can be explained only if we recognize that it is the subject of an experience which we must really call religious. When Hector insults him, Paris readily admits that his brother is just in blaming his cowardice. What he does not accept is the insult to his beauty and his amours. He answers his brother, not without real pride:

[1] *Ibid.*, p. 136.   [2] Book XI, p. 240.

But cast not in my teeth the lovely gifts
Of golden Aphrodite; the rich gifts
Of gods are surely not to be discarded,
Which of their grace they give us, though of choice
Can no man take them.[1]

How the tone of this irresponsible young man has risen! Now it is he who reads Hector a lesson. Man does not 'choose' the gifts he has received from Heaven, they are, properly speaking, 'given'. It is from Aphrodite he has received the mysterious gift of beauty, the desire and the gift of inspiring love. Love and beauty are given gratuitously, they are divine. Paris will not allow them to be disparaged, because that would insult a deity. He has not chosen, but has been the object of a choice; he is aware of being *elect*. The fact that he has received the divine in his flesh should not prevent us from admitting that Paris had undergone a genuine religious experience.

Hence we grasp the perfect coherence of his character. His passion is not that of a mere voluptuary but a kind of consecration. It does not bring him merely sensual pleasure—it certainly does that—but it also brings him near a state that can be called divine. His very lightness and heedlessness border on the serenity of the blessed gods. No questions trouble his soul. Exempt from all cares but those of Aphrodite, he finds, in his consciousness of representing her among men, contentment, plenitude and even authority; and this simplifies his life because it gives it an aim.

Thus he behaves like a coward in the warlike society he lives in, because his will-power is weak or non-existent. But the strength of Aphrodite is able wholly to fill the vacuum of his weakness. In yielding himself to the divine will, Paris has discovered a kind of fatalism which dispenses him from effort and frees him from remorse. His piety justifies his immorality. And what greatness there is in his ardent appeal to Helen, when Aphrodite, after saving him from the spear of Menelaus, transports him to the perfumed bed where his wife is forced to join him:

. . . come, let us go to bed, and take our pleasure;
For never hath desire so lapped my heart,
Not even when I snatched thee first away
From lovely Lacedaemon, and set sail
On my sea-faring ships, and lay with thee
In Cranaë's isle, as I do love thee now
And sweet desire has taken hold of me.[2]

[1] Book III, p. 56.　　　　　　　　[2] Book III.

Aphrodite is here speaking through the mouth of Paris, Aphrodite a cosmic force that confers greatness on the instrument she has chosen, however poor—on this coward whom Hector reproaches in the following words:

> *No, but the men of Troy are very timorous,*
> *Else thou hadst worn a shirt of stone ere this....*[1]

Infinitely far from Paris is Helen. Her character, given to feeling rather than sensuality, is at the opposite pole to that of Paris. Moral in face of her amoral lover, she resists the passion that Aphrodite inflicts on her and would like to refuse the pleasure which the goddess forces her to share. Paris's amorality stemmed from his piety, Helen's morality causes her to rebel against the goddess. Both of them are beautiful and passionate, and this beauty and this passion are gifts which they cannot thrust aside and which constitute their destiny.

Yet Helen's nature was rather for an orderly life. She regrets the time when everything seemed easy in the respect and tenderness of family affections:

> *I ... left my home and kin,*
> *The daughter whom I loved, and the sweet friends*
> *Of mine own age! 'Twas not to be; and so*
> *I waste with tears....*[2]

She judges herself severely and considers that the severe judgment of the Trojan people upon her is quite natural. Helen might still find consolation if only Paris were brave and had a sense of honour, like her husband Menelaus, whom she cites as an example of courage to her lover. With her moral sense, therefore, there is nothing to dispose Helen to appear, glorified by poetry, in the role of the adulterous wife whose infidelity brings ruin on two nations. Paradoxically, Homer has made this guilty woman, on whose account Achaeans and Trojans are slaying each other, a simple creature who asked only to lead the obscure existence of a good wife and tender mother. There is a paradox as soon as the gods enter our lives— at least as soon as these Homeric gods enter them, for they are not very fond of the morals we have invented to defend ourselves. Aphrodite has taken possession of Helen in order to manifest her omnipotence. She bends her victim under the double fatality of beauty and of the furious desire she inspires in men, so that Helen becomes the image of Aphrodite herself.

The troubled feeling that possesses men in her presence is a religious feeling. It immediately throws the Trojan elders into a sort of ecstacy and trembling, and makes experienced men talk nonsense. When they see her coming up on the walls where they are gathered, they utter these strange words:

[1] *Ibid.* [2] *Ibid.*, p. 60.

Small blame that for a woman such as this
Trojans and armed Achaeans should be bearing
Calamity so long; for she to look at
Is wondrous like the immortal goddesses.[1]

Alarming old men, to justify the savage butchery of two nations merely on account of Helen's beauty.

And yet all the Trojans are not mistaken. Neither Priam nor Hector confuse the good and simple Helen who hates herself, who hates her incomprehensible passion and yet loves it as she loves Paris in the sense that she can never detach herself from him—they do not confuse this entirely human Helen with that fatal beauty which is like a destructive flame in her, a manifestation of the divine omnipotence. Priam says:

. . . I find no fault at all with thee;
I hold the gods to blame.[2]

Helen is not mistress of the consequences of her beauty. She had neither desired nor cultivated it. She had received it, a curse as much as a gift of Heaven. Her beauty is her fatality.

◎

And now, after these brilliant but secondary luminaries, come the stars of first magnitude: Hector and Achilles. In these two stars Homer lights up two of the modes of human life so essential that it is hard to live on a certain level without participating in one or the other.

Achilles appears first as an image of youth and strength. He is young in years, about twenty-seven, and especially in his hot-headed movements and passionate angers; his is an untamed youth, he has grown up on battle-fields and has not yet accepted or even known the bridle of social life. Youth and strength are his, a strength sure of itself and of which the weak crave protection against the ill humour of the great. This is what the seer Calchas does at the beginning of the *Iliad*. When Agamemnon questions him regarding the cause of the plague which has broken out in the army, Calchas hesitates to reply, knowing well that it is dangerous to speak truth to powerful men. So he implores Achilles' protection; and the young hero promises unreservedly:

[1] *Ibid.,* p. 59.   [2] *Ibid.*

Ay, ay, be bold . . . For by Apollo whom
Zeus loveth and to whom thou prayest, Calchas,
When thou interpretest the will of heaven
Unto the Danai, there is never a man
While yet I live and see the light on earth . . .
Shall lay a heavy hand on thee, not though
'Twere Agamemnon that thou namedst, who
Now boasts himself far best of all the Achaeans.[1]

Here then is our first vision of Achilles, radiant in strength.

Later when this strength has been defied by Agamemnon and breaks out in threats, it reasserts itself with pride in the great oath—which I only cite in part—that he will cease from action:

'Yea, by this staff of mine,
Which never more shall put out leaf or shoot
Since first it left its stem upon the hills,
Nor yet grow green again, because the axe
Has stripped its leaves and bark—and now the sons
Of the Achaeans, those who sit in judgment
And guard traditions by command of Zeus,
They bear it in their hands—so shall it be
A potent oath to thee: the day shall come
When all the sons of the Achaeans will
Long for Achilles; and in that day thou
In thy distress shalt have no strength to help,
When multitudes fall dying at the hands
Of slaughtering Hector. Thou shalt eat thy heart
Within thee, for remorse that thou didst slight
The noblest of the Achaeans.'
Pelides spoke, and dashed to earth his staff
Studded with golden nails, and sat him down.[2]

From this time and through more than eighteen cantos this strength is immobile. The image of this immobility so fatal to the Achaeans is as striking as that of its release amid the battle-songs of Achilles; because we know that it would be enough, to save the army, for Achilles who has sat down to get up. In the midst of his period of absence, Odysseus says to him: 'Arise and save the army.' Finally this incarnate Force does get up:

[1] Book I, p. 4.   [2] *Ibid.*, p. 9.

And then Achilles, dear to Zeus arose. . . .
So from Achilles' head the splendour shone
To heaven, He left the wall and by the trench
Took stand. . . .
He stood there, and he shouted, while Athene
Called far away; and huge dismay he roused
Among the Trojans.[1]

To describe Achilles' strength, Homer uses similes of great power. Achilles is like a vast fire roaring in the deep gorges of the hills; the dense forest burns, the wind shakes and rolls the flames onward: so rushed on Achilles, like a god, slaying all those he pursued, and the black earth ran with blood. Elsewhere the poet finds an image of the destructive fury of Achilles not in any natural scourge, but in the peaceful work of the farm:

. . . And as a man yokes round-head bulls
To tread white barley in his well-built barn,
And soon beneath the lowing cattle's feet
The grain is trodden, so for fierce Achilles
The whole-hoofed horses trampled in a mass
Dead men and shields. The axle-tree beneath
Was all blood-splashed, and all the rims about
The chariot, for the blood-drops spattered them
Both from the horses' hoofs and from the tires.
But still the son of Peleus hurried on
To win renown, and his resistless hands
Were flecked with blood.[2]

A destructive blood-stained Force—so Achilles appears in the most terrible cantos of the poem. He is atrocious. A poet has rarely pushed horror further than in such scenes as that of the death of the youth Lycaon. The prayers of this child who has been disarmed, the reminder of his first encounter with Achilles in his father's orchard, the story of his unhoped-for salvation—all this touches us deeply and renders Achilles' reply more brutal, the murder more savage and the movement of the poor body which Achilles seizes by the legs and throws with curses to the fishes of the Scamander, more horrible.

Is this son of a goddess a man, or only a brute? He is a man at any rate in his extreme sensitivity to the passions. Herein lies the psychic mechanism of his strength, that he is most acutely sensitive to passion, eaten up with friendship,

[1] Book XVIII, p. 417.   [2] Book XX, p. 464.

self-love, love of glory, and hatred. The strength of this man—most vulnerable of men—becomes manifest only in the flow of passion, but then with incredible violence. Achilles who appears so insensitive, so absolutely inflexible to the terrified eyes of Lycaon, and to our eyes, is inflexible only because his whole being is taut with a passion that hardens him like steel; he is insensitive to everything because he is sensitive only to this.

There is nothing superhuman or divine about this man, if indeed to be divine is to be impassive. Achilles never dominates, he always undergoes. Briseis, Agamemnon, Patroclus, Hector—from the four cardinal points of his emotional horizon life lets loose in him tempests of love or hatred one after the other. His soul is like a sky that is never clear, a sky in which storms are constantly gathering and bursting under the impulse of passion.

His moments of calm are merely apparent. In the scene of reconciliation with Agamemnon, this puppet who has wounded him so deeply and who no longer counts in his mind, Achilles is ready to make every concession, even the most generous. But suddenly, because there is delay in setting out, this new passion that possesses him, this friendship that demands vengeance, bursts the surface-calm. He will not pause to eat and drink, he cries—

> *Because my friend is dead, and there he lies,*
> *Gashed by the biting spear, within my hut,*
> *His feet towards the porch, while round about*
> *His comrades mourn; and so I have no thoughts*
> *For what you say, but only blood and slaughter*
> *And groans of dying men.*[1]

Achilles is a man whose feelings are violently stirred by the single object of their desire, their regret or their hatred at the moment, and which are blind to all else. This object may change: it may be Agamemnon, or Patroclus, or Hector; but as soon as it has taken possession of his soul, it sets his whole being in motion and unleashes the need for action. Passion is something that obsesses him and can only find relief in action.

In this sequence—passion, suffering, action—resides the whole of Achilles' character; even after the death of Hector when it seems that passion should be assuaged—though it is not in Achilles' nature that it ever should be—and should leave him at peace.

> *The gathering was dismissed: the people scattered,*
> *Each troop to its quick ships. While all the rest*

[1] Book XIX, p. 439.

7. *The Voyage of Dionysus (Inside of a drinking cup by Exechias. Last third of the 6th Century)*
8. (Overleaf, left) *Columns of the temple, so-called of Poseidon, at Paestum (5th Century)*
9. (Overleaf, right) *Head of Heracles. Metope at Selinunte (Early 6th Century)*

Turned for relief to food and pleasant sleep,
Achilles wept, remembering his dear friend,
And Sleep that masters all men could not seize him;
From side to side he tossed, as he lamented
Patroclus' manhood and his cheery courage,
The skeins of fate that they had wound together,
The troubles they had borne in passages
Of mortal wars and perilous waves. And as
These memories came to him, he shed big tears,
Now lying upon his side, now on his back,
Now on his face; and then again would he
Rise to his feet and roam distractedly
On the seashore. The Dawn would find him watching
When she appeared across the brine and beach,
And he would yoke swift horses to his car
And tie dead Hector to his chariot-tail
And drag him; and when he had hauled him thrice
Around the barrow of the dead Patroclus,
Would rest again inside the hut, and leave him
Stretched on his face in dust.[1]

These verses show how, especially in the silence of night, the object of passion invades the field of consciousness, calls up every memory and intensifies sorrow to the point where it unleashes action; and this for a time relieves it of anguish. Here then is the first key to his character: strong passions which are relieved by strong actions.

At first sight such a man seems to be a pure individualist. The demon of power, which feeds on and waxes stronger on every victory, seems to have become the only law that governs Achilles. The hero shatters and tramples on all the bonds that have united him with his comrades and with other men. Through its own peculiar destructive and anarchical action, passion annihilates his sense of honour and drives him to the most inhuman cruelty. When Hector, vanquished and dying, in the most heartrending appeal in all the *Iliad*, asks only that his body may be restored to his family, Achilles replies:

Do not entreat me, dog, by knees or parents.
I only wish I had the heart and will
To hack the flesh off thee and eat it raw,
For all that thou hast done to me! there lives

[1] Book XXIV, p. 538.

D

10. *Horseman, in Pentelican marble. Found on the Acropolis (c. 500 B.C.)*

None who shall keep the dogs away from thee;
Not even if they brought and weighed out here
Ransom ten-fold and twenty-fold, and promised
More thereunto; no, not though Priam, son
Of Dardanus, bid pay thy weight in gold;
Not even so thy queenly mother shall
Lay on a bier and mourn the son she bore,
But dogs and birds shall eat thee utterly.[1]

Across this desert of the soul Achilles moves toward the most inhuman solitude. He is preparing his own destruction. This is evident in the scene where he talks of abandoning the army, without thought for the disaster to his friends. He dares to assert that he prefers old age to glory. To grow old while chewing the bitter cud of resentment is to deny the meaning of life; and this he cannot really do.

For the truth is, Achilles loves life, loves it prodigiously, but always in action and in the present moment. Ever ready to grasp what life brings him in emotion and action, living only in the moment, he greedily seizes what is offered by each passing event. Ever ready for murder, wrath, tears, tenderness and even pity, he receives everything, not with an equal indifference in the manner of the sage of old, but in the manner of a robust and hungry nature which feeds on everything with equal ardour, and finds joy even in suffering. From the death of Patroclus he finds joy in carnage, and the poet tells us at one and the same time that 'on his heart lay sorrow hard to bear' and that his armour

Became as though it were wings to him
And bore aloft the shepherd of the people.[2]

This ardour for life is so strong in Achilles that everything in him appears to defy death. He never thinks of death; for him it does not exist, so strongly is he anchored in the present. Twice he is warned: If he kills Hector, he will die. He replies: What matter? Better to die than to remain by the ships, 'a useless burden upon the earth.' To his horse Xanthus who is strangely endowed with human speech to foretell his death in an approaching battle, he replies indifferently:

'Why, Xanthus, dost thou prophesy my death?
'Tis not thy office. Well I know myself
That here it is appointed for me to perish
Far from my mother and my father dear;
But all the same I will not cease, till I
Have driven the Trojans to disgust of war.'

[1] Book XXII, p. 499.　　　　　　　　　　[2] Book XIX, pp. 444, 445.

He spoke, and with a cry along the front
He sent his whole-hoofed horses.[1]

Herein Achilles' wisdom is profound. He loves life enough to prefer an intense life to a long one. This is the meaning of the choice he had made when young. To win glory through action is a form of life that inspires him with a stronger love than a life passed without incidents. After a moment of weakness he firmly maintains his choice. Death in the midst of glory means immortality in the memory of mankind. Achilles chose to live until our times and beyond them.

It is thus, by his love of glory, that Achilles the individual belongs to the community of men in all ages. Glory for him is not only a tomb and monument, but the common fatherland of living men.

There is still a scene, the finest in the *Iliad*, in which Achilles reveals his deep humanity in another way. One evening, when after dragging Hector's body behind his chariot he has brought it back to his tent, he is thinking of his dead friend in the night-silence. Suddenly Priam, the old, bereaved father, appears before him, at the risk of his life

And took Achilles by the knees, and kissed
His hands, the dreadful slaughterous hands that had
Slain many of his sons.[2]

And he speaks to Achilles of his father Peleus, who in his far-off land is still living and rejoicing at the thought that his son is alive. He dares to beg Achilles to restore Hector's body so that it may receive funeral honours. Achilles is touched to the depths of his soul by the memory of his father. He gently raises the old man, and for a few moments the two weep together, one for his father and for Patroclus, the other for Hector. Achilles promises Priam to restore the body of his son.

And thus in a scene of the greatest beauty, of a humanity which is the more striking because we did not expect it of Achilles, Homer completes the portrait of this iron hero of passion and glory.

And now, noble Hector, one would like to speak of you in lyric terms. But Homer who treats all his characters with the same impartiality and never pronounces a judgment on them, forbids it. He wants to be like the quicksilver in the glass, which allows his creations to be reflected in the mirror of art. And yet Homer does not manage to conceal his friendship for Hector. While borrowing

[1] *Ibid.*, p. 446.　　　　　　　　　　　　　[2] Book XXIV, p. 555.

the features of Achilles' character from the oldest traditions of the epic, he has formed Hector with his own hands, using, apart from that, perhaps little more than some earlier rudimentary outline. Hector is his creature of choice: in him more than in any other he expresses his faith in man. We must not forget that in writing a poem within the framework of the Trojan war, which implied the victory of the Greeks and in which he in no way conceals his Hellenic patriotism, Homer none the less chooses the leader of the enemy as an incarnation of the highest nobility he can conceive. This is a token of humanism not really rare among the Greeks.

Like Achilles and most of the other epic characters, Hector is brave and strong. Brilliant similes, not stained with blood, portray his strength and beauty:

> *. . . and as a horse*
> *In stable who has stuffed him at his crib*
> *Breaks halter and goes galloping o' er the plain*
> *To bathe in the fair river that he knows,*
> *Exulting, and he holds his head on high*
> *With streaming mane, flushed with the pride of life,*
> *And bounds with flying leaps to where the mares*
> *Loiter and graze; so lightly Hector plied*
> *His feet. . . .*[1]

He is as brave as Achilles, but his courage is of another quality. It is not natural, but rational; it represents a victory over his own nature, a discipline he has imposed on himself. Achilles' emotions can find pleasure in war; Hector for his part hates it. He says so, quite simply, to Andromache; he has had to learn to be brave and how to fight in the front rank of the Trojans. His is the highest form of courage and, indeed according to Socrates the only one that deserves the name, because, though knowing fear, he surmounts it. When Hector sees Ajax advancing to meet him—

> *giant Aias . . . with a smile on his grim face—*[2]

he cannot repress an instinctive movement of fear. This movement is merely physical; his heart begins to beat more rapidly in his breast. But he overcomes this physical fear by having recourse to his knowledge, one might almost say his science, of fighting:

> *. . . pray do not try*
> *To treat me like a puny boy or woman*
> *Untrained in deeds of war! I know too much*

Book XV, p. 334   [2] Book VII, p. 150.

Of battles and men-slaughterings: I have learned
To swing my hard hide-buckler right and left,
Which tests, I think, the toughness of a soldier:
. . . Or tread wild Ares' dance in the close fray. . . .[1]

Hector is aware of the temptation to cowardice. When he remains before the gates of Troy to meet Achilles and kill or be killed by him, he still finds it fairly easy to brush aside the entreaties of his father and mother, begging him, from the walls above, to return into the city. These entreaties harrow his soul because they picture the burning of the city and the massacre or enslavement of his people which will follow his death. Self-respect, however, is enough to repel the temptation. But then, abandoned to himself and in the silence of his heart, he is troubled by strange thoughts. He reflects that if he fights he will certainly die. Is not there still time to avoid this? Why not, in fact, seek the shelter of the walls? He even thinks for a moment of entreating Achilles, of laying down his arms at the foot of the wall and offering himself defenceless to the enemy. Why not propose terms in the name of the Trojans? (Why not in fact?) For a moment he dwells complacently on this fancy, drawing up in his mind the clauses of a reasonable pact. Then suddenly he starts; his folly and weakness are clear; he recovers himself. 'But why dost thou talk thus with me, my heart?' No, he will not entreat Achilles, or let himself be killed like a woman, or return dishonoured into Troy. The time for dreams is past and gone, like the loves of youth:

No: now there is no room for talk between us
By oak or rock, as lass and lad talk love.[2]

It is a question of looking death in the face and knowing how to die like a brave man. To fight against cowardice, there are not only self-respect and self-love, there is honour higher than life itself.

Achilles has no need to think in order to be brave; Hector is brave in an act of reflection and reasoning.

This firm reason of Hector's sometimes draws splendid words from him. One day when his brother Polydamas, in obedience to a sinister augury—which moreover is true—urges him to desist from battle, Hector, who cannot doubt the soundness of the augury but who will fight in spite of everything, replies: 'The best augury is to fight for one's country.' A surprising remark in an age when auguries enjoyed great authority and were not lightly to be flouted—especially surprising in a very pious man, as Hector is.

But honour and reason do not explain his whole character. The sources from which his courage springs lie deeper. For Hector honour is not an intellectual

---

[1] *Ibid.,* p. 151.   [2] Book XXII, p. 491.

concept or 'ideal', it is to fight for the country he loves, to die if necessary, to fight to save his wife and child from death or slavery. His is not the courage of the sage; it is not founded like Socrates' courage on indifference to earthly things; on the contrary, it is nourished by the love he bears them.

Hector loves his country. He loves

> *Sacred Ilios . . . and the folk*
> *Of Priam, lord of the good ashwood spear.*[1]

He loves them to the point of defending them against all hope; for he knows that Troy is lost:

> *For well I know it in my heart and soul,*
> *Shall come a day when sacred Ilios*
> *Will be laid low.*[2]

But love does not stop short before such certainties: we defend those we love to the last minute. All Hector's actions tend towards the saving of Troy. Achilles is as negligent of social feelings as Hector, on the contrary, is anchored in the love he bears his city, his countrymen and his father who is also his king. To Achilles, the still half-savage chieftain of a tribe at war, a tribe which war uncivilizes still further and sometimes reduces to the level of the brute—to Achilles is opposed Hector, the son of the city who is defending his territory and on whom, even in war, the city imposes its discipline. Achilles is anarchical, Hector civic. Achilles wants to kill in Hector the man he hates; Hector desires only to kill the mortal enemy of Troy. As he hurls his last javelin, he cries:

> *Now in thy turn beware my spear of bronze.*
> *I would have thee take it home into thy flesh!*
> *So should the war be easier for the Trojans*
> *When thou wert dead, who art their greatest bane.*[3]

War does not prevent Hector from being both civic and civilized; his patriotism can abstain from hating the enemy.

He is civilized too in this, that he is always ready to conclude a pact with the enemy; for he has a distinct feeling that what unites men could outweigh what separates them. He says to Ajax:

> *But come, let us give each other famous gifts,*
> *That men may say, Trojans and Greeks alike,*
> *'See, out of soul-consuming rivalry*
> *They fought, and parted in a pact of friendship.'*[4]

[1] Book VI, p. 139.   [2] *Ibid.*   [3] Book XXII, p. 497.   [4] Book VII, p. 153.

In Achilles who hates him, he sees another of his fellow men, to whom it does not seem chimerical to propose terms: he thinks of proposing to restore Helen, and the treasures stolen by Paris, to the Greeks, without meanwhile speaking of the wealth of Troy. And his is not merely the temptation of cowardice; Hector is haunted by the old dream of a treaty which would reconcile enemies. And there is above all the feeling of repulsion from violence which inspires his whole conduct, even at this decisive moment when reason at once condemns his plan as an unpractical dream.

Still later, just before the fight, he suggests a final pact with Achilles, a pact which is human and reasonable. He knows this fight will be the last. 'I will slay thee, or be slain,' he says. But the notion of a pact is still uppermost:

> *Come here, and let us pledge us by our gods,*
> *For they will be the surest witnesses*
> *And guardians of our covenants: I will not*
> *Do thee foul outrage, if Zeus suffers me*
> *To outstay thee, and if I take thy life;*
> *But when I have spoiled thee of thy famous arms*
> *I will give back thy corpse to the Achaeans;*
> *Do thou the like, Achilles.*[1]

Achilles repels him brutally:

> *Hector, thou unforgiven, do not talk*
> *Of pacts to me! there is no truce between*
> *Lions and men, nor yet have wolves and lambs*
> *One mind....*[2]

And his next words bring out the meaning of Hector's proposal, as well as further defining Achilles' character:

> *... so for me and thee*
> *Friendship is out of question.*[3]

While Achilles does not escape from the *particular* in which he is imprisoned by passion, Hector moves in the universal. The understanding he outlined, the project of a treaty, was nothing less than the principle, as yet elementary but certain, of international law.

But the strong love that Hector bears his country, and which already seems to be extending to mankind, rests on a deeper and more vital foundation. He loves

[1] Book XXII, pp. 495–96.   [2] *Ibid.*, p. 496.   [3] *Ibid.*

his own people, and this love is firmly rooted in love for his wife and child. The rest derives from this. The motherland for him is not only the walls and citadel of Troy and the Trojan people (it goes without saying that there is no question of defending a particular conception of the state); it is the lives which above all others are precious to him and which he wishes to save and preserve free. There is nothing more material than Hector's love for his country. Andromache and Astyanax are the clearest and most peremptory images of the motherland. He says to Andromache before leaving her and going to fight:

> *For well I know it in my heart and soul,*
> *Shall come a day when sacred Ilios*
> *Will be laid low, and Priam, and the folk*
> *Of Priam, lord of the good ashwood spear.*
> *But not my sorrow for the Trojans' trouble*
> *And Hecuba herself and Priam king*
> *And all my brothers—that brave company*
> *Who shall go down in dust beneath the hands*
> *Of foes—so moves me as thy suffering doth*
> *When some bronze-clad Achaean leads thee off*
> *Weeping, and takes the day of freedom from thee.*
> *And there, maybe in Argos, shalt thou weave*
> *At some strange woman's bidding, or bear water*
> *From Hypereia or Messeis' stream,*
> *Harshly abused, with strong constraint upon thee....*
>   *... and unto thee will be*
> *Sorrow renewed for lack of one like me*
> *To keep away the day of bondage; only*
> *Let me be dead, with earth heaped on me, ere*
> *I hear thy crying as they drag thee off!*[1]

Just before this, Andromache was begging Hector not to expose himself to battle. Now she cannot, because she knows he is defending their mutual affection. This last conversation between husband and wife offers something very rare in ancient literature: the perfect equality in love which they show each other. They speak, and love, on the same level. Hector does not love Andromache and his son as property that belongs to him; he loves them as beings equal in value to himself.

Such are the 'beloved' whom Hector defends to the last. When face to face with Achilles, the living image of his destiny—when disarmed and lost, he still struggles against all hope, he still makes a pact with hope.

[1] Book VI, pp. 139–40.

This is the moment when the gods abandon him. Hector thought his brother Deiphobus was at his side, but it was Athena who had assumed the form of his brother in order to deceive him. Having thrown his last spear and finding his sword broken, he asks Deiphobus for a weapon. But there is no one there, he is alone. Now he sees his fate in the blinding clarity that precedes death:

> *Ay me,*
> *I see the gods have called me to my death.*
> *I thought that brave Deiphobus was here;*
> *But he is within the wall, and I have been*
> *Deluded by Athene. Therefore now*
> *Is evil death not far away but near,*
> *And no way out . . .*
> *And now my fate has found me.*

Hector is perfectly clear-sighted as regards his fate, he sees death so near that he seems to touch it. But you might say that he is gathering new strength from what he sees, for he immediately adds:

> *And now my fate has found me. Let me not*
> *Die without effort nor ingloriously,*
> *But in the doing of some great deed of arms*
> *For generations yet unborn to hear.*[1]

The moment of death is still the moment of struggle. Hector replies to destiny with a man's act, an act which men everywhere will judge as great.

In this way Homer offers us, in the person of Hector, an image of man which is at once true and elevating. Hector defines his humanity in love of his family, in knowledge of universal values and, up to his last breath, in effort and struggle. While dying he seems to defy death. His cry, which is the cry of a man in travail of a better humanity, he wishes to be heard by 'the men of future times'—ourselves.

◎

In Achilles and Hector we see the opposition not only of two temperaments but of two stages in man's evolution.

The greatness of Achilles is illumined by the conflagration of a world that seems to be passing away, the Achaean world of warfare and pillage. But is this world really dead, does it not survive in our own age?

[1] Book XXII, p. 497.

Hector heralds the world of the city, the community that defends its soil and its rights. He bespeaks the wisdom of pacts, he also expresses the family affections which are a figure of the wider fraternity of mankind.

Herein we see the nobility of the *Iliad* and hear its cry of truth. The contrasting figures of Achilles and Hector express the loftiness and the verity of the poem; their contradiction is part of the development of history and it is still beating in our hearts today.

CHAPTER THREE

ODYSSEUS AND THE SEA

Civilization is a work of liberation and achievement. The second epic that has come down to us under the name of Homer illustrates one of the most important of these achievements. It tells how the Greeks, by dint of daring, patience and intelligence, mastered the art of seafaring; and Odysseus (who gave his name to the *Odyssey*) is the hero of this achievement.

It is not certain, it is indeed very improbable, that the author of the *Iliad* was the author of the *Odyssey*. Some of the Ancients already doubted the ascription. The language of the poem as well as the manners and religious beliefs it portrays are more recent than those of the *Iliad* by perhaps half a century. But the genesis of the poem and the way it was composed by improvisation and by being, at first, orally transmitted by a guild of poets who were called the Homeridae—all this can be explained in the same way as for the *Iliad*. The author who composed it no doubt drew his material from a group of poems which formed the cycle of legends concerning Odysseus. Marshalling the various parts which he selected in accordance with the rules of his art, developing here, omitting there, he conferred a powerful unity on the poem as we now have it, a unity due in the first instance to the hero's personality. Without Odysseus, the *Odyssey* would be no more than a collection of tales and adventures of uneven interest. But in fact not one of these tales and adventures, which are of very diverse origin and the thread of which is sometimes lost in the night of primitive folklore, not one but tells us of the courage and cunning or intelligence or wisdom of Odysseus. The author who arranged, modelled and oriented a still shapeless mass of poetical material, subordinating action, episodes and characters to the one figure of Odysseus, and who also fixed a work he had created anew in writing, was a very great artist—even more than a great poet. The date of composition of the *Odyssey* may be fixed very approximately in the second half or even towards the end of the eighth century before our era. Scholars are far from being agreed as to the date. Written at the time of the discovery and mastery by the Greeks of the western Mediterranean, though it pretends to be unaware of these things, the *Odyssey* was the poem of the rising class of seafarers and merchants before it became the national epic of the Greek people.

The name of the author is of little importance. There is, besides, no inconvenience in giving the same name to the different authors of the *Iliad* and the *Odyssey*, as 'Homer' was perhaps a sort of family name belonging to all the members of the guild of Homeridae. For over twenty-five centuries men have called them by this name and have not thereby been prevented from enjoying the beauty of these masterpieces.

On arriving in their country the Greeks, as we know, were ignorant of the sea and of the use of ships. The Aegeans, who were their masters in the art of navigation, had for centuries used boats with oars and sails; they had also discovered the principal 'sea-routes', as Homer calls them, the routes to the Asiatic shore, to Egypt, and, further away, the routes which from Sicily gave access to the western Mediterranean. On these routes the Aegeans conducted primitive forms of trading, what is called 'mute barter' for instance, by which sailors would deposit on the shore the products they wished to exchange and then, returning to their ship, wait for the natives to deposit products of the same value. After which, and often after several trials, merchandise would be exchanged. But the most primitive and frequent form of Aegean commerce was simple piracy. Pelasgian pirates long remained famous in Greek tradition, but in reality they had formidable successors.

One must repeat that it required centuries for the Greeks, properly so-called, to renew the maritime tradition of the Aegeans. They were primarily landsmen. Without neglecting the hunt or the care of their scanty herds, they had to learn to till the soil before learning to navigate. Soon, a purely agricultural economy was insufficient. They needed and desired the natural and manufactured products which only the East could supply. The nobles wanted gold in bars, jewels, perfumes, and fabrics embroidered or dyed in purple. The West, on the other hand, offered land, very good it was said, to those ready to take it. Here was something to tempt the penniless who were already swarming in these early days. But it appears that the need for certain metals did more than anything else to force the Greeks into a seafaring life. Iron was not abundant in Greece; but tin was completely lacking both in Greece and in the neighbouring countries. Now only this metal, which enters with copper into the composition of bronze, is capable of producing a bronze both fine and resistant.

If, from the time of the Dorian invasion, the iron sword had triumphed over the bronze poignard, bronze still remained in the eighth century and later the favourite metal for defensive armour. This armour was in four pieces: a helmet, body-armour from shoulders to belly, greaves for the legs, and a buckler on the left arm. As long as this noble armour reigned on the battlefield, tin was needed for the soldiery.

So they were bold nobles, members of the old clans, who led the first commercial expeditions. They alone had the means for building and fitting out vessels. These rich landowners were not sorry, either, to lay hands on the new source of wealth, which was commerce. But they did not put to sea alone. They needed rowers, navigators, traffickers and colonists. The crowds of landless and penniless men who swarmed in Greece furnished the nucleus of these profitable expeditions.

But where were they to find this rare tin which exercised a kind of fascination over the men of the eighth century? There were only two places, at least in the Mediterranean region. One was at the far end of the Black Sea, in Colchis, at the foot of the Caucasus. Miletus, the great maritime city of Ionia, followed others in taking this eastern route to the tin mines, and supplied its own metal industry and its neighbours' from the Caucasus. But there was another route to tin mines, much more dangerous and less known than the route through the Dardanelles and the Bosphorus. This one led round the southern coasts of Greece, out into the open sea, then through the dangerous straits of Messina and along the shores of Italy to the tin mines of Etruria. It was the route followed by the great ironmasters from Corinth and from Chalcis in Euboea.

This western route was also the one taken by Odysseus; and no doubt it was for the public of adventurers, sailors and colonists who followed it and also for the military oligarchy of wealthy merchants who were intent on the manufacture of weapons, that the *Odyssey* was composed. Odysseus was the advance-scout of this motley company of sailors, merchants and aristocrat-industrialists.

Our *Odyssey*, however, does not clearly and ostensibly relate the story of the acquisition of tin. It proceeds in the manner of all epic poems, by transferring into a mythical past the adventures that some sailor had had fifty or a hundred years before, or which he might still have, people thought, on the sea-routes of the west. Homer is exploiting the narratives of seafarers who had preceded Odysseus, stories that were current in all the seaports, tales of giants and floating islands and monsters who devour or destroy vessels. Twice Odysseus encounters the island of the witch. Then, too, there is the story of the plant which makes the seaman forget his homeland. The *Odyssey*, like the *Arabian Nights*, is full of such tales. These are stories which, whatever their historical or geographical sources, had in their origin nothing to do with the return of the Achaean chieftain from Troy—which is the real starting-point of the *Odyssey*—and are much more ancient.

The Odysseus of the *Iliad* is a good soldier, a chieftain of great authority who disciplines Thersites and his like, a subtle orator and diplomatist. There is nothing to suggest that he is a great sailor. In the *Odyssey*, on the other hand, all the adventures of the Sindbad or Robinson Crusoe type which had been imagined by seafarers seem to have been fathered on him. He draws them to himself:

Of many men
He saw the cities and he learned the mind;
Ay, and at heart he suffered many woes
Upon the sea, intent to save his life
And bring his comrades home.[1]

He is the adventurer on the ocean, the man 'who wandered far and wide', the hero who has suffered hardship on the 'fearful' sea. And so he becomes the ancestor and patron of the bold adventurers for whom Homer sang.

But there are other elements, more ancient than these stories and even than Mediterranean navigation itself, which go to make up the figure of Odysseus. He is the hero of the folk-tale of the husband's return. A man has set out on a long voyage. Will his wife remain faithful, and will she recognize him on his return? Such is the theme of a story which is found both in the Norse skaldes and in the *Râmâyana*. The husband returns, old or in disguise, and he is recognized by three signs. These vary from version to version. But we can easily distinguish in the *Odyssey* the three signs in the version Homer used. Only the husband can bend the bow which had been his bow. He alone knows how the marriage-bed had been made. Lastly he has a scar which only his wife recognizes—the sign which was to be the last in the story, because it clinched the recognition between husband and wife. Such was the probable order of the signs in the tale followed by Homer. Now the poet uses them in three particularly dramatic scenes, but he inverts their order, modifies their bearing and varies the circumstances. In the folk-tales, the events nearly always take place in groups of three. This repetition in threes maintains the curiosity of a naïve audience. Homer, however, varies the circumstances of the three signs as much as possible, instead of emphasizing the repetition. The sign of the marriage-bed is the only one used for the recognition of husband and wife, in the admirable scene in which Penelope who is still distrustful sets a trap for Odysseus, by ordering Eurycleia to pull the marriage-bed out of the bedchamber. At this, Odysseus gives a start. He himself had made the bedstead by fashioning its base from the trunk of an olive-tree attached by its roots to the ground. He knows that the order cannot be carried out unless some wretch has cut the olive-tree at its base. He says so, and is thus recognized by his wife. The sign of the bow is used in the great scene of the contest between the suitors. By bending the bow which no one has been able to bend and by directing an arrow at Antinoüs, Odysseus is recognized by the suitors; he cries out his name by way of defiance. But the sign of the scar is the first that is used, in a scene quite unexpected by us

---

[1] *The Odyssey of Homer*, translated by Sir William Marris. Oxford University Press, 1925. Book I, p. 1.

and by Odysseus. The scar is recognized by his old servant Eurycleia, in the scene where she is washing his feet, and this provokes a serious and unexpected turn and nearly ruins the skilfully thought-out plan of Odysseus.

Thus the elements, in series of three, of the 'return of the husband', are enriched by Homer with varied, unexpected and vivid circumstances.

Such are a few of the remote sources of the *Odyssey*, which is the story of a man's return to his homeland.

◎

There is no need to describe the plot of this well-known poem. Suffice it to recall that Odysseus is simply a landed proprietor who is greatly attached to his domain, to his wife Penelope who in his absence is being courted by his neighbours, and also to his son Telemachus whom he had left as a small child. When Troy has fallen after a siege of ten years, Odysseus thinks only of a speedy return. But he has to sail round southern Greece in order to reach his island of Ithaca, and when his ship is off Cape Malea, a tempest drives him into the western sea, towards Sicily, Sardinia and north-west Africa. Now in the centuries following the Trojan war, these regions beyond the unknown sea had become peopled with terrors and monsters. So Odysseus the landsman is forced to become a sailor; but his one thought is to return to Ithaca and his family and his land.

The *Odyssey* tells the story of his return, ten years of struggle against the perils of the deep terminating, when he reaches home in disguise, in the battle with the suitors who have installed themselves in his manor and are besieging his wife and devouring his substance. He slays them with the help of his twenty-year-old son and of two faithful servants to whom he has slowly and prudently revealed his identity; and so he regains his family happiness; but after what efforts and struggles!

For the men of that age the western sea was a formidable and unmastered reality. Dangers without number awaited those who ventured into it. Currents might carry away a ship, a storm might break it in some narrow strait or drive it on a rocky headland; or it might be struck by lightning, when the vessel would be filled with sulphur and the crew hurled overboard. At other times the sky would be veiled, the stars that acted as compass would disappear and then one would not know whether one was 'in the realm of gloom where the sun descends beneath the earth, or towards the dawn where he comes up'. Such were a few of the daily risks encountered by Odysseus. But there were also pirates who lay in wait in the straits, pillaged the ship and sold the crew into slavery; or savages who massacred the seamen when they landed on an unknown coast; or, again, cannibals.

And what is the kind of vessel on which Odysseus and his men venture into this fearful sea? A boat without a deck and with one sail which can only be used when there is a tail-wind. Tacking into a head-wind is impossible. If the wind is contrary, there is nothing for it but to row, and this entails an exhausting effort. For most of the time, one tries to hug the coast, in the absence of any chart other than the night sky, but especially on account of provisions; for it is scarcely possible to carry more than a little bread—a sort of pancake—and very little water. This fact necessitates almost daily landings and often a long search to find a spring, in unknown territory; unless one hung from the masthead a sheepskin which would be steeped overnight in dew and then squeezed out to provide a cup of water.

Such was a sailor's life in the eighth century B.C.: it was considered the worst possible kind of existence, a dog's life, in which a man was exposed defenceless to the most terrible of the forces of nature.

Odysseus, who in the legend precedes the masters of the western sea-routes, makes his way like a hero to lands which very soon after were to be planted with Greek cities. But he advances amid the stories the seafarers tell of him, towards fabulous regions, bristling with fantastic perils which greatly enhance in the popular imagination the real perils of the enterprise.

On the Italian shore there are not only man-eating savages, but also the people of the Cyclops, one-eyed giants who live on the cheese and milk of their flocks but also on occasion devour strangers.

On the islands there are fairy-goddesses who hold seamen captive in the toils of love; among them, the goddess Circe who, when about to yield herself to the men who desire her, strikes them with her wand and changes them into lions, wolves, or other animals. This misfortune befalls most of Odysseus's companions, who are changed into swine. But Odysseus never deserts his men. Aided by the god Hermes, he boldly appears before the witch's palace, mounts on to her bed, threatens her with his sword and drags from her the secret of the enchantment. His companions who had thought him lost, greet him on his return:

> *... And just like farmstead calves*
> *About the droves of cattle coming back*
> *To yard when they have had their fill of grazing—*
> *With one accord they frisk in front of them;*
> *The fences cannot hold them any longer,*
> *But round their dams they run with ceaseless lowing—*
> *So these men, when their eyes beheld me, flocked. ...*[1]

Other goddesses, such as the nymph Calypso, dwell in the islands of the sea. Thrown on to the shore near her grotto, Odysseus falls in love with her as a sailor in the Southern Ocean might with a fair Polynesian. But he more quickly wearies

[1] Book X, p. 175.

11. *Dionysus leading his troop. The pine-cones are at the end of the thyrsi carried by the Maenads (Vase painting, c. 500 B.C.)*

of his conquest than the nymph herself who for seven years keeps in her bed every night the audacious mortal she loves and whom shipwreck has deprived of the means of leaving her. But every day Odysseus goes to sit upon a rock on the shore and gaze for hours over the ocean-wastes that separate him from his homeland, from his wife and son and the domain of vineyards and olive-groves. In the end Calypso is commanded by Zeus to let him go. She gives him an axe, a hammer and nails, and with these, not without fear, he builds a simple raft on which to brave the boundless sea.

On another island dwell the Sirens. These are fairy bird-women who attract mariners by the charm of their marvellous voice, and then devour them. Before them on the grass stands a heap of piled-up bones. No seaman passing by that coast can resist the call of the magic voices. Now Odysseus wishes to hear the fabulous song of the Sirens and yet not fall victim to them. After reflecting in his usual manner, he finds a means of getting what he wants and evading what he dreads. He stuffs the ears of his sailors with wax and has himself bound fast and securely to the mast. To enjoy a pleasure forbidden to ordinary men, Odysseus takes a terrible risk and triumphs. He alone among men will have heard the voice of the bird-women and not have perished.

These last stories which are marvellously exploited by the poet show that for the Greeks of the Homeric age the sea might be full of dangers but it was also full of attractions. Odysseus both dreads the sea and loves it and wants to enjoy it. These limitless wastes, the thought of which, as he says, 'breaks his heart,' act also as a magnet. First of all, no doubt, because of the profit one may make. It is beyond the sea, he says, that 'a man gathers much treasure'; it is 'by faring far and wide over the world that he brings back home splendid gold and silver and ivory'.

Sometimes this Odysseus whose one thought is to return home seems nevertheless to be sorry to leave some uninhabited island which he is surprised 'that no one has thought of tilling'. Already in imagination he clears various parts of the still virgin isle. Here he sees moist meadows where the earth is soft, here good vine-gardens, there again fields easy to plough, which would yield fine crops. He picks up a handful of soil and observes that 'there is fatness underground'. He admires the quiet roadstead sheltered from wind and wave, so that the ships would not even need mooring-cables. It is as though the landsman Odysseus has the soul of a colonizer. In these distant lands, still unpeopled or peopled only with monsters, he already sees the cities which his countrymen are going to build—and indeed are beginning to build.

Thus the attraction of the lands beyond the sea is as strong as the fear inspired by the sea. And what appears in the Odyssean legend is not only the desire of profit but the infinite curiosity the Greeks felt regarding the world and its wonders.

E

12. *Young Horseman (Inside of a cup by Euphronios, c. 510 B.C.)*

Odysseus never resists the desire to see strange marvels. Why does he make his way into the Cyclops' cave in spite of his comrades' entreaties? He tells us: it is partly because he hopes to persuade the Cyclops to present him with the gifts which it is customary to offer stranger-guests, but especially because he wants to see this strange creature, this giant who is not 'an eater of bread'; just as he wants to see Circe and to hear the Sirens. There is in Odysseus a feeling of great astonishment regarding the world and the things in it. Like all early men he thinks that nature is full of mysteries; he is afraid of it and this fear peoples it with monsters. But also he wants to see the mystery, and then penetrate it and understand it; last of all, to dominate, and make himself master of it. Therein he is a civilized man.

Before mastering nature, and the sea and the sea-routes, Odysseus has to face it in its terror and its charm. He peoples it with his dreams and hopes as well as with his fears. He in some sort reinvents it, filling it with marvels which it may belong to man one day to discover or invent. This power of reinventing man and the world is what gives so much value and charm to one of the most beautiful episodes in the *Odyssey*, the hero's adventures in the land of the Phaeacians and his meeting with Nausicaa.

Who are the Phaeacians? We need not look for them on a map. They are a happy people who, in the midst of a sea that they can navigate, dwell in wisdom and simplicity in a wondrously fertile land. This land, which is called Scheria, is an Eldorado, an isle of the golden age that time has spared. Here nature vies with art in beauty, splendour and virtue.

Never in the orchards of king Alkinoüs, do the trees cease from yielding fruit in every season:

> *. . . and there the trees grow tall*
> *And thrive, bright-fruited apples, pomegranates,*
> *Pears and sweet figs and olives in their bloom,*
> *Whereof the fruit nor perishes nor fails*
> *Winter or summer throughout all the year;*
> *But evermore the West wind as it blows*
> *Quickens some fruit to life and ripens other.*
> *Pear groweth old on pear, apple on apple,*
> *Cluster on cluster waxes, fig on fig.*[1]

The palace of Alkinoüs shines with a light like that of the sun and moon. Gold, silver and bronze dazzle the beholder's eye. Its doors are guarded by golden dogs

[1] Book VII, pp. 115–16.

which are alive—masterpieces of the divine artificer Hephaestus. It is a fairy-tale palace. In the Phaeacian Eldorado, golden morals prevail, Nausicaa has a heart of gold and her family is worthy of the earthly paradise. Seafaring with these people has remained in that golden age dreamed of by unhappy sailors who toil against billows and hurricanes. Phaeacian ships are thinking ships, which lead the mariner whither he would go, without fear of loss or damage in the mist.

Such is Scheria. It is also the land of singing and dancing. Assuredly there is a fairy-element here; but also, in the mind of the ingenious Greeks, the confused notion, clear enough to the imagination, that man might one day make the earth a marvellous garden, a country of wisdom and peace in which he would lead a happy life.

But the greatest marvel of Scheria is Nausicaa, the king's daughter, so gracious in her simplicity, as capable of washing the family linen as of receiving with dignity the stranger, naked as a savage, who comes out of the bushes to speak to her. Cast up on the shore by a storm the previous night, Odysseus had crouched among the leaves of a thicket on the edge of the wood. Meanwhile, that night, Nausicaa has had a dream in which Athene leads her to suppose that she will soon be married and that, for her wedding-day, she must wash the family linen in the stream that runs down to the beach. Nausicaa seeks her father and says:

> 'Couldst thou not, Daddy, order me a cart,
> A high one, with strong wheels, that I may take
> My nice clothes which are lying dirty by
> To wash them in the river? And besides
> 'Tis right that going to council with the kings
> Thou shouldst be clad in spotless robes thyself:
> And thou hast five sons living in thy halls—
> Two married, and three lusty bachelors—
> And they are always wanting new-washed clothes
> For dances: I must think of all these things.'
>   So said she; for she was ashamed to speak
> Of happy marriage to her father. . . .

But her father guesses this and replies:

> Nor mules I grudge thee, child, nor aught beside.[1]

So Nausicaa leaves with her servants and the linen. They wash it, trampling it in the stream with their feet, and stretch it out on the shingle of the beach. They make a picnic, then begin to play at ball. But the ball falls into the stream. The girls all

[1] Book VI, p. 102.

utter a cry and this awakens Odysseus. He, after breaking off a leafy branch to hide his nakedness, comes out of the wood. The servants run some distance away, in fright. Only Nausicaa awaits the stranger without flinching. And now Odysseus approaches and addresses the maiden whom he wishes, without scaring her, to win over to his plan, with a 'soft and cunning word'. He says:

> *Queen, I entreat thee: art thou of the gods*
> *Or mortal? If indeed thou art of those*
> *Who hold wide heaven, then to Artemis*
> *Child of great Zeus, nearest I liken thee*
> *For comeliness and dignity and breed;*
> *But if thou art of men who live on earth,*
> *Thrice-blessèd are thy sire and lady mother,*
> *Thrice-blessèd are thy brothers: well I wot*
> *Their heart is ever warm with joy of thee,*
> *Oft as they see thee entering the dance,*
> *So fair a flower. But over all men blest*
> *In heart is he, who shall prevail with gifts*
> *Of wooing and shall lead thee to his home.*
> > *. . . yet of a truth,*
> *In Delos once I saw a thing as fair,*
> *A young palm springing by Apollo's altar—*
> > *. . . so, when I saw that,*
> *I marvelled long at heart, for never yet*
> *Shot such a tree, so goodly, from the ground.*
> *So, lady, likewise do I marvel at thee*
> *And am amazed and greatly fear to touch*
> *Thy knees.*[1]

After this, he relates some part of his misfortunes, without however divulging his name, and asks Nausicaa to take him to her father. The rest happens as it ought to happen. The unknown stranger is generously entertained by the Phaeacians. He tells them his story and his name. They take him back to his country, where he will still have hard battles to fight against the lords who are pillaging his palace under pretext of courting his wife. And so at last, by courage, intelligence and affection, he rebuilds his threatened happiness.

Such are a few aspects of the *Odyssey* which became the most popular poem of a seafaring people, the poem in which Greek children, who learned to swim as soon as they knew how to walk, also learned to read, by construing and reciting it to-

---

[1] *Ibid.*, p. 105.

gether. Composed out of the still fresh experiences which a nation of landsmen had of the sea, this sailor's poem, full of combats and dreams, is also a poem of action. In the person of Odysseus it launched a brave and curious people toward the mastery of the sea. A few generations after the *Odyssey*, the Mediterranean from east to west was to become a Greek lake on which the main routes were mapped out and known. Thus Greek poetry is always connected with action; it springs from action and guides action by imparting a greater precision to it.

◎

It is not enough to say that the *Odyssey* is simply the poem of the sailor. Odysseus is much more than that. He incarnates one of man's essential attitudes in the face of nature and of what he still calls destiny. Faced by the various obstacles that confront him, Odysseus always meditates; before acting, he reflects. This is his first movement in the moment of greatest peril. Cunning as a savage, one might suggest. No; because on the primitive level of intelligence which is the level of cunning, he attains a pitch of refinement which is his alone. An artifice of Odysseus is the neat and simple solution of a problem, a solution that entirely satisfies the mind.

Here, for example, is a problem. Some men are imprisoned in a cave sealed by a rock which they cannot move. With them is a one-eyed giant who means to eat them; and some sheep which must go out to pasture. The reasoning is as follows: only the giant can remove the rock, therefore one must not kill the giant but make use of him by removing his power to harm. He has only one eye, therefore blind him: for that purpose, plunge him into sleep; therefore make him drunk. One must foresee the event of his calling for succour: therefore, whisper to him, without his suspecting, a negative reply to the question his comrades will probably ask him. Lastly, escape from the cavern by means of the only given factor which must inevitably leave the cavern, which the Cyclops cannot but allow to leave, namely the sheep. To reach this solution Odysseus forgets none of the data of the problem, material or psychological: he not only uses the stake of olive-wood and the wine-skin, but—what is his surest weapon—subtle words. Thus the short speech in which he addresses the Cyclops when offering to let him drink wine contains exactly the right words: words of reproach and the moral considerations of a man who has been wronged—all likely enough to blind the Cyclops to the unlikelihood of a gift. So, by making use of all the factors, Odysseus neatly arrives at the only possible solution of the problem. The whole thing works out like a theorem. But the mathematical nature of the artifice does not exclude a wealth of detail. The operation is conducted in masterly fashion. Under the hands of Odysseus and his men a stake which has been hardened in the fire is joyously twirled round in the Cyclops' eye. The roots of the eye shrivel. The story is adorned with a few artistic lies and gratuitous details; and Odysseus takes care not to forget the sheep but carries them off in his ship; especially does he greatly enjoy his artifice, both during and after the adventure. While he is still in the cave the invention of the name of 'Noman' which he has given himself for what it is worth, delights him.

> . . . *and my heart laughed*
> *That the smart trick I played them with my name*
> *Had so misled them. . . .*[1]

And at the moment when he is putting to sea, he cannot, despite his comrades' terror, resist the pleasure of calling out to the Cyclops and, so to speak, signing his stratagem. He sends him by word of mouth a sort of visiting card:

> *Say that it was Odysseus made thee blind,*
> *Sacker of fortresses, Laertes' son,*
> *Who dwells in Ithaca.*[2]

On another occasion, far more moving than the adventure with the Cyclops— which is not without a touch of humour—Odysseus remains most impressively master of himself. The occasion is that of the tempest which is finally to cast him up on the isle of the Phaeacians. Already Notus and Boreas, Eurus and Zephyrus are playing with his broken raft as if it were a toy. He is clinging to a plank, which is his only support, when there suddenly appears to him the goddess Ino, emerging from the waves and offering divine help in the form of a sail which will bear him up while swimming, if he trusts himself to the water. Wait! says Odysseus to himself. Is this a trap? Is the goddess really offering me safety? He thinks of what remains of his raft and concludes:

> *This will I do; it seems to me the best.*
> *So long as to their joints the timbers hold*
> *I will abide here and endure my troubles,*
> *But when the waves have smashed the raft to pieces*
> *Then will I swim: I see no better plan.*[3]

So Odysseus who believes in the gods, while knowing that they can be perfidious as well as favourable, trusts in the first place only to himself. When thrown into the sea, he swims on for two days, with all his might, and finally makes land at the mouth of a stream. His efforts have been rewarded.

[1] Book IX, pp. 154–55.   [2] *Ibid.*, p. 158.   [3] Book V, p. 95.

In the desperate struggle he wages against the sea, against destiny, to snatch from them his share of happiness, Odysseus' weapon is, along with courage, intelligence. It is of an entirely practical kind, a superior art of turning men and things to his advantage, while not forgetting the gods; an intelligence that wins to safety by means of a full wine-skin and an olive-pole placed in the right spot; or of some beams, planks and nails assembled with hammer-blows; and especially that wins to safety through that subtle knowledge of men in which he excels, with a well-turned compliment, a cunning speech, a lie which the poet calls 'faultless'; and also through the feelings he inspires: the beginning of love in Nausicaa, the youthful attachment of his son, the tender fidelity of his wife, the unswerving loyalty of his old servants, the swine-herd Eumaeus and the nurse Eurycleia, and others.

Odysseus represents practical, inventive intelligence: not a disinterested knowledge of the world, but the power and the will to find an answer to difficult circumstances by inventing 'devices', as the Greeks called them, devices to counter nature and the hostility of fate and the obstacles of every kind which the gods and his enemies place in his path and which separate him from happiness. One of the principal epithets of Odysseus is 'much-devising'.

He has made up his mind to recover or reconstruct his happiness, just as formerly he had constructed the marriage-bed with his own hands. He is the 'homo faber' or artisan-intelligence. In the course of the *Odyssey* we see him as carpenter, pilot, mason and saddler. He handles axe, plough and rudder as skilfully as he handles the sword. But the masterpiece of this good workman is his family happiness, and the patriarchal happiness of his subjects who are also his friends—a happiness he reconstructs by means of his 'faultless intelligence', as Homer says.

Odysseus, then, incarnates the struggle of mind to organize men's happiness in a world of which the laws seem like Scylla and Charybdis. It is an effort that heralds the effort of science to preserve man's life and increase his power over the world. By creating the personage of Odysseus, Homer and the Greek people performed an act of confidence in the power and value of intelligence.

CHAPTER FOUR

ARCHILOCHUS,
POET AND CITIZEN

There was a brilliant and continuous flowering of lyric poetry through the seventh and sixth centuries, so bright that even the rise of tragedy did not cause it to fade. It was lyric in both senses; in the old sense of a poetry that creates many forms of verse and stanza for the purpose of song; and in the modern sense, in that for the first time it directly expresses the poet's emotions, it responds in song to the events of his life, and is therefore personal. These two senses were united. The variety and mobility of emotional life, associated with the present, ordained both supple rhythms and a close connection with song. Even without musical accompaniment, modern lyric poetry remains song.

This lyric poetry, which was extraordinarily rich and abundant, is now one of the most devastated areas in Greek literature. One has to make a long search among the débris of philology to salvage a few fragments, sometimes a single verse or a word cited by a grammarian on account of a dialectical form or a metrical peculiarity to which it bears witness; sometimes a little more, but very little except for the great Pindar and the wearisome Theognis (how unjust!) who was recopied, revised and amplified for the use of schoolboys.

Leaving them aside, let us choose two flowers of extreme rarity. Archilochus was the first in date of the great European lyrists. His work is much mutilated. Not more than ten verses of any one piece of his have been preserved: but from these fragments the rest seem to derive. He rejected the manner and matter of epic, and the long verse-narratives in which Homer's successors became entangled. The novelty of his own verse is that it seems to dance to a measure in three-time; and in this he wrote love-poetry and satire, and denounced the old heroic values. And yet, despite his anarchical bent, he was fully engaged in the service of his city. The other flower of early lyric was Sappho, of whom one can only say that she was and remains unique.

◎

Archilochus was born in Paros. This island is a block of marble emerging from the Aegean. Immense wealth lay under a thin layer of earth, but it was still unproductive because in the seventh century sculptors and architects worked only in soft rock. For Archilochus, Paros was bare and bald, carrying a few goats that browsed among the rocks, a few fig-trees and vineyards, some meagre corn in the valley-bottoms, and a few fishing villages. Later on, when he left his birthplace, the poet wrote:

Heed not Paros and those figs and the life of the sea.[1]

In this poverty-stricken land, as everywhere else at that time in Greece, there were social distinctions. Nobles, who were slightly less poor than the rest, held the lands that were worth cultivating; they exploited the poorer folk. From time to time the latter rebelled. This social situation together with the barrenness of the soil forced the Parians from early times to emigrate. There was much talk of colonial expeditions in seventh-century Greece, and tales were current of gold-mines to be exploited and fertile land for farming in Thrace, to the north of the Aegean. Thrace was still occupied by savages unaware of the value of gold. Now Paros was connected, by religious cult, with Thasos, an island near the Thracian coast. Here, as often happens, the missionaries had opened the way for the colonists by introducing, two generations before the time of Archilochus, the cult of the goddess Demeter.

It was Archilochus' own father, Telesicles, who assembled the first company of emigrants. These men proposed to found a new city on Thasos and, no doubt, to conquer the island from the natives and from other colonists who had already arrived in large numbers. Later on, one would see about crossing the straits and exploiting Thrace. Telesicles did not forget to have his company and his plan blessed according to custom by the god of Delphi; at Delphi in fact the priests of Apollo maintained a kind of information service for emigrants. This took place in 684 B.C., when Archilochus was about twenty; but he did not accompany his father.

Archilochus was a bastard. His mother was a slave named Enipo, as he tells us in his verses. Indeed, far from denying his servile blood, he boasts of it. Son of a slave and a noble adventurer, he was none the less a citizen of Paros: for that purpose (we are still in the seventh century) it was enough for his father to have recognized him. The only legal consequence of his half-servile birth was that he

[1] This and the following passages from Archilochus are taken from *Elegy and Iambus* . . . edited and translated by J. M. Edmonds. London and New York, 1931, Vol. II. This quotation is fragment 51, p. 123.

had lost any right in the paternal succession. So this son of a slave, recognized by his father, was reduced either to vegetating on Paros or to seeking his fortune at the point of the sword. He tried each way in succession.

Remaining first on Paros, Archilochus fed not only on figs and fish, but on Homer's verses. Even though he was to make a quite different use of poetry, it was in contact with Homer, as the language proves, that Enipo's son became aware of his poetic vocation. It may be admitted that the substance of his early poems was furnished by the events of his life on Paros and also by the news he received from the colonists on Thasos.

The poem *On the Shipwreck* was inspired by a disaster at sea in which perished many of the first citizens of Paros, including his sister's husband. It is a poem of consolation but also of energetic comfort:

If he keeps complaining of woeful misfortunes, Pericles, no citizen will take pleasure in feasting, nay, nor city neither. 'Tis true these noble souls have been whelmed in the roaring sea and our hearts swell with grief; yet to woes incurable, my friend, the Gods have ordained the remedy of staunch endurance. Such things possess one man today, another tomorrow; and now they have turned our way and we bewail a bloody wound, but soon they will pass to others. Then quickly put thou womanish grief away, thou and thine, and endure.[1]

Further on the poet forces the accent to the point of provocation, in a conclusion which drew reproaches from the moralist Plutarch:

. . . for I shall no more heal a wound by weeping than make it worse by pursuing joys and feasts.[2]

The whole of Archilochus is in these lines, in this way of looking bereavement frankly in the face, even though it costs him the blame of men of principle. And here is the beginning and even the clear outline of satire in the poem he wrote about this time to a courtesan known by the name of 'Doll':

As the fig-tree on its rock feeds many crows, so doth the simple Pasiphilé (friend-of-all) receive strangers.[3]

It was apparently on Paros that Archilochus loved Neoboulé; and then, when the engagement was broken off, took the cruellest poetic vengeance on her. The

---

[1] *Elegy and Iambus*, II: Archilochus, No. 9, p. 103.   [2] *Ibid.*, No. 13, p. 105.
[3] *Ibid.*, No. 17, p. 107.

prospective father-in-law, Lycambes, had promised the poet his daughter in marriage; but later, for some reason that remains unknown, he repelled the suitor and even brought an action, accusing him, on what pretext we do not know, of being an outlaw and of having sought Neoboulé for her money. The poet's vengeance was terrible. He wreaked it in, among others, the poems known as epodes, which usually relate animal fables or fables with a key, and which are always directed against one or other of his enemies, and sometimes of his friends. First of all he settles his account with Lycambes:

Father Lycambes, what, pray, is this thou hast imagined? Who hath perverted the wits thou wast endowed with? Thou seem'st matter for much laughter to thy fellows now.[1]

And hast thou turned thy back on a great oath made by salt and table?[2]

O Father Zeus, 'twas no wedding I feasted at![3]

And he shall not come off scot-free for what he hath done unto me.[4]

Meanwhile, the poet served his one time prospective father-in-law with an appropriate fable. The eagle and the fox, although of different standing, like Lycambes and Archilochus, have made a treaty of friendship. But the eagle breaks the treaty; he feeds his eaglets on the fox's cubs and boasts that he is safe against reprisal. The fox knows he cannot grow wings and so take vengeance, but he prays Zeus to come to his aid:

O Zeus, Father Zeus, Thine is the rule of Heaven. Thou overseest the deeds of men, alike knavish and lawful: Thou takest account of the right-doing or wrong-doing of beasts.[5]

Dost thou see that high rock yonder, rough and malignant? Therein I sit preparing battle against thee.[6]

Zeus listens to the fox. One day when the eagle steals from the altar a sacrificial offering, he carries off, mingled with his prey, a burning brand which sets fire to his nest. The eaglets are burned and the fox avenged.

---

[1] No. 94, p. 147.   [2] No. 96, p. 149.   [3] No. 99, p. 153.
[4] No. 92, p. 147.   [5] No. 88, p. 145.
[6] No. 87, p. 143, ed. J. M. Edmonds. These are separate fragments which different editors arrange and *interpret* differently. It is not certain that No. 88 belongs to the poem of the fox and the eagle, although Professor Bonnard so interprets it—and very plausibly. The meaning of No. 87 is not perfectly clear. Professor Bonnard translates it into French as: 'Dost thou see that high rock . . . etc. 'Tis there he perches, the white-backed eagle, inaccessible to thy assault.' (Translator's note.)

The bitterest of Archilochus' epodes are directed against Neoboulé herself. It seems as though he will never have done insulting her, and in the coarsest manner. Now she is depicted as an old woman reputedly depraved, now as a stale courtesan or even as a 'fat harlot' from whom the men, including Archilochus, turn away in disgust. All this is seasoned with animal and other fables, in one of which Neoboulé is an amorous old lioness in quest of strong young lovers.

And yet at a previous time Archilochus had felt for Neoboulé a love exquisitely fresh and even keenly sensual. He depicted his beloved by means of a quite novel art, without literary idealizing or sentimental excuses:

She rejoiced with a branch of myrtle and the fair flower of the rose-tree in her hands, while her hair veiled her shoulders and her back.[1]

Or again:

. . . perfumed so of hair and bosom that e' en an old man would have loved them.[2]

Or again:

she is 'like a crow carried away with pleasure';

and

(she) flapped her wings like a halcyon on a jutting rock.[3]

Of himself he writes:

Wretched I lie, dead with desire, pierced through my bones with the bitter pains the Gods have given me.[4]

Or else:

but Desire that looseth our limbs, my comrade, overwhelmeth me.[5]
and I care neither for iambi *nor for rejoicings.*[6]

The nature of Archilochus is that of a passionate lover. Desire overwhelms him, and for a moment he is carried away by pleasure; or would be, at least, if he could grasp it. But let the object of desire elude him, then love is quick to change to hatred. His nature is at once sensitive and furious, vulnerable and violent and he appears to have found as much enjoyment in vengeance as in possession, in hatred as in love. His hatred is, moreover, more tenacious than his love. So when he is deprived of the love of Neoboulé, his rage is immediately, and for years, let loose against the flesh he had desired and is now insulting. In the same poem, one of the epodes, he says:

[1] No. 29, p. 113.   [2] No. 30, p. 113.   [3] No. 102, p. 155.
[4] No. 84, p. 141.   [5] No. 85, p. 141.   [6] No. 22, p. 109.

For such was the desire of love that twisted itself beneath thy (?)[1] heart and poured a thick mist over thine eyes, stealing the gentle wits from thy head.[2]

But he also, and in the same poem, mocks and insults her:

No longer doth thy soft skin bloom as it did; 'tis withering now.[3]

This is the poem which contains the lowest insults to the woman he had loved so violently; the grossest obscenities. Here, side by side, are the two movements:

I would that so I might be granted to touch Neoboulé's hand. . . .[4]

and throw myself on this eager vessel . . . . pressing thigh to thigh.[5]

In various passages the amplitude of hatred corresponds to the extent of the love experienced and bears witness to it. No doubt this obstinacy in rending those who have wounded him is what makes Archilochus the father of satiric poetry.

Having exhausted the delights of loving and insulting, our poet decided to answer an appeal from the colonists on Thasos to their countrymen of Paros, and to leave his native island. Military life in the service of a new city might perhaps cure him. The verses addressed to those he would persuade to follow him to Thasos are traversed with images of this wooded island:

but this isle stands like the backbone of an ass, crowned with savage wood.[6]

One must read the Greek to enjoy the charm of this 'pointed' rhythm, which, although in three-time, is really binary. Archilochus perhaps invented, if he did not borrow (and perfect) it from the tradition of his country's dances.

Our poet, then, set out with a new company of Parians for Thasos, about 664 B.C., some twenty years after his father; and from this time onward he fought for Thasos, with sword and pen.

But I am a servitor of Lord Enyalius, and yet I am skilled in the lovely gift of the Muses.[7]

He is now the War God's man-at-arms, and at the same time mouthpiece of the Muses. He says:

In the spear in my kneaded bread, in the spear my Ismarian wine, I recline, when I drink, on the spear——.[8]

an image of the hard and harassing life which was now to be his.

[1] Professor Bonnard construes this as 'my' and believes it refers to the poet himself.
[2] No. 103, p. 155.   [3] No. 100, p. 153.   [4] No. 71, p. 135.   [5] No. 72, p. 135.
[6] No. 21, p. 109.   [7] No. 1, p. 99.   [8] No. 2, p. 99.

But satire quickly resumes its sway. Archilochus loves military life. If his tongue is harsh to his comrades and biting as regards one or other of his leaders, it seems that this violence in satire stems only from an ardent love of soldiering. He has his knife into those who exploit and into those who ridicule the profession of arms. The vain and bedizened general and the braggart soldier are implacably caricatured by this brave fighting man. Here is a satire of the comrades who have been boasting of some ridiculous victory:

Of seven that lie dead whom we overtook in the pursuit, we are the thousand slayers.[1]

How far we are now from Homer! There is no question of 'singing the exploits of heroes', but of 'debunking' sham heroes.

Here is the would-be dictator, whether of Paros or Thasos:

But now the rule is with Leophilus, the power is with Leophilus, all belongeth to Leophilus, and I address Leophilus.[2]

Leophilus means 'Friend of the populace'—no doubt a sobriquet.

Here are the friends who have been promoted generals. There is the satire of Glaucus, one of the poet's oldest comrades with whom he had crossed land and sea, and shared perils and fears in common:

Look, Glaucus; the waves e'en now run high, and upright about the tops of the Gyrae stands a cloud, the token of a storm; fear cometh of the unexpected.[3]

And yet, when appointed general, this same Glaucus is rather too proud of his curls!

'*Sing of Glaucus the horn-fashioner*'[4] (referring, according to the Scholiast, to 'the hornlike bunching-together of the hair'—Translator).

I love not a tall general nor a straddling, nor one proud of his hair nor one part-shaven; for me a man should be short and bow-legged to behold, set firm on his feet, full of heart.[5]

Glaucus again is the timid but conceited deer of one of the epodes, the horned personage whom Neoboulé, now a courtesan, draws into her cave on the ground that, because of his beauty, he must succeed to her throne—and whom she ends by devouring. She looks for the heart, that choicest of morsels. Alas! the deer has no heart.

Others of the poet's friends are treated to virulent sallies; among them, that very

---

[1] No. 59, p. 129.   [2] No. 69, p. 133.   [3] No. 54, p. 125.
[4] No. 57, p. 127.   [5] No. 58, p. 127.

dear Pericles whom Archilochus reproaches in a violent diatribe with indulging his gluttony at the meals they take in common:

drinking much and unmingled wine, neither contributing thy cost; nor yet enterest thou invited as a friend unto friends, but thy belly hath sore beguiled thy mind and thy wits to have no shame. (Athenaeus, *Doctors at Dinner*, to whom we owe this fragment, says: 'Archilochus speaks of Pericles as breaking into banquets uninvited like the Myconians'.)[1]

After which he observes that his friend's family, on the father's side, is descended from a line famed for greed.

This Pericles was the hero of a fable celebrated in the ancient world, the fable of 'The Ape of Archilochus'. The ape who has been unsuccessful in his candidacy for a certain throne, wishes to retire into solitude. The fox (Archilochus), when travelling with him, prepares one of his tricks. While the two are passing a cemetery, the ape, who is merely a parvenu, pretends he recognizes the tombs of his ancestors' serving-men; whereupon the fox replies with a current proverb: 'The men of Carpathus refer to the hare.' Now everyone knew that there had never been hares in Carpathus. The fox meanwhile declares he has found a buried treasure and on this pretext takes the ape to a trap. The ape touches it so clumsily that he loosens the catch and is caught behind. The fox laughs at his hairless buttocks. 'What! Thou a king!' he cries, 'with such a rump, thou Ape....'[2]

Archilochus' satire spares neither friend nor foe. Was it a friend or an enemy who drew upon himself the ever sinister curse of the dog-star?

Many of them I hope the Dog-Star will wither up with his keen rays.[3]

Another terrible verse may be cited:

favouring the foe with woesome guest-gifts.[4]

Among other butts for satire are the soothsayer, who is scarcely or only just satirized in Homer; and the homo-sexual who appears now for the first time in Greek literature—to be flogged in the cruellest and crudest fashion. Other pictures, of boasters, prostitutes and procuresses, vigorously delineate the features which these types of future comedy were destined to take on; although with Archilochus there is as yet no question of traditional comic types, or 'masks', but of every kind of person whom he has met and known and who has wounded him in his feeling for human dignity. For in the poet's heart the fibres of tenderness and anger are so closely interwoven that they make his satire harder on those who are most dear to him.

[1] No. 78, p. 137. See Mr. Edmond's edition (Translator).
[2] No. 91, p. 145.   [3] No. 61, p. 129.   [4] No. 7, p. 101.

Yet in this mixture of friendship and hatred, the satiric note always prevails. When defining his art and comparing himself with the hedgehog, he writes:

The Fox knoweth many things, the Hedgehog one great thing.[1]

And elsewhere:

One great thing I know, how to recompense with evil reproaches him that doeth me evil.[2]

Albeit, this vulnerable man has to be the first to be wounded.

◉

But now comes a kind of satire which goes beyond that of fellow-soldiers and enemies, and yet is sharper than any—a satire of values.

The first step taken by the middle class in its attack on the nobility had been to claim not only the material goods but the cultural riches which were vaunted by the still-improvised aristocratic poetry. They were no doubt bourgeois poets, the men who composed the *Iliad* and the *Odyssey* on noble themes. But that had been a half century or more earlier. Since that time the humbler bourgeoisie had become aware of its strength. Archilochus belongs to this age and this rising class. He wants to be 'free', which means that he asserts his liberty of judgment regarding the moral traditions and poetical forms of the still dominant aristocracy. To create satire is, for Archilochus, to furnish an outlet for the claims of a new social class. This is not to say that Archilochus's satire contains any precise political claims. But concurrently with these claims which in his time gave rise to a class-war, the birth of a satiric vein in poetry is the affirmation of a new right: the right of the individual to pronounce his own judgment on the ideological foundations of society.

The use Archilochus makes of this right is liberal and even anarchical. He mocks a certain kind of life, the 'ideal' kind which was celebrated in epic but which Archilochus, in the age in which *he* is living, regards as an evasion from the virtues which the new type of man should display. What he hates and attacks are the values which have become false values.

He especially assails the exaggerated sense of honour which characterized Homeric poetry, as indeed it characterizes all feudal societies. Over against this honour ('aidos') which is merely submission to public opinion, Archilochus sets the demand of his individual nature which wishes to be sure of getting 'pleasure' out of life.

[1] No. 118, p. 175.   [2] No. 65, p. 131.

13. *Young Woman's head. Parian marble. This statue was erected on the Acropolis towards the end of the 6th Century; overthrown by the Persians in 480; then buried by the Athenians. It was rediscovered on the Acropolis at the time of the excavations of 1885–1889. It still bears · · ·es of paint*

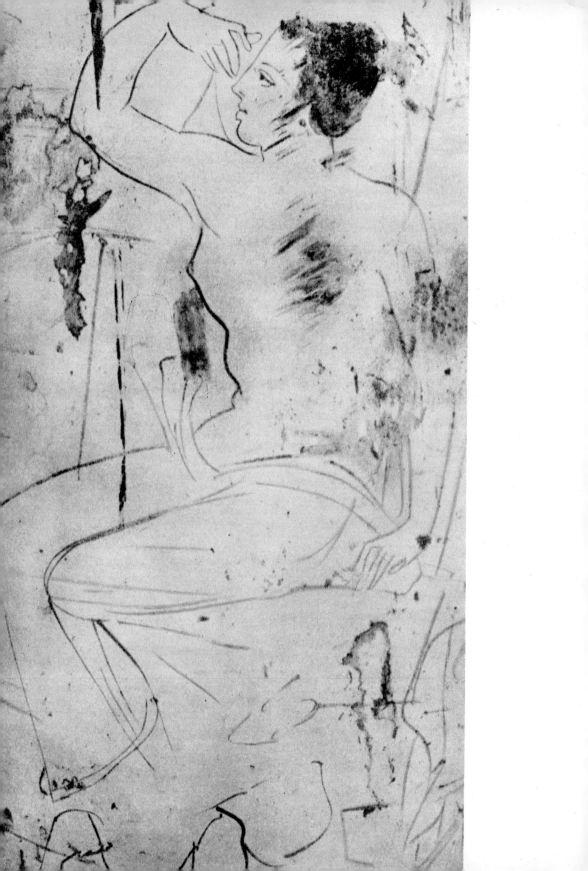

So he writes:

No man, Aesimides, would enjoy very many delights who heeded the censure of the people.[1]

What a difference, and how novel is the attitude when we compare it with a hundred or more appeals in the *Iliad*: 'Come now, cowards! In a moment ye will have made matters worse by yielding ground. Set honour in your hearts, and sense of shame.' The ethics that are defended by Archilochus, whatever their laws, reserve him pleasure in the first instance, and this he considers the principal justification for life and for its struggles.

In epic poetry, the hero's life and death were justified by glory. By glory Achilles, Hector and even Helen assure their existence in this world and win security against death through that kind of personal survival which the memory of future generations will confer on them. Archilochus, for his part, asserts that, however great the dead man has been, he is doomed to oblivion and even to insult:

No man getteth honour or glory of his countrymen once he be dead; rather do we pursue the favour of the living while we live; the dead getteth ever the worst part.[2]

Archilochus may not approve this base desertion of the dead, and yet he notes with a kind of harsh though indubitable pleasure that the attachment of the living only to the living is one of the laws of existence. This quiet negation of glory, which had been the highest value for the Homeric world, shows how vigorously his satire has freed itself from the trammels of tradition.

By making realism a basis for poetry as he does in this passage, Archilochus created a place for the feelings and beliefs of himself and his contemporaries. This satire of the outmoded Homeric virtues—what may be called the rejection of heroism as a source of inspiration—was the instrument for liberating men.

It is remarkable moreover that the liberty regarding social traditions which he strives to obtain is first of all exercised within himself and in respect of his own feelings. Let me recall the striking example of the 'Shipwreck' poem. In this elegy of consolation, the poet most sincerely associates himself and his city with the mourning that has come upon his friends and his sister. But a moment arrives when he wrenches himself free of the sincere affection he has expressed, but in which he does not wish to remain imprisoned. He decisively and in an almost provocative tone rejects a social constraint which is rooted in his own feelings but which would prevent him from living a life of pleasure. He says so, frankly, and in a manner once more to scandalize the moralists.

No. 8, p. 101.   [2] No. 63, p. 131.

F

14. *Woman at dressing-table. White lekythos (End of 5th Century)*

But there is another and more famous example of this anarchical attitude that overturns social conventions. This is the story which has caused many honest patriots, both in ancient and modern times, to blush for shame—patriots of whom many have never wielded a deadlier weapon than the pen—the story of the abandoned shield.

The shield I left because I must, poor blameless armament! beside a bush, gives joy now to some Saian, but myself I have saved. What care I for that shield? It shall go with a curse. I'll get me another e'en as good.[1]

It is clear Archilochus knows how to fight. But if it is necessary to leave his shield in order to save his life, he leaves it; and he says so, without boastfulness but with a sense of triumph: he has succeeded in 'remaining alive'! Observe, too, what follows: 'I'll get me another e'en as good.' For what purpose, except to fight another day? This soldier who saves his skin with the intention of resuming the fight is not a coward, but merely a sensible man. He does not take himself, either, for an epic hero. The poet who laughs over his misadventure, who laughs with joy at remaining alive, is no Homer. It is impossible not to feel, in the deliberate levity of these verses, how far Homer's heroism and the whole future poetical tradition that flows from it, have been audaciously rejected by the poet, in so far as they are conventional.

But if Archilochus had taken as sustenance for his verse the conventional, heroic themes, he would not be the founder of lyrism. He could only base this new poetry on the rebellion of the new type of man against the heroism which a caste was tending to reserve to itself and which was being celebrated in his time by a poetry now already academic. Archilochus wants to express himself as he is; whether brave or not is of little moment—but truthful.

It is not surprising that this emancipated individual should have been the first in ancient literature to relate the fable of the wolf 'of fierce nature' who refuses to wear the collar that has marked the neck of the dog with a shameful sore (Vide La Fontaine). 'To heal a sore of that kind', Archilochus knows a 'good cure'. This is freedom.

In this freedom which is apparently congenital in the poet, while at the same time connected with his contemporaries' efforts to liberate the individual—herein lies the new force of his genius as satirist.

But the wolf 'of fierce nature' is doomed to solitude. In one of his finest poems, of which only part has been preserved, Archilochus feelingly describes the bitterness of this solitude which is a necessary consequence of the satirical battle of which he is in the very forefront:

[1] No. 6, p. 101.

Soul, my soul, that art confounded with hopeless troubles, look up and defend thyself against thy enemies, setting a bold front against ambushes and standing nigh unto the foe firm-planted; and exult not openly if thou prevail, nor if thou prevail not lie wailing at home; but rejoice not overmuch in delightful things nor be vexed overmuch in ill, knowing what sort of temper possesseth man.[1]

For 'tis thy friends make thee choke thyself.[2]

Solitude, yes; but also valour in facing other men's viciousness, and wisdom in bending before the strokes of fortune. The poet is far from taking a romantic pleasure in his solitude; he fights against it and, to destroy it and also give a far wider meaning to his own emancipation, he constructs a moral system of his own.

The anarchical individualism that we found in Archilochus at the outset was not his final attitude: he was not a rebel against every rule. In his experience of life he finds the elements of an ethic, of a 'knowledge' of the 'rhythm of human life', which will allow him to express his individuality as well as possible, and, once this rule is discovered, to communicate it to his fellow-citizens.

The ancient poet rarely forgets that he is writing verse within the framework of a community of which he feels himself a member. It is no paradox to say that this anarchical individualist is an individual who has freely engaged himself. He was never sparing of his strength in the service of Thasos, a city he passionately adored. He fought for it like any other citizen. But in addition to this, he was a poet, that is, he had received the 'lovely gift of the Muses' to describe, for the benefit of his companions in arms, the hardships and the greatness of the struggle they waged in common.

Archilochus knows the soldier's toil and the seaman's thirst:

Come, go then with a cup all along the benches of the swift ship and draw drink from the hollow tuns, draining the red wine to the lees; for we no more than other men can stay sober on this watch.[3]

He has also faced the ordeal of hand-to-hand fighting, he describes 'the woeful work of the sword'.[4] He knows the terror that strikes the soldier at the approach of danger.

The purely military verse of Archilochus, describing battles between the rival cities that were disputing the mastery of Thasos and Thrace, was important enough for an historiographer of Paros to attempt later on to engrave an image of these struggles in stone, with the help of quotations from the poet. This monument, though much damaged, has been discovered. It was a kind of temple of Archilochus, such as used to be raised in honour of great men. Its mere existence

[1] No. 66, p. 131.　　　[2] No. 67, p. 133.　　　[3] No. 4, p. 99.　　　[4] No. 3, p. 99.

shows that our poet's verses were not those of an outlaw, but of a citizen devoted to the state and performing a double service, that of an esquire of the war-god and an artisan of the Muses.

This warlike poetry very rarely expresses the glory of arms. It would seem to be, above all, an exhortation to courage; it strives to be effective, a poetry of action. The old adventurer who has faced so many ordeals knows that in the last resort there is a virtue that triumphs over danger, when one loves one's country and leaves the rest to the gods, even if Archilochus himself has little belief in them and scarcely speaks of them. This virtue is courage.

It is not bestowed by man's 'heroic' nature, but is the kind acquired by the citizen who refuses to flinch. It is supported by the deep feeling of comradeship that unites soldiers who face death, which is the same for all men; but it refuses to share the risk of battle in the company of cowards.

Few feelings appear to me more profoundly Greek. Courage was the very foundation of ancient society, although it was oriented in different ways in different ages. It may or may not escape an attempt to transcend or 'idealize' it; but it is always there, common to Hector and Socrates, and Archilochus. It matters little whether it incline toward glory or toward wisdom, provided only that it maintain him, as he ought to be, standing upright.

Nor must we forget that it was not merely on the battlefield that Archilochus placed his courage and his muse at the service of the state. Certain fragments of his work, badly mutilated as it is, show that he took part in the political struggles of Thasos. 'In the very midst of discord', when 'even the scoundrel gains his meed of honour', Archilochus seems to have appealed to his fellow citizens in 'the thrice miserable city of Thasos'[1] to put to sea once more and found a city more just, one in which the wicked will not reign. This was to be the subject of his last epode.

But, even if this conjecture cannot be verified, we at least know from several isolated verses that Archilochus never begrudged his countrymen the resources of his heart. The servile blood which he never denied sometimes wrings from him a desperate cry, in an accent like that of Solon, such as this verse:

Ah ye, who die of hunger in my city, understand my words. . . .

It is certain that, once and for all, Archilochus had chosen the side of those who are 'dying of hunger'.

Tradition has it that he himself died in a battle between the men of Thasos and the men of Naxos, about 640 B.C.. Solon was born about then. In less than half a century his great voice was to resound in Athens.

---

[1] No. 129, p. 181.

◎

By virtue of his ardour in winning and defending new values against the feudal caste which was no longer in a position to maintain its dominance without having recourse to a now out-of-date ideology, Archilochus may be regarded as the first spokesman of the efforts that were to end in the fall of the aristocracies and the expansion of human personality within the framework of popular sovereignty; and finally in the new struggle which the first philosophers who were adepts of rational thought were to undertake against the old traditions.

With him, then, the poetry of heroism gives place to the poetry of wisdom and action.

CHAPTER FIVE

SAPPHO OF LESBOS,
TENTH OF THE MUSES

Sappho's heart is like a strange country, full of wonders. An 'enigma', a 'marvel', said the ancients. The terms are appropriate in their simplicity. An enigma her life and character certainly were, however variously they have been interpreted. Enigmatic and marvellous are words that apply still better to her poetry, mutilated though it may be.

At Mitylene on Lesbos, towards 600 B.C., Sappho presided over a sorority of young girls, which was devoted to Aphrodite, the Graces and the Muses. 'The home of the servants of the Muses' was what she called her house; later on, among the Pythagoreans and in Alexandria, the term 'Museum' was to be used. Sappho's institution was simply a school under the patronage of the feminine deities of love, beauty and culture. That this school should have had the form of a religious association is a fact not to be ignored. Community of worship established very strong links between the girls and their instructress. Sappho's poetry is in a sense a poetry of the mutual love which the devotees of the goddess bore each other. But it must not be supposed that the object she set before the girls under her charge was consecration to the deity. Sappho was in no way a priestess of Aphrodite. The fact was simply that in this period all educational establishments took the form of religious associations. The first philosophical, and medical, schools were in like manner religious fraternities. They did not for that reason educate priests of Aesculapius. But just as physicians educated the devotees of that god in the art of healing, so Sappho, with the help of the goddess, tried to teach the girls of Mitylene an art of living—the art of being women.

Music, dancing and poetry were much cultivated in Sappho's circle. Yet the house of the Muses was no more a conservatorium or an academy than it was a seminary. The arts were not taught for their own sake, still less for professional purposes. Sappho's object was to assist the girls who lived with her, through this life in common and through the practice of the arts, the cult of Aphrodite and of the Muses, to realize in the society in which they were shortly to take their place an ideal of feminine beauty which the goddesses they honoured had been the first to incarnate.

These young girls would marry. Herself married and mother of a little girl whom she compares to 'a golden flower', it was simply for marriage regarded as the full realization of woman in beauty and joy, that Sappho prepared the girls who were committed to her charge.

This implies that the status of woman in Lesbos was very different from her status in most of the other Greek cities—a point we shall return to. It is certain that at Mitylene woman animated the life of the city with her charm, her dresses and her wit. As in all the Aeolian lands, marriage brought her into men's society as an equal; one recalls the example of Andromache. She shared in the musical and poetic culture of the time. She was man's rival in the field of the arts. Now if Aeolian customs reserved a position of this kind for the wife, it is not surprising that they should also have required schools in which girls were educated to play the part that was expected of women.

The pupils of the Muses prepared themselves, under the instruction of their senior, to incarnate in the city of Mitylene the perfections of Aphrodite. All Sappho's verses are illumined by the brilliance of feminine beauty. Woman's face, according to Sappho, should be bathed in moving gleams of light; her eyes should be filled with grace, her steps should inspire love. The aim of culture is the acquisition of beauty. Attentive to the gifts and lessons of Aphrodite, her guide and model, the goddess who teaches her to love the flowers and the sea, who reveals the charm of the outer world and above all the captivating beauty of woman's body, the young girl grows in nobility and grace, while beauty exalts her features, makes her happy and spreads over her whole person that abundant joy which Sappho hails as a stellar light.

In a festal atmosphere and, as it were, under the eyes of the goddess of whose coming power over their lives they were now growing aware, the girls led a semi-monastic existence, rigorous and also fervent; but instead of being directed towards celibacy, their thoughts were inclined towards meeting the bridegroom. The poetic culture that Sappho inculcated in the ardent stanzas expressing the omnipotence of Aphrodite, which the chorus of young girls sang in unison, was what the ancients called an 'erotic', or culture of love. Side by side with their senior in whom Aphrodite had long had her dwelling, the girls were slowly, and through joy and sorrow, initiated into their vocation as women. They began to feel their hearts and senses developing and, if their destiny called them to it, they awakened to passion.

How ardent was the affection which this kind of education aroused between Sappho and her friends, under that burning sky where Cypris reigned supreme, we learn from her verses. For it was in poetry that this lovely heart found freedom, in presence of the beauty she had tended and reared.

> *Je le vis: je rougis, je pâlis à sa vue;*
> *Un trouble s'éleva dans mon âme éperdue;*
> *Mes yeux ne voyaient plus, je ne pouvais parler.*
> *Je sentis tout mon corps et transir et brûler.*

In these matchless verses Racine, after many others, sounds an echo of Sappho's cruellest poem. Here is a translation of it, as literal as our language will allow:

It is to be a god, methinks, to sit before you and listen close by to the sweet accents and winning laughter which have made the heart in my breast beat so fast and high. When I look on you, Brocheo, my speech comes short or fails me quite, I am tongue-tied; in a moment a delicate fire has over-run my flesh, my eyes grow dim and my ears sing, the sweat runs down me and a trembling takes me altogether, till I am as green and pale as the grass, and death itself seems not very far away....[1]

We are in the circle of passion, where Eros is lord. Desire strikes and Sappho counts the blows. This poem describes a combat. Attacked in her flesh by Eros, the assurance Sappho had had in the control of her organism, she now sees crumbling a little more after each assault. All the sensations that bind us to the world around, that assure us of our existence, of images and sounds, of the regular beating of the heart and the flow of blood to the face—all these escape her in succession. She loses control over her organs, one after the other, and, beside herself, as it were, she dies with each of them. She dies with her swooning heart, with her throat deprived of the power of sound, with her tongue which is suddenly dry; the fire spreads through her veins, her eyes refuse their office, her ears now hear only the throb of the arteries, her whole body begins to tremble; she is as livid as a corpse. But now, having seen her various organs deprived by passion of their power, having, so to say, experienced these partial deaths, she must now undergo the death of her inmost being. The malady which is invading her is faced, in its triumphant advance, only by the consciousness of the self, deprived of its natural means of support. This in turn it submerges; and the subject becomes paradoxically aware that she is dead—a 'not very far' removes the absurdity, though only by a hair's breadth. The concluding verses read:

> *and death itself seems not very far away.*

[1] Fragment 2. This and the following translations of Sappho are taken from *Lyra Graeca*, edited and translated by J. M. Edmonds ... in three volumes. London and New York, 1922, Vol. I, pp. 140–307.

Nowhere is Sappho's art more bare than in this ode; nowhere are her verses more strangely physiological. Here we have nothing but facts—the strict and exact notation of the physical effects of desire. There are very few adjectives, or the adjectives which contrive, in the love-lyric, to clothe physical phenomena with sentiment. Here we meet verbs and nouns; it is an art that deals with things and events.

In all this the soul has little or no share. The body might summon it to help, might throw the burden of its suffering on the soul; but in fact it would be enough for Sappho to take refuge, for her physical pain, in some such alibi as jealousy, hatred or the sadness due to separation. Sorrow serves as a kind of morphine. At the origin of this poem a philologist has detected the departure of a girl friend, who is to be married, from the house of the servants of the Muses. The man whom the first verses show seated beside the object[1] of Sappho's passion is no doubt the fiancé. But the poem says nothing about the grief of the parting. Sappho does not brood complacently over this feeling, or abandon herself to grief in order to escape her torment. It is solely and wholly the suffering of the body that occupies her; all she knows of her love is this deafening and blinding storm which has been let loose in her body.

She has nothing to conceal; her art is candid, straightforward, and true. She blushes for none of the things that are happening to her. She says: *tongue* and *ears*; *sweat* and *trembling*. Such poetry is poles apart from the pleasant. It is not pleasant to be sweating. Sappho streams with sweat; she is neither ashamed of it nor does she glory in it, she simply notes it.

Sappho does not describe the object of her desire. This remains outside our grasp; all that she notes—and this in a word and with unflinching accuracy—are the events that centre round this object. But in what does the dramatic action culminate? Simply and indubitably in the destruction of the organism by passion.

A fire is burning in the darkness. The poetess places it at the heart of a broad zone of shadow. In her art there is nothing—no feeling whatsoever, no description of the beloved object—to turn us away from the flame, but it must burn in solitary triumph and so accomplish its work of destruction. This light in the midst of darkness is Sappho's passion.

The literary historian can marvel, for here he is in presence of a beginning. Euripides, Catullus and Racine have spoken of love in Sappho's accent, but Sappho in her own. She is new. In vain one listens to other and older voices, such as Andromache to Hector:

[1] Mr. Edmonds' translation appears to regard the object as a man (Translator).

> *...No, Hector, thou to me*
> *Art father, mother, brother, as thou art*
> *My husband full of life.*[1]

Paris to Helen:

> *...come, let us go to bed and take our pleasure:*
> *For never hath desire so lapped my heart,*
> *Not even when I snatched thee first away*
> *From lovely Lacedaemon ...*
> *   ...and lay with thee*
> *In Cranaë's isle, as I do love thee now*
> *And sweet desire has taken hold of me.*[2]

Archilochus says of Neoboulé:

> *...her hair veiled her shoulders and her back ... (she) was perfumed so of hair and*
> *bosom that e'en an old man would have loved them.*[3]

This is Mimnermus remembering Nanno:

> *But what life would there be, what joy, without golden Aphrodite? May I die when I*
> *be no more concerned with secret love and suasive gifts and the bed, such things as are*
> *the very flowers of youth....*[4]

Each of these voices has its personal accent; yet how strangely distinct from all of them is the resonance of Sappho's voice! Less individual are the tenderness of Andromache, or Paris's sensual invitation to scornful Helen, or the straight, bold, self-contained glance of Archilochus at Neoboulé, or Mimnermus' melancholy when remembering Nanno. No, Sappho is unique, Sappho burning and grave.

Never before this had Eros burned. He had heated the blood and warmed the heart; had persuaded to self-sacrifice, to enjoyment, to tenderness; he had never burned and destroyed. To each of his victims he gave something, courage, pleasure or the sweetness of regret. But to Sappho he gives nothing, he takes everything away.

A god without senses. 'Invincible' and 'indiscernible' are the notions conveyed by a word she elsewhere applies to him. He cannot be trapped; he both disconcerts and discourages. He invites opposites, for his sweetness is bitter. His shape cannot be imagined. Whereas the figure of Aphrodite shines clearly in Sappho's verse, Eros is clothed in no human form; the vigorous young archer with the unerring

---

[1] *Iliad*, Book VI. Trans. Sir William Marris.   [2] *Ibid.*, Book III.
[3] Trans. J. M. Edmonds. *Elegy and Iambus*, Fragments 29 and 30, *ed. cit.* Vol. II, p. 113.
[4] Trans. J. M. Edmonds, *Ibid., ed. cit.*, I, 89.

aim does not appear in any of her surviving verses. One would think that the type had not been invented, though this is not certain; in any case, Sappho was not free so to represent him. For her Eros is a mysterious force that invades one's limbs and 'undoes' them. She perceives him only through the torment he inflicts on her, and her mind labours to discover his face. The secret and invisible being who is now in her can only be expressed by metaphor, and the images that confer poetical existence on him reveal his brutal and insidious nature. They are borrowed from the blind forces of the physical world or from the alarming movements of a wild beast:

Lo! Love the looser of limbs stirs me, that creature irresistible, bitter-sweet. . . .[1]

The translation here is almost crushed beneath the heaviness of the words. A single adjective conveys the sweetness and bitterness of Eros and thus points to his incomprehensible nature. The word translated by 'creature' means a creeping animal. 'Love' for Sappho has no wings, he is a snake. As to the word 'irresistible' (that is, 'devices' fail against it) one feels in the Greek word the impotence of *homo faber* to reduce this untamed force. The words rendered by 'irresistible creature' mean more or less: 'Eros, the beast who cannot be trapped.'

A creeping animal, a monstrous creature, an imperious as much as an unthinkable force, such is Eros making his way through Sappho's limbs. Here is another metaphor taken from the natural world:

As for me, love has shaken my heart as a downrushing whirlwind that falls upon the oaks.[2]

Sappho's experience of love is of a whirlwind which leaves her lying prostrate, understanding nothing. This force, without thought or feeling, threatens to uproot her soul. As formidable to man as savage beast or tempest, passion is known to its victim only as a destructive deity.

And yet she confronts these storms. Beyond the zone of tempests she preserves within herself a sky immutably serene. A golden dream dwells in this ravaged heart.

◎

Every passion has an object. The pleasure or pain with which it pierces us drives us towards or away from it. We yield ourselves to suffering as we do to the night which will bring back the day. But what *was* the object of Sappho's passion? This enquiry leads us into the most mysterious regions of her poetry, and also the least

---

[1] *Ibid.*, No. 81, p. 239.　　　　　　　[2] No. 54, p. 223.

explored, despite the uncouth hypotheses which unpoetical philology has scattered along the way.

There can be no question of specifying the name or sex of this object. What Sappho does not divulge and what we sometimes learn only by a chance gender (when some philologist's zeal for virtue has not corrected the revealing termination), is not for us to trace beyond the text or, as it were, by breaking into the text. And the text, speaking by itself, reveals poetical horizons far wider than any historical consideration that might arise from knowledge of civic status or from observation of a sexual perversion.

What was there in this object to inspire passion? Let us recall a few verses of the poem we have already analysed:

. . . and listen close by to the sweet accents and winning laughter which have made the heart in my breast beat so fast and high.

Nothing else and nothing less. A sound breaks on the ear and no more than this is needed to set body and soul on fire.

When I look on you . . . in a moment. . . .

The most fleeting perception, that of a sound, or a mere glimpse of the beloved object, are enough to unleash passion in its fullest extent.

How astounding is the contrast between the exiguity of the cause and the intensity of the effect! The area of passion which this poem traverses is as vast as the view which it gives us of the object is limited. We know everything about her suffering, we exhaust it in detail; but of the beloved object we know only of the voice and the laughter. Yet this object without being described imposes its authority. 'What!' you will say, 'so much suffering for so slight a cause!' But we know that the cause was not slight.

In all the fragments of Sappho's verse which express passion, however little the length or richness of the passage allow us to detect the process of poetical creation, the movement of passion and the poetry that communicates it arise always at the opposite pole from any description or enumeration of the qualities of the beloved. It is enough, every time, for a single quality of the beloved to utter its appeal, and the whole organism is overthrown. In the midst of this confusion and in response to this appeal, poetry gushes as from a fountain.

The appeal arises from a simple gesture; the steps of an absent woman, the brightness of a vanished face, the delicacy of a girl's throat, a head crowned with flowers, the gracefulness of an arm that is being raised. It can even be the lack of grace:

I loved you, Atthis, long ago, when my own girlhood was still all flowers, and you—you seemed to me a small ungainly child.[1]

The departure of this ungainly child, who leaves Sappho's house for the rival school of Andromeda, is enough to provoke the outburst we have already cited but must now refer to the occasion that gave rise to it:

Lo! Love the looser of limbs stirs me, that creature irresistible, bitter-sweet, but you, Atthis, have come to hate the thought of me, and run after Andromeda in my stead.[2]

Thus Sappho's passion and poetry obey calls which are so tenuous that they may be called 'signs'. This poetry of signs—a symbolism in the first meaning of the word—is at the opposite pole to descriptive poetry. A sign is not a description. Descriptive poetry has something of the style of a passport. After enumerating the features of a face or the elements of a landscape, it often forgets that things and persons declare themselves to us in an unforeseen gesture or an accidental appearance more fundamentally than by an analysis of their elements. The tone of a voice or the memory of the way a friend walks pierces Sappho with pleasure or suffering. By such signs is the lover assured that the beloved is irreplaceable; and that is why they can convey her to him entirely, as though the vital presence obeys the call of the particular sign. This sign binds and subjects us to the object, and in this subjection we find pleasure.

There is nothing that increases the power of the beloved object over Sappho more than absence:

See to it then that you remember us, Anactoria, now that we are parted from one of whom I would rather the sweet sound of her footfall and the sight of the brightness of her beaming face than all the chariots . . . of Lydia.[3]

Anactoria is absent. Two images of her strike the poetess who loves her. Of course a swarm of images fly round her, but a poet does not register them all. One or a very few suffice to evoke the being whom the poet desires. Two images present Anactoria: the sound of her footfall, and a face beaming with the light of stars, a face of stellar brightness.

So, by two signs, absence becomes presence. There are nights when the call of the absent one grows stranger, more mysterious. In the stillness of night, when the outer world lies hushed, and body and soul in the lonely bed grow heavy with longing and regret, a voice, at once voice and light, approaches on invisible waves, penetrating the darkness. To perceive its presence, the blind senses feel as it were into the shadows and strain towards the beloved object.

[1] No. 48, p 221.   [2] No. 81, p. 239.   [3] No. 38, p. 209.

A certain Arignota[1] had once lived in Mitylene among the girls in Sappho's establishment. She had loved the tender Atthis who was another of the poetess's friends; and then, later, had gone to live in Lydia on the opposite coast. Sappho shares the sorrow of Atthis to whom she addresses the following poem. She recalls the joys of the life they had shared with Arignota; with her she listens to the voice of the absent friend which from distant Sardis is trying to reach them. By the very nature of the emotions expressed, this poem is very difficult to interpret:

Atthis, our beloved [Arignota[2]] dwells in far-off Sardis, but she often sends her thoughts hither, thinking how once we used to live in the days when you were like a glorious goddess to her and she loved your song the best. And now she shines among the dames of Lydia as after sunset the rosy-fingered Moon beside the stars that are about her, when she spreads her light o'er briny sea and eke o'er flowery field, while the dew lies so fair on the ground and the roses revive and the dainty anthryse and the melilot with all its blooms. And oftentime while our beloved wanders abroad, when she calls to mind the love of gentle Atthis, her tender breast, for sure, is weighed down deep with longing; and she cries aloud for us to come hither; and what she says we know full well, you and I, for Night that hath the many ears calls it to us across the dividing sea.[3]

One hesitates to speak further of this poem. No commentary can retain such fluid beauty in its meshes. And yet, by dwelling further on it, we may hope to enjoy the pleasure twice over.

Like other poems of Sappho's, this one is associated with silence and starlight. The smallest gleam of light acquires more value in the darkness, the sense of hearing grows more acute. At the same time the inner world of memory and longing and regret, liberated now by the stillness and the dark, confers a secret meaning on every sound or gleam that reaches us. The moon has sailed up over the sea, like a rose-pink shape risen out of Asia. Is it the moon? Or maybe a sign from Arignota?

A light spreads over the wavelets and the fields. Is it indeed the moonlight or the brightness of our friend's beauty? It is as though the poetess's mind were hovering, hesitant, before this lunar vision; it is as though Sappho could see a phantom mounting into the sky, reaching to her feet, touching the flowers in her garden.

[1] Or possibly the 'Anactoria' mentioned above (Translator's note).

[2] The correct reading of the first three verses is doubtful. Mr. J. M. Edmonds whose translation is quoted here, follows W. von Wilamowitz-Moellendorff in reading 'Anactoria'. Monsieur Bonnard may have better authority for Arignota (Translator's note).

[3] No. 86 (A letter to Atthis), ed. cit., p. 247.

The vision lingers an instant among the flowers, and they awaken to new life in the coolness of dawn.

Then suddenly the vision is effaced, and something else more precise and insistent takes its place. The call of the moon-ray becomes the call of a voice, and a cry is heard, high and tenuous like the cries heard in dreams; for the atmosphere of the poem is that of a dream. Strange words are seeking to traverse space and penetrate the soundless zone in which the dreamer is isolated. Arignota is speaking, heavy with desire for Atthis, heavy with regret. Her words have an unmistakable meaning; she is commanding Atthis and Sappho to rejoin her. But—and here the dream-like character of the poem is most striking—if the message the words transmit is certain, they cannot be understood *as words*; they are imperceptible and mysterious. It is as though they carried a second meaning which is unattainable. The ear strains to catch them in the night-silence, or rather the night itself becomes 'many ears' to hear and convey the message; and yet what it hears is incomprehensible.

In these verses Sappho's poetry has become detached from the material world to which she seemed to be chained when telling of her physical torments, and takes up its dwelling among dreams. And it is the absence of the friend that enables this to happen. The beings who move in the poetic world to which she admits us exist in the ineffable manner of those who people our dreams. There is nothing vagu about them; on the contrary, we have an extremely precise feeling about their existence, we are more certain of their presence than of the presence of ordinary beings. The message they send us is in no wise ambiguous. And yet the very strong feeling we have regarding their reality is almost entirely detached from the perceptions which usually assure us of the existence of objects. If to make themselves heard they borrow the language of the senses, show themselves and speak to us, this sensory appearance is a sort of disguise and it is not by this disguise that we recognize and understand them. Arignota is not recognized and understood in the lunar form she takes on or in the incomprehensible words she utters. It is beyond the language of the senses that her presence is perceived. Sappho's poetry seems here to have accomplished the miracle of enabling us to reach out, beyond the world of appearances, to what one is tempted to call pure presences.

This, in any event, is becoming clear, that Sappho has discovered a new kind of reality. The moon and the silence of night—a silence full of voices—is both distinct from Arignota and connected with her by a close and secret bond. And this bond between Arignota and the moonbeams, between the friend and the voice in the night, is at the very heart of Sappho's verse. To be more precise, the meeting point of these objects of sensibility—Arignota and the visions of the night—is the real object of Sappho's passion.

◎

Let us read a few more fragments.

> *The moon is gone*
> *And the Pleiads set,*
> > *Midnight is nigh;*
> *Time passes on,*
> *And passes; yet*
> > *Alone I lie.*[1]

Around the fair moon the bright beauty of the stars is lost them when her silver light illumines the world at its fullest.[2]

The Moon rose full, and the maidens, taking their stand about the altar. . . .[3]

. . . and we maidens spend all the night at this door, singing of the love that is between thee, thrice happy bridegroom, and a bride, whose breast is sweet as violets. But get thee up and go when the dawn shall come. . . .[4]

. . . and [the cricket] pours down a sweet shrill song from beneath his wings when the Sun-god illumines the earth with his down-shed flame outspread.[5]

Thus of old did the dainty feet of Cretan maidens dance pat to the music beside some lovely altar, pressing the soft smooth bloom of the grass.[6]

And as for [the doves] their heart grows light and they slacken the labour of their pinions.[7]

> *. . . and crowned with a wreath of flowers tied about your head. . . .*[8]

. . . but do you, Dica, let your dainty fingers twine a wreath of anise-sprays and bind your lovely locks; for it may well be that the blessed Graces, too, are more apt to look with favour on that which is adorned with flowers, whereas they turn away from all that goes ungarlanded.[9]

I have a pretty little daughter who looks like a golden flower, my darling Cleis, for whom I would not take all Lydia, nay nor lovely [Lesbos].[10]

Sappho's marriage songs, which we have not yet touched on, were chanted at

---

[1] Trans. J. M. Edmonds. No. 111, p. 263.   [2] No. 3, p. 189.   [3] No. 112, p. 263.
[4] No. 47, p. 219.   [5] No. 94, p. 253.   [6] No. 114, p. 265.   [7] No. 16, p. 195.
[8] No. 82, p. 241.   [9] No. 117, pp. 265, 267.   [10] No. 130, p. 273.

15. *Woman's head and coiffure (Archaic sculpture, 6th Century)*
16. (Overleaf, left) *Maenad carrying thyrsus, in the troop of Dionysus (Detail of vase-painting, c. 500 B.C.)*
17. (Overleaf, right) *Solon (Copy dating from the first century A.D. after a bronze original later than 300 B.C.)*

festivals in the city or neighbouring villages by the girls of her school. These verses show how sensitive she was to the pleasant aspects of nature; how deeply the mystery of trees and animals affected her. Thus:

Evening Star that bringest back all that lightsome Dawn hath scattered afar, thou bringest the sheep, thou bringest the goat, thou bringest her child home to the mother....[1]

Or again:

*Like the pippin blushing high
On the tree-top beneath the sky,
Where the pickers forgot it—nay,
Could not reach it so far away.*[2]

Or again:

Thy form, O bride, is all delight; thy eyes are of a gentle hue; thy fair face is overspread with love; Aphrodite hath done thee exceeding honour.[3]

Nature is omnipresent in Sappho. The spectacle of the starry firmament, the sight of a branch shaken by the wind, awoke in her soul echoes that no other Greek has given us. Since her time neither Aristophanes, rich and varied as are the concerts in which the swans on the banks of Hebrus, or the Muses on Olympus, the nightingale in the bush or that other bird on the ash-tree bough, are his performers; nor Theocritus dreaming the city man's golden dream of country holidays —neither poet has touched those delicate threads that link the world of trees and wild things and wind and sea so strangely to the movements of the human heart. Theocritus, at most, in *The Witches*, or Euripides, who is always in the vanguard of ancient poetry, in his portrayal of the torments of Phaedra, had perhaps a glimpse of this connection; but in these instances it is a question of verses that are reminiscent of Sappho.

Before her time there was, of course, as always at the sources of Greek poetry, the inexhaustible genius of Homer. He assuredly loved nature; or rather he *knew* her, he saw right through her inflexible laws, he perceived in her an order essentially foreign to man. But the abysses of ocean, the cruel rocks and shattering storms which make up Homer's nature, a nature full of gods, and, it is true, of gods in human form who express the swarming multiplicity of life, are not only hostile to man but impenetrable. This nature is so fundamentally inhuman that man's heart can find no attachment in her, can seek no consolation from her, can even hear no echo of his torments.

---

[1] No. 149, pp. 285, 287.　　　[2] No. 150, p. 287.　　　[3] No. 158, p. 293.

G

18. *Gathering Olives (6th Century Amphora)*

In Sappho on the contrary, nature, emptied now of mythical beings, has suddenly become full of presences, friendly presences, sensitive to the movements of the soul. Sappho lies awake, alone with her passion:

> *The Moon is gone*
> *And the Pleiads set. . . .*
> *Alone I lie.*

The moon sets, familiar stars go out, time passes. . . . No, Sappho is not alone because she still has the night. In this presence of night and stars, of flowers and songs of birds, and tender young bodies—in this presence of all the strange and blooming loveliness of things—we now catch a glimpse of what lies beyond the desolate regions of love poetry, a glimpse of new poetical worlds in which the cult of nature restores joy to the poet's heart.

So the desert blooms and Love is now evoked in the midst of roses, or stars, at the heart of the world's splendour. Beyond the sphere of bitterness, Sappho's poetry knows the sweetness of Eros. The god who tortures her has been placed by her in the centre of a magic circle. Her verses conjure up the passion confronted without flinching and the cruelty of desires laid bare, by the magic of natural presences. Eros is now crowned with flowers. Thus enwreathed he does not appear less cruel; but his cruelty is at least adorned with beauty. It is as though the poetess is growing more attentive; as though Nature and Love are listening to each other.

We are on the threshold of the mystery. This nameless form that looses the limbs and threatens life itself, lo, is suddenly changed to delight. The desire for the enigmatic absence-presence of the young girl, longed for in secret, is now fulfilled with dainty gestures, graceful dances and music and innocent games. Heavy was the flesh in the lonely night-watches, but there came an hour when, under the beauty of the spangled firmament, it was at length consumed; when the fire that burned it was converted into light. Linked to the peace of night-time and the glittering constellations, the image of the absent one now raises up the too heavy flesh and turns into sudden joy the long disquietude of Eros. Song of birds, brightness of flowers, rustling of branches—what are these but responses to the call of desire? The beauty you seek, I give you. So in the end poetry becomes a plenitude of the soul; and it is as though the sensual sound it emitted were suddenly and by magic resolved into the harmonics of chastity that accompanied it—and that were already perceptible in the sensual phase.

The work of Sappho is a meeting place, where nature and love join and are interpenetrated; where the fire of love and the freshness of the world mingle in one movement.

You are come; it is well; I was longing for you, and now you have made my heart to flame up and burn with love. Bless you, I say, thrice bless you, and for just so long as you and I have been parted.[1]

◎

Sappho grasps and expresses the correspondences that exist in our hearts between nature and love. The emotion she receives from the beauty of the outer world and the tenderness she feels for her friends are woven together into the same poetical fabric. One may judge of this from a rather longer fragment in which, however much the papyrus which preserves it has been damaged, the pleasure given by flowers and the melancholy that attaches to the departure of loved ones are heard echoing, as it were, together.

So I shall never see Atthis more, and in sooth I might as well be dead. And yet she wept full sore to leave me behind and said 'Alas! how sad our lot; Sappho I swear 'tis all against my will I leave thee'; and I answered her 'Go your way rejoicing and remember me, for you know how I doted upon you. And if you remember not, O then I will remind you of what you forget, how dear and beautiful was the life we led together. For with many a garland of violets and sweet roses mingled you have decked your flowing locks by my side, and with many a woven necklet made of a hundred blossoms your dainty throat; and with many a jar of myrrh, both of the precious and of the royal, have you anointed your fair young skin....[2]

In a poem like this Sappho seems to have caught the invisible waves that run from the world to our hearts, from our hearts to the world; for poetry now knows, what chemistry knows in a different way, that between our being and the world there is an affinity of substance.

Herein lies the poetic discovery peculiar to Sappho, the one that shows us in her poetry an anticipation of modern poetry. Her dream participates simultaneously in the two worlds which our mind is always questioning: what we call the outer world on one side, and on the other the world of feelings within ourselves. Whereas the majority of ancient poets, when evoking nature or describing love, evoke them successively or in parallel, as though they thought these two universes were different, Sappho is aware that physical nature and the human consciousness are one and the same thing, identical in substance as in properties, because there is nothing in the movements of passion that is not sensitive to natural phenomena. The world of the heart which stands at the finest, extremest point of the natural world, experiences and echoes every oscillation of it. In Sappho's poetry these two

[1] No. 89, p. 249.   [2] No. 83, pp. 241, 243.

worlds are interpenetrated one by the other and, at one and the same time, speak the same language.

What is this language and what is the name of this single reality that Sappho seeks to know and strives to reveal? What, in short, is the ultimate object of her passion? After the many passages that have been quoted, we can scarcely doubt its nature or be uncertain of the point at which the converging planes of reality in its dual aspect unite in her poetry. A figure sits waiting on the crest of consciousness: Sappho springs toward this figure as toward a priceless possession. This thing that wounds her, that makes a sign, and suddenly discovers itself to her in the grace of a gesture or the brightness of a flower, what name can we give it, but that of Beauty?

All kinds of created beauty inspire longing in Sappho, and especially that interlacing of beauty when youthful bodies and wreaths of blossom, the flower of the body and the graces of nature are mingled in the joy of sunlight, when the beautiful is incarnated in the fragility of youth and springtime:

. . . I love delicacy, and the bright and the beautiful belong for me to the desire of the sunlight.[1]

[1] No. 118, p. 267.

CHAPTER SIX

SOLON AND THE
APPROACH OF DEMOCRACY

Greek civilization came into being along the fringes of Asia Minor where for some centuries past Hellenic cities had been springing up. Homer was an Ionian, so was Archilochus; Sappho was an Aeolian. These are a few examples only. It was also in the cities of Ionia and about the same time that the first scientists and philosophers appeared, that the first marble statues and some of the first temples were raised.

Now in the same era but in Sicily and Magna Graecia, on the extreme western fringe of the Hellenic world, other scientists and philosophers, and other temples which were often splendid edifices like the one called the temple of Poseidon at Paestum—the finest perhaps of all the Greek sanctuaries—testified to the vigour of this nascent civilization.

There was more than one cause for the birth of Greek civilization on the periphery of the Greek world. It points for one thing to the dependence of the Greeks on the neighbouring civilizations which they called 'barbarian'; because in the area between Asia and Sicily, that is, in Greece proper, nothing or almost nothing that looked like civilization existed at that time.

This is a rough generalization. One ought at least to mention the peasant poet Hesiod and to remember that at the outset Sparta was a city of dance and song. And there were a few other facts to belie the 'nothing or almost nothing' we spoke of.

But now comes the ascendancy of Athens. For three centuries and more Athens, which had at first been a small country town, became 'the school of Greece', and the 'Hellas of Hellas'. The first of these expressions, which comes from the historian Thucydides, should be read in its context; this gives it a strictly political meaning. Athens was the school of Greece in the sense that she prepared the most enlightened cities for democracy. Not that she was the first of the democracies; there had been others before her, in Ionia. But by her prestige as a great democratic city that provided her people with the most splendid festivals and the finest dramas both tragic and comic, by the brilliance of the temples and other monuments she raised to confer lustre on the Athenian people, finally by the way in which her historians and philosophers formulated, attacked or defended the rights of the people, Athens occupies the foremost place. Here for two centuries beat the heart of Hellas. Here comedy, in quips absurd or grotesque, told home truths to all and sundry. Here the tragic conflict between man and destiny was portrayed most poignantly in drama. Here Socrates, Plato and many others established the dialogue of philosophic enquiry—in the street, in the shop or the stadium—and carried the enquiry from earthly to heavenly things.

Before indulging in the luxury of an *Antigone* or a Parthenon, the first problem eighth-century Athens had to solve was the problem of living. About two centuries were needed to find a provisional solution for this basic problem. The result was the invention of democracy. This is a fine word, but one that may be a little deceptive. 'Democracy' means 'power of the people'. But of what people? One suspects the answer. We have already indicated a few elements of the problem that seems to be solved by a word, whereas a word never solves anything.

Let us summarize the main points. In the struggle which took place in Attica and elsewhere in the eighth century, two classes were at grips, the class in possession and the class of the dispossessed. Those in possession owned the great estates; the dispossessed had very little land, but they had their hands and arms, and superior numbers. The solution proposed by Solon was to consist of a body of laws which gradually assured all the *citizens* of equality in civil and political rights. Thus democracy was never more than the power exercised in the city by the 'citizens'.

It will be seen at once that there was no question of the whole body of the workers, of the producing population; but only of the citizens. In the ancient city-state the majority of the producers were slaves; and herein we see the limits of democratic advance. It never comprised the slave population.

When this reservation has been made—and it is a very serious one because it contributed to the disappearance of ancient civilization—it is still true that in the course of the eighth and seventh centuries there arose in most of the Greek cities, in Ionia first and then at Athens, a great number of exceptionally violent social struggles in which the poorest section of the citizens sought to wrest equality of rights from the most powerful section and to have this equality registered in written law; in fact, to seize that share that was due to it in the city-government. So it was here, though the slaves always remained outside the conflict, that a first form of democracy took shape, vague as a promise that was some day or other to be fulfilled.

For a long time, of course, the city was composed of two kinds of citizens. There were the nobles descended from the first occupiers of the land; they were members of the clans, called 'gentes' in Latin, and they were also the rich citizens who, for the most part, cultivated their own lands along with the members of their 'houses'. By this time, however, the original ancestral domain had ceased to belong collectively to the clan. The land was shared among relatives and was inalienable. It could not pass to another family either by donation or sale or as a dowry. It was an absolute principle that 'property remains in the family'.

Proud of their blood, the Eupatridae alone had access to the magistrature, they alone were 'kings', judges and generals. They spoke to the gods on behalf of the city, they offered up the necessary sacrifices, they were the priests of this civic religion which had no regular clergy. These nobles represented some fifty families in Athens or rather in Attica.

But, still inside the city-state, there were also a crowd of men who had set up on their own account, free workers, if the word free still had any meaning. These included the small peasants who owned only their shacks and the implements—and what implements!—with which they scratched the hillsides still half-covered with brushwood—men who were always on the confines of slavery, with nothing better than their two hands to help them, men who died in numbers in springtime, 'the season when', as an aristocratic and realistic poet puts it, 'one has nothing to eat.' There were all kinds of artisans who had no materials, but what were supplied by the Eupatridae, to repair their roofs, make their shoes or leather shields or bronze weapons, or to find the gold that was placed on the heads of the animals offered as sacrifices. They were too poor to have a workshop of their own; only the potter worked at home, and there was a potter's oven in every village. Lastly, there were the seafaring men who, in the eighth century which saw so many colonial expeditions, were beginning to gain in importance; these comprised shipbuilders and rowers, sailors and, before long, shipowners. Now these plebeians formed a very numerous body, but they were divided. The interests of the sailors and merchants were not the same as those of the artisans or the poor peasant proprietors. And they only began to 'think collectively' out of opposition to 'the big men' who exploited them. Only the nobles were armed, and they taught the rest of the community 'to think aright'. In the eighth and seventh centuries a state of civil war was, so to speak, normal in all the Greek cities.

But towards the end of the eighth century an invention of well-nigh incalculable importance suddenly modified and aggravated an economic situation that was still just bearable. This was the invention of coinage. It exasperated the class-war, in two opposite ways. A section of the poor became poorer, but another section of the 'dispossessed' class was now to enrich itself in commerce, to demand a share in the administration of the city and to open an attack on the privileges which still belonged to the aristocracy.

Until that time, according to the Homeric poems, trade had been conducted by barter. Wine was exchanged for cereals, oil for raw metal and so on. People also calculated in 'values of oxen'. Gradually, ingots of gold and silver were adopted as tokens of exchange. But these ingots were not stamped or certified by the state; they had to be weighed every time, and for this purpose the money-changers had their scales in the market-place.

Money in the proper sense of a coinage struck by each city and of a guaranteed weight, was invented in Lydia, that region of Asia Minor through which the Pactolus flowed over sands shining with gold. But the Greek cities of the Ionian shore took over this invention and spread it over the known world in the course of the vast colonial movement of the same era.

This was no doubt profitable for purposes of exchanges, but profitable to whom? The men already rich hastened to put their hands on this new form of wealth, which was not perishable. Now it is clear that in the *natural* economy the great rural proprietors had scarcely any means of accumulating wealth. One could not pile up treasure in corn, oil or wine. They might slightly increase their luxury by purchasing cushions, carpets or finely-wrought weapons from the East, but in this primitive economy the big landowner preferred to employ his surplus by extending the circle of his clients. Thus, in a bad year, the small 'free' farmer and even the artisan might appeal for help to the lord of the region; and the latter would take pride in being 'a citadel or a rampart' of the poor, as the epic poems expressed it. So the small worker was still in some sort protected by the great.

The appearance of coinage created a quite different situation, because it allowed a man to capitalize his surplus production by turning it into money. Furthermore, the rich man learned how to make his money bear fruit, he maintained that it would produce 'little ones' (his name for interest). Thus, pride of birth was intensified by rapacity. Whereas formerly a noble would hand over the surplus he could not use, as a gift, now he lent, and the rate of interest he demanded was very high, because he liked to place part of his capital in maritime enterprises in which the risk was very heavy. He lent and speculated. The wealth amassed was now simply a capital sum to be used to acquire further wealth.

There came into being in this way what Aristotle calls 'Chrematistiké', which means the art of money, the capacity to amass and make money fructify. It can be seen that this was not far from being a first form of capitalism. Now the invention of coined money affected the relations between the classes in important ways.

In the first place the lower class, especially the small peasants, being obliged to borrow on very unfavourable terms, were slowly pushed in the direction of slavery. What indeed could the little landowner give as security to the big man? His land which he could mortgage; then his labour. Which meant that in default of repaying the loan and once his land was seized, he would remain as a tenant or rather a serf, and would be obliged to hand over the greater part of his harvest to his creditor. In Athens the amazing figure has been recorded, of five-sixths. In the last instance he would have only his own body as security; that is, he could be sold into slavery, and so could his wife and children who were sold even before him and by him, as the last forms of movable property he possessed.

Thus it can be seen that the existence of slavery and the inferior status of woman now operated against the citizen's interests and blocked the way to any true kind of democracy. Such were the horrible consequences of 'Chrematistiké' in Athens at the moment when civilization in its most brilliant forms was about to flower there.

But the consequences of an invention are never as simple as one supposes. The invention of coinage was not merely a new instrument of oppression in the hands of the nobles; there came a moment in the course of long and bloody conflicts when it became an instrument of liberation in the hands of the people.

We must not in this connection forget the merchants, who belonged to the lower class. Some of these commoners grew rich, first in the great Asiatic seaports of Smyrna, Miletus and Ephesus, and then in Greece proper at Corinth, Megara and Athens. The nobility despised them, but now had to reckon with them. These commercial parvenus began to buy land from the poor peasants, who preferred selling to these men rather than borrowing at exorbitant rates of interest. Having thus acquired landed property, the wealthy plebeians now demanded a share in the administration, in public offices, in the magistracy, in military command, in fact in all the rights hitherto reserved to the blue-blooded aristocracy.

But how could they succeed except by allying themselves with the multitude of the dispossessed, by leaning for support on the rabble of the exploited? Thus the class-war was greatly intensified by the alliance of poverty and ambition against aristocracy.

It was the struggle between the 'kalokagathoi' and the 'kakoi', according to the vocabulary used by the nobles. The 'kalokagathoi' were, in their own language, the men who had been trained to every virtue by the practice of sport and the cult of the Muses: they were both well-favoured and full of nobility; they were noble in both senses of the word, being at once of good birth and ready to perform every kind of exploit. The 'kakoi' on the other hand were the bad and the wretched— the 'villeins', who owing to the meanness of their birth belonged to the people and were capable only of mean actions. It was a strange vocabulary and one which the issue of the conflict was to belie.

◎

It would be difficult here to follow step by step the progress of the conflict which was to lead, in a large number of cities, to a democratic liberation or at least to what ancient society understood by this term. Let us confine ourselves to Athens and associate our narrative with the story of the poet-legislator Solon.

Solon was of noble birth. The 'gens' or clan to which he belonged had given Athens the last of her kings. But in the mid-seventh century this family had, for reasons of which we are ignorant, become greatly impoverished. Solon, who grew up in the second half of the century at a time when industry and commerce were beginning suddenly and vigorously to expand, decided to restore his fortune by travelling abroad and marketing the olive-oil produced in Attica.

Here then was a young noble—a poet also—taking to the oil-trade. The desire to visit new countries like young Ionia, and old civilizations like Egypt whose history went back four or five thousand years, no doubt had a lot to do with Solon's decision to earn his living by travel. Much later, when he was an old man and had completed his legislative work, he took to the sea again. This appetite for new knowledge was his way of growing old or perhaps of remaining young. 'I grow old', he wrote, 'learning many things.'[1]

Solon had returned to Athens in the prime of life after restoring his fortune by commerce, as he had planned. His fellow-citizens regarded him as a man free of prejudice and above all fundamentally honest; and he had become a popular figure with each of the two classes which were then engaged in a war to the knife. Plutarch, who places him in his gallery of famous men, says very justly: 'The great esteemed him because he was rich, and the poor because he was honest.'

One day Solon had the courage to render his country a great service. The story, which may have been slightly improved in the telling but which rests on a basis of fact, because a mutilated poem of Solon's refers to it, is also related by Plutarch.

At the period in question Athens and Megara which were neighbouring cities and both in a fair way to becoming great commercial seaports, were disputing the possession of Salamis. This island lies off Athens and is the key to its port. Whoever possessed it could hold or blockade Athens. Now the men of Megara occupied it in spite of every effort to prevent them; whereupon the Athenians in their vexation passed a law forbidding anyone, under pain of death, to speak of Megara in public.

---

[1] A saying recorded by Plato.

Solon conceived the notion of passing for a madman. When belief in his madness was well established, he appeared one day in the Agora, mounted the rostrum and to the assembled citizens recited a poem he had written on the beauty of Salamis and the shame for the city to have surrendered it to Megara. The people listened (after all, he was mad!), then they became enthusiastic; they moved on Salamis, Solon directed the attack, and the island was recaptured from Megara. We possess a few isolated verses of this poem, which read:

Then may I change my country and be a man of Pholegandros or Sicinus[1] instead of an Athenian, for full soon would this be the report among men: This is an Athenian of the tribe of Salaminaphetae or Letters-go of Salamis. . . .
    Let us go to Salamis, to fight for a lovely isle and put away from us dishonour hard to bear.[2]

The tone, which is at once bold and appealing, pleased the Athenians. Even if the story has been somewhat touched up, it is clear that Solon instigated the reconquest of Salamis. And it was this event that, with the general esteem he inspired, accounts for his being chosen as arbiter and legislator in the conflict which was dividing his country.

◎

In recalling the composition of the opposing camps, we must now add a few supplementary details.

The great landowning nobles had by this time monopolized the whole or nearly the whole of the Attic plain. They cultivated these vast estates by means of their kinsfolk, their clients and their slaves. Barley and wheat were rare, and these were imported from the shores of the Black Sea. Vines, fig-trees and olive-trees were abundant; part of this produce was for export. Meanwhile, these vast estates were increasing through the liquidation of the small ones.

The landowner, or Eupatrid, supervised the farming from a distance, like a feudal lord. In the course of time he had acquired the habit of living in the city and now his main occupation was politics. He governed, he made war; and he judged in the courts, according to a law which was still only partly written and which he alone, with his peers, was in a position to interpret.

In face of these nobles were the people, and first of all the peasant proletariat. There were some free landowners, but their numbers were dwindling; there were

[1] These were small hamlets on islets in the Aegean.
[2] *Elegy and Iambus* . . . with the *Anacreontea*. Newly edited and translated by J. M. Edmonds. London and New York, 1931, Vol. I, Solon, Fragments 2 and 3, p. 117.

tenant-farmers, except on the mountain slopes where the soil was so poor that there was little to be got out of it. And there were serfs, peasants who were riddled with debt. Whether the harvest was good or bad, five-sixths of it always went to the master, one sixth only for the wretched peasant—a rate of payment that provoked cries of rage for a whole century through the countryside of Attica. One must add that manufactured objects, such as the implements which the peasant, bound down to the overwhelming conditions of his life, had to buy in the city or get made for him by the local smith, were relatively very dear, whereas the agricultural produce he offered was cheap, as the landowner could put quantities on the market.

A short time, and all the small peasant proprietors would be slaves. Suppose this man sells his mortgaged land; he will now be a country workman, a labourer or unemployed. There is no work for a free man owing to the number of slaves. Suppose that, as a tenant-farmer, he cannot pay his five-sixths: he becomes a slave. Suppose that, in the same circumstances, he abandons his illusory property and tries to go into exile; he is pursued as a fugitive slave. Slavery lies in wait for him at every exit.

It was in truth a terrible drama that was being enacted in seventh-century Attica. All round the great estates the land was bristling with boundary posts. These marked the Eupatrid's right of possession over the mortgaged land; they indicated the mortgage and the sum due. They meant that the nobles were proceeding to turn the Athenian people into a people of slaves. Land and power were to belong to a few; the rest were to be excluded from the community of citizens. Were the Eupatridae indeed going to make the Athenians a people of helots? Was Athens to become another Sparta?

How far we seem now from democracy! and yet salvation is near.

Geography had made Attica a country of seamen and merchants. Observe this long triangle of which the two longer sides, extending some hundred and twelve miles, are washed by the sea. Consider all these creeks and shore lines, some of them low and sandy for light craft, others providing deep-water ports for more modern vessels. And note the chain of islands from Attica to Asia, beckoning and reassuring the sailor.

Round the shores of Attica, as in Athens at the foot of the Acropolis and before long at the Piraeus, there is a swarming population of fishermen, sailors, small shipowners, artisans and merchants. Some are in rags, but others are growing rich and gradually escaping from dependence on the landed aristocracy. Many of them travel and most of them are resourceful.

Now the nobles need these sailors and merchants to handle the produce they sell abroad. They also need the potters, who live in a rapidly growing suburb of Athens, to manufacture the great red and black jars in which they export the wines and especially the precious oil—those fine Attic vases which have been discovered in places as far afield as Egypt and the shores of the Black Sea, in Sicily, at Cumae and even in Etruria, from a time as early as Solon's.

The nobles might end by enslaving the impoverished peasants; but with the artisans and merchants, poor or rich, they had to come to terms.

Now the poor peasants formed what looked like the most helpless portion of the plebs; but it was also the most rebellious portion, and the largest numerically. Some of them, appealing to an ancient usage, purely and simply demanded the equal redistribution of the whole territory. At a time when reforms could only be effected by violence, this numerous class was to be used by Peisistratus, the tyrant who was so much hated but who, in the logic of historical evolution, really continued the work of Solon and realized his reforms.

The merchants were the most moderate and the shrewdest section of the population; they were the most inclined to negotiate and also the most determined to take a hand in civic affairs. They had had enough of being compelled, in private as in public life, to accept decisions made over their heads by the Eupatridae. They were citizens, and they did not wish their civic rights to be a dead letter.

What insured the victory of the lower class in its age-long struggle with the landed nobility was, ultimately, the alliance between the two sections of the plebs, the artisans and merchants with the small peasants and country workmen.

We pass over the bloody disorders which forced a compromise. This consisted of an agreement to nominate, between the two parties—the nobility of the clans, and the people—an arbiter commissioned to proceed to a vast economic, social and political reform. The arbiter in whom, at this moment of mortal peril, Athens placed her confidence—the oppressed because they counted on his love of justice, and the oppressors no doubt because he was a man of their own caste—was Solon. The nobles were deceived. Solon was not the man of a caste; he was a citizen of Athens.

Solon then was appointed Archon in 594 B.C. with extraordinary powers to reform the state. He immediately adopted very bold measures, moderate as they may appear to us; some of them were economic and social, others were political.

The first and most indispensable of his reforms, the one which saved the half-serf peasantry from complete serfdom, was the unreserved freeing both of lands and persons. The land was freed; all the boundary posts in the fields which marked the enslavement of land that had fallen into the hands of the Eupatridae were pulled up, and the land was restored to the debtors who had become tenants or slaves. Men were freed. Insolvent debtors recovered their liberty together with their land, and their debts were cancelled. Furthermore, those who had been sold abroad as slaves were sought out, redeemed and freed by the state, and re-established in their properties.

Solon celebrates this freeing of land and persons in verses we still possess, verses that testify to his deep love both of the land and of men. He invokes Earth herself, oldest of the gods, and prays that she will bear witness in his favour before the judgment-seat of history:

Right good witness shall I have in the court of Time, to wit the Great Mother of the Olympian Gods, dark Earth, whose so many fixed landmarks I once removed, and have made her free that was once a slave. Aye, many brought I back to their God-built birthplace, many that had been sold, some justly, some unjustly, and others that had been exiled through urgent penury, men that no longer spake the Attic speech because they had wandered so far and wide; and those that suffered shameful servitude at home, trembling before the whims of their owners, these made I free men.[1]

Magnificent verses of the oldest of Athenian poets, expressing the love he bore his oppressed people, a people he had restored to liberty and to the just possession of its goods.

It may be said that such a measure, involving the cancellation of debts, despoiled the rich. No doubt it did. But the rich had abused their power. Solon made them disgorge what they had taken. This bold measure which liquidated the past and saved the Athenian people was completed by a statute that prevented the return of any such situation in the future. Solon suppressed slavery for debt. Henceforth, it was forbidden to take a man's person as security for a loan. This statute safeguarded individual liberty; it was the corner-stone of Attic law. Such a law existed in no other Greek city.

Space obliges us to pass over many other reforms, economic and social, important as they may have been. One such was the monetary reform, which Solon successfully carried out. Several of these new laws put in check the hitherto exorbitant power of the 'gentes'. Such was the provision imposed by Solon which required the division of a noble patrimony, on the father's death, among all the heirs—a measure that weakened the territorial nobility. Such also was the facility now granted to a man who had no legitimate son, permitting him to adopt an heir by will, from a family outside the 'gens'. This was a direct blow to the old family law. Finally, there was the right granted to any citizen to purchase such land as was called noble. The effect of these laws was to strengthen the people as a whole, to divide up property and to increase the number of small landowners.

[1] Fragment 36. Translation cited, pp. 149, 151.

Other laws boldly freed the individual by limiting paternal authority as far as was possible at that time. There could be no question of venturing to forbid a father to expose his new-born child. But from the moment when he had recognized his child by presenting it to the city, he lost the power of life and death. He could no longer sell his daughter except on account of notorious immorality, nor could he get rid of his son unless for serious reasons. When the son came of age, the state regarded him as his father's equal.

◎

What especially marks the reforms of Solon, once he had carried out that part of his task that required boldness and severity, was their equity and moderation. He in fact had the hardihood, in the revolutionary crisis that he was handling, to wage war on two fronts. In the midst of a serious conflict no policy is more difficult to pursue than this policy of 'justice'—a word that is constantly recurring in his poems.

Thus, in one of the rare passages of his work that have come down to us, Solon depicts himself as covering each party in turn with his shield. He had protected the nobles against the extreme demands of the mountain folk. He is alluding to all this when he writes:

... *Nay, I stood with a strong shield thrown before the both sorts, and would have neither to prevail unrighteously over the other.*[1]

Elsewhere he writes:

... *And ordinances I wrote, that made straight justice for each man, good and bad alike. Had another than I taken the goad in hand, a foolish man and a covetous, he had not restrained the people; for had I been willing to do now what pleased this party and now what pleased the other, this city had been bereft of many men. Wherefore mingling myself strength from all quarters I turned at bay like a wolf among many hounds.*[2]

There is another image expressive of his courage, that noble courage of moderation that resists the extreme demands of either camp:

... *I set a mark as it were in the midway betwixt the two hosts of them.*[3]

Here again we have an example of the raciness of Solon's poetry.

Such is the importance and such the spirit of the economic and social reforms of this great Athenian.

[1] Fragment 5. Translation cited, p. 121.   [2] Fragment 36. Translation cited, p. 151.
[3] Fragment 37. Translation cited, p. 153.

◎

No less important were his political reforms, inspired, as we shall see, by the same spirit of boldness and moderation which in a few generations was to bear fruit in democracy.

In the allocation of public offices Solon was careful not to advance at one leap from a system in which these functions remained the exclusive privilege of the nobles, to a democratic régime which would have opened them to every citizen. Neither Solon nor any other Athenian could have done this at the beginning of the sixth century; the balance of forces in the class-struggle absolutely excluded such a thing.

Solon proceeded as follows. He withdrew exclusive political rights, such as the privilege of occupying all magisterial posts, from those of noble birth. It was not now birth that decided, but financial position. He divided the people into four classes according to their wealth. The citizens belonging to the more well-to-do class had the right to occupy the more important positions; they also bore the heaviest burdens. In the other classes the burdens, whether in taxation or military service, diminished in proporton to the rights enjoyed. Thus in the fourth and lowest class the citizens paid no tax and they were only recruited on rare occasions as rowers or light-armed soldiers.

It will be seen that Solon's constitution established a kind of democracy of electoral qualifications. The important point was that the right conferred by noble birth was rejected because birth cannot be acquired. This right was transferred to personal fortune, because fortune can be acquired, at least in theory. For the rest, this kind of system which is based on financial qualification is never more than a stage on the road to complete democracy. The distinctions that had been established, the barriers that had been raised against the advancing tide of democracy, would soon disappear. After about a century of conflicts, far less violent, however, than those which had preceded Solon's reforms, political rights would belong equally to all the free citizens. So this was how, with a mixture of great boldness and rare prudence, Solon opened the way to democracy.

Already, however, in Solon's system there was a right that belonged to everyone—the most important of all rights. All the citizens, from the highest to the lowest, had the right of voting in the popular Assembly. This was of capital importance. In the Assembly rich and poor were equal. Anyone could vote, anyone could speak. No doubt in Solon's time the powers of the Assembly were still limited. But at least Solon recognized the principle of equality of rights, in voting and speaking. In the course of time the popular Assembly was to become the fundamental organ of public life. The poor who are always the more numerous

19. *Cobbler (6th Century vase)*
20. (Overleaf, left) (a) *Line fishing. On the sand at the bottom, a lobster basket. At the right, a cuttlefish (6th Century cup)*
    (b) *Digging out clay, or perhaps mining. The hanging amphora contains water (Corinthian plaque in earthenware. 6th Century)*
21. (Overleaf, right) *Women pounding grain (6th Century Crater or two-handled cup)*

would have no difficulty in carrying their views against the views of the rich. The limiting qualifications would be abolished, though only as a consequence of further crises and reforms, and Athens would then be the most democratic city in Greece. This development was clearly in germ in Solon's constitution.

Another and very important institution in the public life of Athens was also thrown open by Solon to the citizens as a whole. This was the tribunal of the Heliasts, a large popular court of law which later on was to number as many as six thousand judges, divided into ten sections. Now Solon had decided that any citizen was eligible for membership, and he also extended its jurisdiction by making it a court of appeal from the decisions of the individual magistrates. Later on, the Heliasts were to judge nearly all cases of public and private law.

It is clear therefore that from the time of Solon the people, who now sat in the Assembly and in the Court of the Heliasts, were in a fair way to establishing popular sovereignty. Now the sovereignty of the people is nothing less than democracy. As Aristotle says: 'When the people are masters of the vote, they are masters of the government.'

As early then as the beginning of the sixth century something can be seen taking shape—that image of the people who, under the impulse of their orators, discussed everything and decided everything, from treaties of peace to the building of the Parthenon, the Propylaea and the rest—the people of whom Fénelon observed in a striking epigram: 'Tout en Grèce dépendait du peuple (he should have said: in Athens), et le peuple dépendait de la parole.'[1]

◎

If, in conclusion, we ask what source of inspiration, what inner fire enabled Solon to accomplish so great a work, the answer, I think, will be that he loved his people and he loved justice. He believed in it as one believes in God. Solon's God had as his attribute not only power, but justice.

Solon loved his people. The reader will recall the passage in which we saw him, when speaking of his reforms, receiving the exiles on their return to Athens: 'those men that no longer spake the Attic speech, because they had wandered so far and wide.' There is something like a sob in this verse. And the following one contains, at least implicitly, one of the only protests—and perhaps the most moving protest —ever uttered by a Greek against the inhumanity of slavery: '. . . and those that suffered shameful servitude at home, trembling before the whims of their owners, these made I free men.'

It is the love he bears his people that here draws from Solon, as it were in spite of himself, a movement of revolt against a condition that abases a man to the point

[1] 'In Greece, everything depended on the people, and the people depended on the spoken word.'

H

of making him tremble before the caprice of another man. It was in this spirit that he loved his people.

And how he loved Justice! Justice was the very countenance of the God in whom he believed. He set the rich at the head of the state; but what responsibility he placed on their shoulders! He expected them to exercise justice. And there is a violent and even sacred anger in the pamphlet which he wrote against certain evil and wealthy men who were corrupting the fair order desired by the legislator and by the gods.

So then (if I may summarize this poetical fragment), the rich men whom he has called to be leaders of the people have yielded to injustice and have been using their power only to purloin! They who should be the guardians of religion have been thieves, even in the sanctuaries of the gods! They whose whole conduct should be obedience to the laws of Justice, have offended against it by their un-bridled appetite for gain! At first Justice endures the outrage in silence; but she lays up the memory in her heart, and prepares a chastisement. Now the tone rises. We see the injustice of the rich spreading like a relentless ulcer over the whole city. Again the flames of civil war are kindled, the young men perish, and the poor in thousands, loaded with chains and doomed to slavery, take once more the path of the exile. At last, however, this scourge which the rich have let loose turns against them. Solon personifies it as the Evil Genius to which evil Wealth has given birth. No obstacle can now stay it in its work of avenging Justice. It leaps the walls of the villas where the rich have sought refuge; it can find and seize them even in the corners of the rooms where they are hiding.

Such, the poet shows, is the catastrophe that befalls a state where the rich are workers of iniquity. The concluding verses celebrate in fervent tones the beauty of the law which the legislator has tried to establish in his motherland:

Good rule maketh all things orderly and perfect.[1]

And further on, he says:

And of her all is made wise and perfect in the world of men.[2]

It will be seen from these fragments that Solon is a great legislator and statesman only because he is first of all a living conscience, a man in whom a warm heart is united with sound reason: a poet, an 'enthusiast', as the Greeks would say. Justice has her dwelling in him; his desire is to cause Justice to reign in the young demo-cracy of Athens.

But was this truly the democracy of a sovereign people? Here we shall find our-selves faced with the grave restrictions inherent in it, and first of all that of slavery.

[1] Fragment 4. Translation cited, p. 121. [2] *Ibid.*

CHAPTER SEVEN

SLAVERY AND
THE STATUS OF WOMAN

The Greeks invented democracy; but they did this within certain limitations which must now be defined. From the outset these limitations seriously impaired the value and efficacy of that 'popular sovereignty' for which the peoples have struggled for so long. They did worse: they prevented democracy from progressing, they blocked its development. We may even ask ourselves whether some one of them should not be counted among the main causes of the failure of ancient civilization.

Two of these limitations, the principal ones, should be emphasized; they were slavery and the inferior status of woman. Others existed that were almost as serious.

◎

Democracy, of course, means equality between all the citizens. These were, no doubt, numerous, but not numerous enough. Thus in Athens, although such calculations are difficult and uncertain, it is generally agreed that there were, in the fifth century, about 130,000 citizens (including the women and children, which is far from making 130,000 electors), 70,000 resident aliens—Greeks from other cities who were more or less permanently established there but who did not enjoy political rights; and finally 200,000 slaves. This means that out of a population of 400,000, half were slaves. It also means that, although Athenian democracy was very egalitarian in all that concerned the political rights of the citizens, it subsisted and maintained itself in large measure through the work of the slaves.

Slavery, then, constituted a definite limitation of Greek democracy. No ancient society indeed seems to have been able to dispense with slavery. It was the primitive form of what is today called 'the exploitation of man by man'; and it was also the severest. Medieval society did not permit slavery, but it had serfdom. In modern society we have the wage-earning system, not to forget colonial exploitation. The freeing of man from the oppressive forces which the stronger exercise over the weaker is very slow in coming; but it has been on the march ever since society has existed.

◎

What were the reasons for slavery? At the outset, however paradoxical this may appear, slavery seems to have marked a stage in progress. The primitive Greek tribes had no slaves. When they made war on each other, they killed their prisoners. In very ancient times, of which traces can be detected in the *Iliad,* the prisoners were eaten, raw or roasted. Slavery appeared when men preferred to keep a prisoner alive, not from any feeling of humanity, but for what he would produce as a worker; or again, in the early days of commerce, they began to sell prisoners in exchange for money or for some commodity. It is probable that when people began to trade, one of the first objects of merchandise consisted of men. But still it was a step in progress, a kind of softening, dictated by self-interest, of the primitive brutalities of war.

Slavery was in fact an outcome of war, and in Greek society the majority of slaves were former prisoners of war. After a battle the prisoners who could not redeem themselves were sold. After an assault the men of a captured city were generally put to the sword, but the victors drew lots for the women and children and either kept or sold them as slaves. These customs were not strictly applied between one Greek city and another. They felt scruples in selling Greeks as slaves, the more so as Greek slaves were regarded as rather poor workers. But in a war between Greeks on the one side and Persians or other non-Greek peoples on the other, the rule was strict. There is record of a Greek victory over the Persians, as a consequence of which twenty thousand Persian prisoners were thrown on to the slave-market.

Dealers in slaves followed the armies. The slave-trade was very active and lucrative. Great fairs for the sale of slaves were held in the Greek cities that bordered on barbarian lands, and notably at Ephesus in Ionia, at Byzantium and in the Greek cities of Sicily. The slave-market was held in Athens once in the year. Some slave-dealers amassed considerable fortunes.

There were, however, other ways of becoming a slave than through being a prisoner of war. The first was birth. The child of a slave-woman was a slave; he was not the property of his mother, but of the owner of his mother. Often, and indeed in the majority of cases, he was exposed by the roadside at birth and died. The master considered it too costly to let the child live, which would mean feeding him until he was old enough to work. This rule was not however universal. Many of the slaves who figure in tragedy boast of being born in the master's house; but we must not rely over much on what the tragedies say.

Another source of supply was piracy. Piratical traders made raids into the so-called barbarian lands north of the Balkans and in southern Russia, and brought back much human merchandise. These were excellent slaves. Raids were also made into certain Greek lands, such as Thessaly and Etolia, where the state and the police were not strong enough to prevent this kind of man-hunting.

In the last place, private law was also a source of supply. It must not be forgotten that in most of the Greek states the insolvent debtor could be sold as a slave. Athens alone, as far as we know, was an exception, from the day when Solon forbade slavery for debt. Yet even in philanthropical Athens the father had the right to expose his new-born children by the wayside—at least until he had presented them to the city in a ceremony analogous to our baptism. Sometimes they were picked up by the slave-dealers. Worse still, in all the Greek cities except Athens, the father who was considered the absolute master and owner of his children, could at any time, even when they were grown up, get rid of them and sell them as slaves. In times of extreme poverty this was a terrible temptation for the poor. Such sales, however, were forbidden in Athens, except in the case of girls who were shamelessly profligate.

War, birth, piracy and private law were therefore the principal sources for the supply of slaves.

◎

It will be seen that the slave not only had no part in the city but that he was not regarded as a person. Juridically speaking he was an object of property which could be sold, bequeathed, hired or given. One of the ancient philosophers defined his position exactly when he said that the slave was an 'animated tool'—a kind of machine that had the advantage of being able to understand and execute the orders given it. The slave was an instrument belonging to another man; he was his 'thing'.

But the law did not accord him any legal existence; or, to be exact, he bore the name of the place he came from, or else a kind of general nick-name. His marriage was not legal. Two slaves could of course cohabit, and their union might be recognized by the master, but it was not a marriage. The master could therefore sell the man and woman separately. Their offspring did not belong to them but to their master, and he could get rid of it if he so desired.

The slave, being an object of property, could not himself enjoy the right of property. If, from gratuities or some other source, he happened to save a little hoard, he kept it only on sufferance. There was nothing to prevent his master from taking it.

The master also had the right to punish his slave in various ways. He could throw him into prison, beat him, put him in the pillory—a very painful punishment—have him marked with a hot iron, or even put him to death, though not in Athens; but of course this was not to the master's advantage.

The master's interests indeed were the only guarantee the slave possessed. The master will take care not to spoil his tool. Aristotle says in this connection: 'One should take care of one's tool as far as this is appropriate to the work.' So, when the slave is a good instrument for work, it is wise to feed him adequately, to dress him better, to give him proper hours of rest, to allow him to raise a family, even to give him a glimpse of the supreme, though very rare, reward of freedom. Plato insists that it is to the master's interest to treat his slave well. He regards the slave simply as a kind of 'animal', but this 'animal' should not rebel against a condition which, according to the philosopher, springs from an inequality in the nature of things. He therefore admits that one should treat the 'animal' well, and he specifies that it is 'in our interest more than in his'. A fine philosophy of 'idealism', as people call it.

The slave's legal position is therefore inhuman; or rather, it should be repeated, he has no juridical status, because he is not regarded as a human being; he is simply an 'instrument' which is used by citizens and others.

One must add, however, that all this was rather theoretical, and that in the practice of daily life the Athenians, for instance, did not conform to a doctrine which would have turned slaves into a servile species, doomed by nature to remain servile and to work for man, just as there are bovine and equine species, domesticated by man and quite distinct from the human species.

The Athenians were in fact much less strict and doctrinaire than the philosophers in relation to their slaves. They were more human, and they usually treated their slaves as men. We shall meet with a few examples by and by, but it must be remembered that here it is only a question of the Athenians.

Other Greeks, though we are now speaking only of the Spartans, continued to be extremely ferocious in their treatment of the helots, who were their slaves. Now these helots, and others who lived in the same region as the Spartans, outnumbered their masters by nine or ten to one. The Spartans greatly feared them; and in order to keep them in a state of obedience, they had established a reign of terror. The helots were forbidden, under pain of death, to leave their cabins after sunset. Many other things were prohibited. In addition to this, and in order to keep down the numbers, the Spartans from time to time—apparently once a year—organized man-hunts, which were neither more nor less than expeditions for the purpose of massacre. The young men lay in ambush in the country districts and hunted and murdered these cursed beasts who were called helots. This was said to be an excellent training for the horrors of war. It is strange to think that such abominable practices can have existed in a civilization which, at the very same time, was making the most wonderful, agreeable and beautiful inventions—for the use of a small number of privileged persons. Civilization is a very complex affair, and in speaking of Greek civilization it is wise not to forget that, with all its merits, it was the culture of a slave-owning society. Perhaps this should lead us to think that a civilization that is not organized for all the human beings composing it, either does not deserve the name or is in constant danger of relapsing into barbarism.

Let us return to Athens. Here the slave wore the same clothes as the citizen, at any rate as the poor citizen. There was no outward sign to distinguish a slave from a free man. At home in the family-circle he enjoyed freedom of speech with the master; many passages in Attic comedy show that slaves were not afraid of speaking home truths. The Athenian slave was admitted on the same footing as the citizen to a large number of religious ceremonies. He could even be initiated into the Eleusinian mysteries, in which the faithful were instructed in the rites and beliefs that enabled them to attain eternal life. Then, too, the master, in Athens, no longer possessed power of life and death over his slave; and if he punished him too brutally, the slave could take refuge in certain sanctuaries where, under the protection of the God, he could demand that his master sell him to someone else.

In the other cities of Greece the slave was exposed to the violence of any free man. Any citizen could flout or strike him in the street. Plato thought this practice all right; but nothing like it was permitted in Athens, where the aristocrats were furious that they could not thrash their slaves without rhyme or reason.

Athens even gave the slave guarantees against the brutality of the magistrate or the policeman, guarantees which mark the beginnings of a legal status. Thus, in Greece as a whole, the sanction established by police regulations was a fine for free men, and the whip for slaves (who had no money). Now in states other than Attica the amount of the flogging was left to the discretion of the magistrate or the executioner; but in Athens, where the maximum fine for citizens was fixed at fifty drachmae, the maximum number of lashes was also fixed at fifty. Thus the law recognized that the slave possessed a right as against the representatives of the state. This may not have been much, but still it was a beginning of legal revolution. The example of Athens, as a matter of fact, was not followed in this matter by the other cities, because this legal recognition of a slave's rights seemed very dangerous to a society wholly founded on slavery.

We should not represent even Athens in colours too idyllic. In the lower stratum of Athenian slavery thousands of poor wretches were vegetating or dying, in the mines for instance, men who were fed just enough and often barely enough for them to work and whose labour was interrupted only by the rod. The philosophers were perfectly aware that the Athenians' treatment of their slaves was full of inconsistencies. We hear Aristotle scornfully grumbling between his teeth that 'democracy puts up with anarchy in the slave population'.

◎

But what did the slaves work at? It would be a great error to accept Taine's picture of Greece; to suppose, in brief, that the citizens folded their arms or engaged simply in public life, while all the work and production fell to the slaves. These idle citizens occupied merely with politics, while the slaves produced everything for them, may have been presented by certain philosophers as a kind of ideal; but the reality was quite different.

Athenian citizens for the most part had a trade; they were peasants, businessmen, artisans or sailors. And the slaves were employed, always as 'animated tools', on the lower levels of production.

In the first place they did the greater part of the house-work. Here almost everything depended on the service of female slaves. They pounded or ground the corn which, with the old-fashioned mills, was a painful business. Homer shows us the women setting to work on it at night, 'their knees sagging with fatigue'. Theirs, too, were the tasks of baking, cooking, weaving cloth and making clothes. Women-slaves spun and wove and embroidered under the eye of the mistress who, for that matter, did the same. These slaves sometimes filled a considerable place in the family life in which they shared, as both comedies and tragedies bear witness. Thus it was with the nurses and the 'pedagogues', a name which does not carry the modern sense but simply means that they took the youngsters to school and back, that they were a sort of children's nurse but that they also taught the small boys to behave properly. In the plays, nurses and pedagogues are full of good advice and reprimands and also of affection—an affection which the children reciprocate when they are grown up. Witness the picturesque fondness that little Orestes' nurse shows for him twenty years after she has fed and reared him, when she is told the news—a false report, indeed—of the death of 'her heart's torment'. The nurse has to carry this news to Aegisthus who, with Clytaemnestra, has killed Agamemnon, Orestes' father. Here are a few lines from the nurse's speech in Aeschylus' tragedy, *The Choephoroi*:

> *And sure his heart will be uplifted too*
> *To hear that message. Oh my heavy grief,*

How many bitter agonies of old
And all confused this breast of mine has borne
Within these walls of Atreus, and yet none,
No sorrow so insufferable as this!
All else I bore with patiently, but now
My dear Orestes, my life's long loving care,
Entrusted from his mother's arms to mine,
Breaking my sleep with many a summons shrill,
With daily troubles multiplied in vain:
For sure, a witless babe, like a dumb beast,
Must needs have nurse's wit to nourish it.
A child in swaddling-clothes cannot declare
His wants, that he would eat, or drink, or make
Water, and childish bellies will not wait
Upon attendance. Of all this prophetess
And often falsified—a laundress then
To wash the linen shining-white again,
Fuller and nurse set on a common task—
Such was the double trade I plied, as I
Nursed young Orestes, his father's son and heir.
And now, alas, they tell me he is dead,
And I must take to him whose wickedness
Infects the house news that will make him glad.[1]

It matters little that this is a character from tragedy, a nurse attached to a royal household. Aeschylus obviously took his model from ordinary family life in the fifth century and scarcely altered it.

A citizen of Athens or any other city had in fact to be very wretchedly off not to own at least one slave. The ordinary citizen had a manservant and two maid-servants. A prosperous burgher had several of both sexes; and there were great houses which employed a score, though that is pointed out as rare. We should remember also that private houses in Greece were very simple, and the food to be prepared very sober, except on fête days. But even in the city there was always a piece of land to be tilled and there were clothes to be made. In a large measure, therefore, slavery was connected with household work.

There were, on the other hand, few slaves in the country, on the farms and even on the great estates. For ages past the estates had been cultivated collectively by the

---

[1] Translated by George Thomson, in *The Oresteia of Aeschylus*. Cambridge University Press, 1938, Vol. I. pp. 257–59.

members of the family, in the broad sense of the term, with a few slaves certainly, but rather with country workmen—poor freemen—who were engaged for the corn-harvest and the grape-harvest. In cases where the land had been divided up and the holding was small, the soil was often too barren to permit the peasant to maintain several slaves all the year round; he would therefore make do with one or two slaves as general labourers. Apart from this, the cultivation of vine and olive required expert attention, and so the small farmer preferred to look after it, as far as possible, himself. He kept very little slave-labour because it was too expensive.

In brief the proportion of slaves in agricultural districts was always small, not to say insignificant. As the early ages of Greek history were mainly agricultural, the extension of slavery came late. It came naturally with the development of industrial labour. Every kind of industry required a large number of slaves owing to the lack of machines or, as Aristotle calls them, 'instruments that work by themselves.' The slave was 'an animated tool', but to perform a piece of work which a quite simple machine would do now, several slaves were needed. A team of slaves was a machine with men for parts.

The building-trade employed both free labour and slave-labour. The building of a temple, for example, was no small enterprise. We possess the actual accounts for the construction, by the State, of one of the temples on the Acropolis. Now these show us that for various tasks requiring ordinary labourers or skilled work-men, the state enrolled both slaves hired out by heir owners and also freemen. For the same work the wages were the same, whether for slaves or citizens, with this difference that the owner of the slaves, who often worked along with them, pocketed their wages, though of course he had the obligation of feeding them. It was the same in the various categories of private industry, which were organized in workshops or little factories. Some industries, however, had been separated from the family-organization; thus there were mills that turned out cloaks, large shoe-factories, musical-instrument works, factories for beds, and naturally for weapons. Slave-labour was preferred for most of these industries.

But it should be observed that, however great in the aggregate was the number of industrial slaves, they were never employed in considerable groups. Nothing resembling our great factories existed; first, because there were no machines, and secondly, because the supervision required for large numbers of unpaid workers would have been difficult to organize. As a big establishment, we know of an arms-factory owned by a certain Cephalos who employed a hundred and twenty men. Now the only enterprises that employed much larger numbers were the mines. The Athenian state owned valuable silver mines at Laurion. We must admit of course that their exploitation had been organized by Peisistratus, a dictator who, subsequently to the time of Solon, had been raised to power by the mass of small evicted peasants; and that Peisistratus had first of all wanted to provide work for the unemployed, and at the same time do a stroke of business. So the first miners at Laurion were free citizens. But the working conditions were abominable. When the unemployed were once more absorbed as a result of various circumstances, including a measure of land reform, the State offered these mines as concessions to contractors who worked them with slave-labour. We know instances of rich men who obtained several concessions and worked them with as many as 300, 600 and even 1,000 miners.

The number of industrial slaves in Athens towards the end of the fifth century must have been very considerable. When the Spartans invaded Attica and established a stronghold, twenty thousand fugitive slaves sought refuge with them. There is no doubt that most of these were industrial workers; and the mass escape naturally means that their working conditions had become severe.

It is perfectly clear that slavery was a very dangerous ulcer at the heart of society, an ulcer which threatened its very existence. We must also observe in this connection that, if the absence of machine-production was one of the causes of slavery, the existence of slavery, on the other hand, the very ease with which people could obtain a sufficient amount of slave-labour, also explain why they did not try to invent mechanical modes of manufacture. These were never developed because one disposed of slaves; conversely, the fact that there were no machines meant that one absolutely had to preserve slavery.

But this vicious circle was more mischievous than it looks. It was not enough that the existence of slavery should render the invention of mechanical production unnecessary; slavery also tended to put a brake on the kinds of scientific research which would have permitted the creation of machinery.

Slavery, in short, put an obstacle in the way of scientific progress. It is a fact, even if scientists are not always aware of it themselves and sometimes deny it, that science develops and progresses in large measure only in order to be useful to man, only in order to make him freer as regards the forces of nature and of social oppression. We may say, at any rate, that that is one of the principal *raisons d'être* for science. The kind of science which does not place its research and discoveries at the service of man and of his progress and liberation, that kind of science loses its conscience and soon perishes.

This is what happened to Greek science. Because it was not stimulated by the necessity for discovering and working out means of mechanical production— which were replaced by slavery—Greek science went to sleep, or rather died, for centuries, and with it one of the essential agents of man's progress; or, if this did not happen in every respect, science confined itself to theoretical speculation, and, as far as progress was concerned, the result was the same.

The evil effects of slavery in the societies of the ancient world suggest many other reflections. I will only observe that a society so thoroughly imbued with slave-owning, one in which a majority of human beings were oppressed by the others, was in no position to defend itself against the threat of what has been called the barbarian invasion. It was beaten in advance, and ancient civilization perished, owing, in part, to the existence of slavery.

◎

Before concluding these reflections, one would like to explain why, in the ancient world, there was practically no one to condemn and fight against slavery. One is struck, and at first sight scandalized, by the fact that the greatest philosophers of antiquity, when speaking of slavery, are so far from condemning it that they try to justify it. This is true of Plato and Aristotle, especially Aristotle who strives to demonstrate that in order that there should be freemen and that these freemen, or citizens, should govern the cities, it is absolutely necessary that there should be slaves, that is, a class of men forcibly doomed to produce the necessities of life. In Aristotle's view, the existence of slavery is a corollary to the existence of free men; and therefore the reduction of a portion of mankind to slavery is a natural right. There are beings who are slaves by nature and it is normal to constrain them to this condition by means of war; war being, he thinks, 'a kind of hunting that allows one to obtain men who, though born to obey, have refused to submit.' Such reflections, coming as they do from one of the greatest 'thinkers' of the ancient world, show how far our ways of thinking are constantly dictated by the social conditions in which we happen to live.

They also show how deeply at that time society was imbued with the practice of slavery, because there were men of great intelligence who justified it and even worked out in connection with it a theory that is nothing more nor less than a race-mysticism. Now such mysticisms are deadly in their effect on the peoples who adopt them. Many examples could be cited, but I will limit myself to that of antiquity. The scorn in which a part of mankind was held was a fundamental cause of the degradation of ancient humanism and of the collapse of civilization.

Nevertheless, in a society so deeply ravaged from top to bottom by the ulcer of slavery, there were protests here and there. I am not speaking of the slaves' revolts: such revolts took place and were harshly repressed. But they were more especially numerous in the Roman period than in the Greek. There were practically none in Athens, because Athenian customs and the way slaves were treated were in fact more human than the laws regulating them or the theories justifying slavery. There was the one mass-escape I mentioned, at the time of the Peloponnesian War. I do not therefore propose to speak of risings, but of the protests uttered by free citizens speaking to a people of freemen. There were such protests, in spite of everything, and one is greatly impressed by meeting them in that most popular of the arts cultivated by the Greeks, namely on the stage, in tragedy and comedy.

It was Euripides, the last of the great tragedians, who uttered the first protests against slavery. In several of his tragedies the poet shows free women who fall into slavery. Some of them commit suicide. Why should they prefer death to slavery? Because, as they tell us, they will become the master's property, they will be obliged not only to endure his caresses, but, because of the promiscuity of living conditions, anyone else's. So they prefer to die. Euripides was the first writer who refused to distinguish between the nobility of the freeman and the so-called baseness of the slave. 'Many slaves', he wrote, 'bear that name which is a dishonour to them, but their souls are freer than those of freemen.' This is genuine humanism, not racial mysticism.

In comedy we meet with a large number of slaves, some of whom venture to tell their owner that there is no natural difference between master and slave. Thus in a comedy of the fourth century we find a slave speaking as follows: 'One is no less a man for being a slave, than are you, my master. We are made of the same flesh and bones. No one is a slave by nature; it is fate that makes the bondsman.' This maxim actually goes back to the fifth century, when Alcidamas, a disciple of the Sophist Gorgias, raised the revolutionary cry: 'God made us all free: nature does not make slaves.'

The Christian revolution, one can now see, was prepared from far in advance and from lowly origins. It was because Christianity offered salvation to all men, poor and rich, bond and free—all equal in the eyes of God—that it undermined ancient society from within, through its foundation in slavery. Christianity took root at the outset among the poor, the slaves, and especially among women. But the disintegration was slow, and when the ancient world as a whole became Christian, it did not abolish slavery. The scourge of slavery, as the ancient world had practised it, gave way only before violence, and it was the inrush of the barbarian invasions that carried away slavery together with the social structure as a whole. Even then it did not entirely perish, because it was to reappear and maintain itself under the attenuated form of serfdom.

The evolutionary progress of civilizations, the progress of human liberty, are certainties. But real, concrete liberties are not born overnight. Oppressive systems are strong in their own defence. When Philip of Macedonia subjugated Greece, he imposed on the Greeks an attitude which forbade the freeing of the slaves. He knew what he was doing.

◎

The slave was not, however, the only human creature who had no part in Athenian democracy. Side by side with him, and despised almost as much, was woman. Athenian democracy was strictly and fiercely masculine; and it suffered in respect to woman, as it did in respect to the slave, from a grave discrimination which, though not racial, had the distorting effects of racial mysticism.

It had not always been so. In the primitive Greek communities woman was highly venerated. While the man devoted himself to hunting, the woman not only brought up the children, man's 'young' which took so long to grow, but she tamed wild beasts, gathered health-giving plants, supervised the precious reserves of the household. Being, as she was, in close contact with the life of nature, she held the first secrets which had been wrested from nature and she fixed the taboos which the tribe had to respect if it wanted to live. All this was prior to the settling of the Greeks in the country that was to take their name.

In the life of the couple, the woman enjoyed equality and even primacy. One should not, for that matter, speak of a 'couple'; marriage in those days was not monogamous, it was a matter of successive and temporary unions in which the woman chose the man who would give her a child.

When the Greeks, in successive waves, occupied the southern part of the Balkan peninsula and the Asiatic shores of the Aegean, they found peoples who were living for the most part under a matriarchal régime. The head of the family was the mother—the 'mater familias'—and relationship was reckoned on the distaff side. The greatest deities were feminine deities, who presided over fertility. The Greeks adopted at least two of them: the Great Mother or Cybele, and Demeter, whose name means Mother Earth or Mother of Corn. The importance of these cults in the classical period reminds us of the pre-eminence of woman in primitive Greek society.

The so-called Aegean peoples, the Pelasgians, Lydians and many others, preserved either a matriarchal régime or matriarchal customs. These people were peace-loving; the palace of Cnossos was unfortified. They practised agriculture, and this reminds us that it was woman who, by establishing agriculture, had brought mankind to a sedentary life, which is an essential stage in man's progress. Among the Cretan peoples, women enjoyed great prestige and still dominated the community.

Greek literature preserved a great number of legends in which woman is painted in the fairest colours. This is especially true of the oldest literature. Andromache and Hecuba in the *Iliad*, Penelope in the *Odyssey*, not forgetting Nausicaa or Areta, queen of the Phaeacians who is sister of the king her husband and also mistress of his decisions, all these women live on a footing of perfect equality with the men, are often the senior partners, and figure as the inspirers and controllers of men's lives. In certain Greek countries, like Sappho's Aeolis, woman maintained her position of eminence over a long period.

Very different was the situation in democratic Athens and, generally speaking, in Ionian lands. Literature, it is true, preserved the image of noble women; but it was only in the theatre that Athens applauded the Antigones and Iphigeneias. In this respect, indeed, a great gulf had opened between literature and life. Antigone was henceforth to be confined to the gynaeceum or the opisthodomos of the Parthenon; or, if she were permitted ever to emerge, it was on such rare occasions as when she figured in the procession that carried the new veil to Pallas Athene, the veil she and her companions had woven during the long months of their cloistered confinement.

Meanwhile, and side by side with the image of ideal women, literature was beginning to offer a distorted and, at first sight, caricatural picture of the sex. There is a vein of misogyny running through Greek poetry and going back as far as Hesiod, who was almost a contemporary of the author of the *Odyssey*. Hesiod, that grumbling old peasant, tells how, in order to punish men for having received from Prometheus the gift of fire which Prometheus had stolen from Zeus, Zeus ordered the gods and goddesses to set to work, three or four of them together, to mould out of wet clay, and grievous desire, and guile, and impudence—woman, that fair monster, that 'deep pitfall with steep sides and no means of escape'. It is to woman that man owes all the miseries of his existence as a frightened animal. Hesiod is tireless in dilating on the cunning, coquetry and sensuality of woman.

No less eloquent is Simonides of Amorgos who grossly insults the sex in a poem which is only too famous. This poet divides women pedantically into ten categories, each type being likened to an animal or some other creature. Thus we have the woman whose mother was a sow:

. . . all that is in her house lies disorderly, defiled with dirt, and rolling upon the floor, and she groweth fat a-sitting among the middens in garments as unwashed as herself.[1]

Then there is the fox-woman, full of underhand tricks; there is the chatterbox with her scandal and tittle-tattle, true daughter of a bitch, barking all day long; her

---

[1] *Elegy and Iambus . . . with the Anacreontea.* Newly edited and translated by J. M. Edmonds. London and New York, 1931, Vol. II, p. 217.

husband cannot keep her quiet, even by breaking her teeth with a stone. Consider also the idle-back, as heavy and hard to shift as the earth she springs from; and the child of water, changeable and capricious as her mother; at one moment furious and uncontrolled, at another gentle and smiling as the summer sea. There is the she-ass, obstinate, gluttonous and profligate; and the weasel-type, thieving and vicious. And there is the handsome mare; too proud to lower herself to any sort of work, she refuses even to throw the sweepings out of doors; vain of her beauty, she bathes twice or thrice a day, anoints herself with perfumes, and sticks flowers in her hair: 'Such a wife may be a fair sight for other men, but she's an ill to her husband.'[1] And there is the monkey-woman, so hideous and repulsive that one must pity her husband—'alas for the wretched man that claspeth such a mischief!'[2] The last type, which is the busy bee, can scarcely console us for so many detestable kinds of women.

This brutal anti-feminine poetry reflects the revolutionary change which had taken place in the status of woman between primitive and historic times.

Monogamy at the outset was not favourable to woman. The man was now the master. The woman never chose her future husband and in most cases had not even seen him. A man married simply for the 'procreation of legitimate children'; love-marriages were non-existent. The man was at least thirty years old, the woman only fifteen—a little girl who on the eve of her marriage dedicated her doll to Artemis. Marriage was a contract which put hardly more than one of the two parties under obligation. The husband could repudiate his wife and keep the children, without other formality than a declaration in presence of witnesses, provided that he returned the dowry or repaid the interest on it. If on the other hand the woman asked for divorce, it was very rarely granted and then only by virtue of a legal decision on the ground of gross ill-treatment or notorious infidelity. But infidelity was in the manners of the time. The husband did not deny himself either concubines or courtesans. Demosthenes is reported to have declared in one of his speeches: 'We have courtesans for our pleasure, concubines for our comfort, and wives to give us legitimate children.'

A legitimate wife had to be the daughter of a citizen. She had been brought up, like a little white goose, in the gynaeceum which was her sphere and almost her prison. A minor from the day of her birth to the day of her death, she only changed one guardian for another when she married. If she became a widow, she became the ward of her eldest son. In the gynaeceum she supervised the work of the slaves, and she shared in it; and rarely did she leave the gynaeceum, except to visit her parents or go to the baths, and then always under the close guard of a slave. She might sometimes go out with her lord and master; but she did not go to market.

[1] *Ibid.,* p. 221.　　　　　　　　　　　　　　　[2] *Ibid.,* p. 223.

23. Eleusis. The column in the foreground is in imitation of the torch used in the ritual

She did not know her husband's friends, nor did she accompany him to the banquets where he met them and to which he might on occasion bring his concubines. Her only business was to give her husband the children he desired and to bring up his sons until they were seven, at which age she ceased to have control of them. She kept her daughters and trained them in the gynaeceum for the life she had led herself, the melancholy life of a child-bearing housekeeper. The wife of an Athenian citizen was simply an 'oïkourema', an 'object (the word is neuter) whose purpose is to look after the household'. For the Athenian she was merely the first of his servants.

Concubinage developed on a large scale during the classical era in Athens. It was a sort of half-marriage, half-prostitution; and it was on this ground which, though not recognized, was tolerated and favoured by the state, that the only notable Athenian women whose memory has come down to us grew up. The fair and brilliant Aspasia, brilliant with all the charms of wit and learning, was the daughter of a Milesian. She is said to have been expert in the new art of sophistry. Pericles, after repudiating his legitimate wife, a noble, installed Aspasia in his own house. Here she held a salon and, despite a whole campaign of insults, her pseudo-husband managed to impose her on Athenian society. This man who, according to Thucydides, declared in an official discourse that the best thing women could do 'was to cause men to say as little as possible about them, whether of good or ill'— this man paraded his liaison with the high-class 'hetaira', a word that simply means female friend. Thus the case of Aspasia and others like her shows that to acquire any real personality a woman had to begin by being half a courtesan, a fact which constitutes the severest possible condemnation of the Athenian family.

Plato in his ideal state tolerates concubinage, provided that men conceal their 'friends' and that the latter cause no scandal.

We say nothing of the so-called low-class prostitutes who filled the brothels of Athens and the Piraeus—slaves for the most part, though not all of them. The young men could have one for an obol. This kind of prostitution was officially established in houses which Solon had founded with a view to public order and morality.

But how, we may ask, and at what moment had so complete a revolution taken place in the status of woman? How had the Andromaches and Alcestises of legend become the Aspasias of reality, how had they become either the nameless wives or concubines, mere slaves of man's pleasure or agents for procreation? One thing is certain: there was a time when the female sex suffered its gravest defeat. From being mistress of the family community in matriarchal times, woman had fallen, in classical Greece, into the most humiliating situation. When did this 'great historical defeat of woman' take place? We are reduced here to the field of conjecture, but

I

24. *Head of woman or goddess from the Artemisium (temple of Artemis) of Croesus, at Ephesus (c. 550 B.C.)*

the most likely is that it was connected with the discovery of metals and the development of war as a profitable industry.

Men discovered copper and by alloying it with tin, forged the first weapons of bronze. Then they discovered iron and made themselves new weapons, very formidable in that age. Once in possession of these arms, they turned war into an immensely profitable business. The Achaean brigands piled up gold in the tombs of the Mycenaean kings. And the Dorians destroyed what remained of the peaceful civilization of the Aegean peoples. This took place at the very beginning of the historical period.

With the fall of Aegean civilization, woman lost her position of primacy and the so-called monogamous marriage was established. This was because man, the lord of war, wished to transmit the wealth that war procured him to children of whom he was certain of being the father. Hence monogamous marriage, which made the legitimate wife an agent of procreation, and other women objects of amusement or pleasure.

As a matter of fact the remnants of matriarchy took some time to disappear. Apart from the legends which conveyed a memory of them, in tragic poetry, down to the middle of the classical era, woman for long preserved rights which she afterwards lost and did not everywhere recover. An instance of these was the right of voting which, according to a learned English hellenist, Athenian women possessed in the time of Cecrops, that is, about the tenth century B.C.

What really seems the limit is that when Euripides began to treat tragedy realistically and to depict women either with the very real faults that the social pressure they had undergone had bred in them, or else in the noble yet perfectly true manner in which legend presented them, yet also in colours so close and familiar that they *really* became the wives, sisters and daughters of the spectators— when he did that, Euripides caused the whole of Athens to cry shame on him and even to treat him as a misogynist. Whether he spoke too well of women, or too ill, it came to the same thing, it was still misogyny. In the eyes of his contemporaries Euripides paid a heavy price for not respecting Pericles' dictatorial instructions: 'Silence regarding women, silence about their virtues, silence about their misfortune.' Euripides felt too keenly for them, to be silent.

But this unnatural attitude to woman had social consequences that were much more serious. We know how the sentiment of love became perverted in this way, that as man was incapable of feeling love for a being as socially degraded as woman, the feeling became what is called Greek love—the paederasty of which ancient literature, and mythology and life, were full.

The status of woman in the ancient Greek world was therefore an ulcer as serious as slavery. Excluded as she was from civic life, woman, as much as the

exercise

slave, called for a society and civilization which would restore not only equality between the sexes, but the dignity and humanity which were her right.

And that is why, as I have said, it was among women as much as among slaves that Christianity extended its sway. But the promises of early Christianity—promises of liberation for both classes—were only imperfectly fulfilled, at least in this world we live in. How many revolutions were needed and will still be needed, since the Christian revolution, to rescue woman from the abyss into which her 'great historical defeat' plunged her?

◎

It was in these ways that Athenian democracy became degraded. Confined solely to male citizens of full age, it was so unrepresentative of the 'popular power' its name indicated, that one can reckon the number of citizens composing it at approximately 30,000 men out of a total population of 400,000—a small crumb of good earth which one storm would be enough to wash into the sea.

If the Greeks invented democracy, it was in the fashion of a child growing his first teeth. These teeth have to grow, and then they have to drop out. But others will appear after them. *exercise*

131
1.5
1.6

CHAPTER EIGHT

MEN AND GODS

Greek religion seems at first glance very primitive; and primitive it is. Some of the notions most prominent in the classical epoch, notably the ideas of 'hubris' and 'nemesis', are to be found among populations as backward as the Moïs tribes of southern Indo-China. It is a mistake, in trying to understand this religion, to look for points of comparison with Christianity.

In the course of its existence which extended over a period of more than a thousand years, the religious life of the Greeks assumed a number of varied forms; but it never took on a dogmatic form, which would have simplified our understanding of it. There is nothing in Greek religion to resemble a catechism or anything like a sermon, unless indeed the tragic or comic representations can be called 'preaching'. Now they can, in a sense I shall make clear. But I must add that in ancient Greece there were virtually no clergy, or in any case no influential clergy, aside from the oracles in the great sanctuaries. It was the city magistrates who, in addition to their other functions, performed certain sacrifices and pronounced certain prayers. These ritual acts were part of an ancestral tradition which we should do wrong to ignore. But actual beliefs were extremely free, even wavering and changeable. A belief counted less than the ritual gesture that accompanied the belief: it was like saying good-morning by raising your hand, or throwing a kiss to the great powers whose importance in daily life both the masses, and the intellectuals who were rarely far apart from the masses, agreed in recognizing.

Greek religion presents the intricate medley of beliefs we find in folklore; in fact it is a folklore. If the distinction between religion and folklore, which we make today, has any meaning when applied to a dogmatic religion like Christianity, it has no meaning when applied to the ancient religions. It was from the chaotic yet vital traditions of folklore that the ancient poets and artists took the material with which they constantly created and recreated their conceptions of the gods. They remained believers as long as their art spoke directly to the people, and thus they refashioned the popular faith, making the gods more human. This progressive humanizing of the divine is one of the most striking features of Greek religion. It has other features no less important, but as I am obliged to choose, I shall insist most of all on this one.

◎

Greek religion, like all primitive religions, reflects at the outset simply man's weakness in the face of 'powers' whose presence he detects in nature and later in society and in himself, powers that seem to impede his action and to constitute a threat to his existence all the more formidable in that he fails to grasp its source. What interests primitive man is not nature or the forces of nature in themselves, but only nature in the measure in which she intervenes in his life and fixes its conditions.

Man, even primitive man, knows himself to be capable of reflection—witness Odysseus—capable also of undertaking actions and calculating their consequences. But now he is constantly running his head against obstacles, making errors, or missing his aim, his aim being simply to satisfy some elementary needs. Hence he arrives quite naturally at admitting that there exist around him wills much more powerful than his, wills whose behaviour is altogether impossible to foresee.

Primitive man therefore records, by empirical reasoning, the action of deity as the action of a 'power' that intervenes unexpectedly in his life. It usually intervenes to his detriment but sometimes to his advantage. It may be beneficent or maleficent, but it is at first unexpected, arbitrary, foreign to himself both in its nature and conduct. A god in the first instance is something that surprises. Its action inspires astonishment, fear and also respect. To express these complex feelings, Greek uses the word 'aidôs', English the word 'awe'. Man does not hold this 'power' to be supernatural, he rather has the feeling of having encountered something 'other' than himself.

The religious feeling of primitive man can be almost wholly defined as a feeling of the presence of 'Otherness'.[1]

The divine may exist everywhere, in a stone, in water, in a tree or an animal. Not that everything in nature is god, but everything can be, by luck or mischance; everything can manifest itself as deity.

Let us imagine a peasant walking across the mountains. At the edge of the track he comes upon a pile of stones. Now this pile in the course of time has been formed of stones that peasants like himself have thrown there as they passed. These piles,

[1] . . . le sentiment de la présence de l'Autre.'

which he calls 'hermes', are reassuring landmarks in districts that are little known. A god dwells in them; later on he will acquire human form and will be called Hermes, the god who protects travellers and who conducts the souls of the departed on the difficult paths that lead to the nether world. For the moment he is only a pile of stones, but this pile is divine and therefore 'powerful'. Sometimes a traveller who needs to be calmed and protected lays a food-offering at the spot; if the next traveller is hungry, he will take it, calling his find a 'hermaion'.

At the outset and over a long period the Greeks were peasants, and later sailors. Their gods were the same. They dwelt in the fields, woods, rivers and springs, and later in the sea. Now the Greek lands did not receive all the rain they needed, or it fell capriciously. Rivers were few and sacred. One should not cross a stream without saying a prayer and washing one's hands in the water. One should not urinate at the mouth of a stream or near its source: this is the advice of the peasant Hesiod. Rivers are regarded as fertilizing not only the fields but also the human species. When a boy grows up and for the first time cuts his long hair, he devotes it to some stream in his native region.

Each stream has its deity, a river-god who has the form of a bull with human face. In the European folklore of today we still find river genii appearing as bulls. In Greece the water-spirit also figures as a horse. Poseidon, who became one of the great gods of classical Greece, is associated as much with a horse as with water. One day with a blow of his trident he caused a pool—pompously called a sea—of salt water to splash as high as the Athenian acropolis, just as, with a blow of his hoof on Mount Helicon, the winged horse Pegasus caused the spring of Hippocrene to gush out. Now the form and functions of Poseidon depended on the trades pursued by the populations who worshipped him. Among the sailors of Ionia he was god of the sea; on dry land and particularly in the Peloponnese, he was both the horse-god and the god of earthquakes. The many streams that disappear underground, and sometimes emerge much further on, were popularly believed to erode the earth and provoke seismic disturbances.

The Greeks also peopled the countryside with many other genii to whom they attributed a semi-animal and semi-human form. The Centaurs, who had the body of a horse and the head and torso of a man, belong to the realm of poetry and art; but they are certainly of popular origin. The name appears to mean 'those who lash the waters'. They were probably at the outset tutelary spirits of the mountain torrents of Pelion and Arcadia, where poets placed their habitat. In Ionia inscriptions testify to the belief in Silens: they had a horse's legs and tail and a rather ugly human body, and they expressed the wilder aspects of nature. They were also ithyphallic, a feature which was not originally intended to provoke mirth but expressed the great fertilizing powers of nature. The same remark applies to the

Satyrs, who had the feet, ears and tail of a goat and were likewise ithyphallic. They were later to be enrolled in the fierce and joyous troop of Dionysus, with whom they helped to make plants and trees grow, and herds and families multiply. They also assisted him in bringing back the Spring, as primitive peoples always doubted whether Spring would succeed Winter.

Like all the European peoples, the Greeks also expressed the fertility of nature in the form of numerous feminine deities. The most popular of these and the nearest to mankind—although, like all divine beings, very dangerous to approach—were those amiable spirits who were as affable and graceful as young women and whose name of 'nymphs' simply, in fact, means young women. They were enchanting creatures, benevolent, joyous, ever ready to dance; but they might suddenly grow angry and threatening, and then they became that something 'other' which characterizes the whole of deity. Supposing a man goes mad before your eyes: people say: 'the nymphs have taken him.' It was to them, however, that men addressed the most intimate worship, the worship inspired by our deepest feelings, namely our love for our wife and children. When, after an absence of twenty years, he returns to Ithaca and before he, with Telemachus, undertakes the stern battle with the suitors which will give him back Penelope and his kingdom, Odysseus approaches the deep, vaulted cavern of the Nymphs, by the sea-shore. To them, of old, he had offered many sacrifices. To their care he now confides the treasure he has brought back from his voyages. But especially does he wish to entrust to them the safety of his present enterprise. He bows himself to the ground, he kisses that great rustic deity, 'the corn-yielding Earth,' and then, raising his hands to heaven, he begs the familiar, protecting nymphs, as well as Athena, to grant him victory.

There was a queen of wild nature, very like the nymphs who escorted her. She was at first called simply the 'Lady of the wild beasts', but in the religious life of Greece she later became the great goddess Artemis. She haunted forests and high mountain-tops, and her worship was connected with the cult of trees, springs and streams. She was called, according to the locality, *Lygodesmos*, which means that she lived among willow-trees, or sometimes *Caryatis*, because of walnuts, or sometimes *Cedreatis*, because of cedars. She was the most popular goddess in the whole of Greece. The Greek peasant of today has not entirely forgotten her, because he calls the queen of the nymphs—in whom he still believes—'The beautiful Lady' or 'The Queen of the Mountains'. This survival of Artemis after two thousand years of Christian faith is one of the most striking instances of the popular and universal character of this ancient peasant-religion. And there has been another survival, this time of the cult of nymphs. Scarcely a century ago, in a rock-dwelling on a hillside in the heart of the city of Athens, women who were with child used to make offerings to the nymphs from whom they expected a happy delivery and conjugal happiness.

Then there was 'the corn-yielding Earth', a deity who, with the sky, is as old as any in the world. Alive under our feet as under the peasant's pick or plough, she is also the mother of all living things, beasts, men and gods, whom she feeds with her grain. In fact her Greek name, Demeter, probably means 'Mother of Corn'. Homer says that one day Demeter was united with a mortal named Iasion, and that a field ploughed three times over served as their couch. She gave birth to Ploutos, whose name means wealth.

Now in the ancient economic system, wealth consisted of the provision of corn which men stored up in their silos and lived on during the seasons when the fruits of the earth are rare. Pluto, king of the underworld, is simply a name derived from 'ploutos'; it means 'he who possesses wealth'. This wealth consisted not only of the countless multitude of the dead, of whom Pluto was lord, but in the first instance of the seeds stored in the silo.

Demeter was the goddess of seeds. Her daughter, who was always associated with her cult, bore several names of which the commonest was Coré, which means 'The Maiden of the Grain'. From as early as prehellenic times Demeter and Coré had been the two great goddesses of the peasant population of Attica: later, this cult spread to the whole of the Athenian community. The legend tells us how Pluto, king of the dead and of silos, carried off Coré to the nether world. In order to calm her mother's grief, Zeus ordered him to restore her. So he restores her every year. The Mysteries of Eleusis in Attica celebrated the return to the light of day of 'The Maiden of the Grain', and the reunion of the two goddesses who pass eight months together and are separated for four months.

According to an attractive theory, the eight months of reunion were calculated from the time when the silos were reopened for the autumn sowing. All plants spring up very quickly in Attica; cereals planted in October grow during the winter, apart from a short interruption in January. They begin to ripen at the end of April, are harvested in May, and threshed in June. Then the seed reserved for the next sowing is stored in the silos: the Maiden of the Grain returns to the under-world, to the realm of Pluto. But by a very natural confusion, Coré's sojourn underground was also related to the period when the seed that has been sown comes up as a young ear of corn. 'Except a grain of wheat fall into the earth and die, it abideth by itself alone', we read in the Gospel: 'but if it die, it beareth much fruit.'[1]

A little before the time when the silos were opened, the Mysteries of Demeter and Coré were celebrated at Eleusis. Here, though in what form we do not exactly

[1] John XII, 24.

know, the initiate attended the reunion of the Mother of Corn and the Maiden of the Grain. In any event, the ceremony of initiation offered the believers a spectacle which was no doubt very simple. In fact a Christian writer who appears to be reliable declares that the highest mystery in the initiation consisted of the display by the high-priest of Eleusis of an ear of corn.

If the origin of this cult was agrarian and very simple, it is nevertheless true that in the course of centuries it acquired deeper meanings.

The life-giving Earth nourishes the grain of corn. She nourishes us while we live. When we die she takes us back into herself and we in our turn nourish the plants of the earth. Corn that nourishest us, we are also thy nourishment. As then we must return into the bosom of the living Earth, the death which awaits us loses its terror; and the springing up of the new harvest may symbolize the eternity of life.

There thus grew up, on the foundation of an ancient rural cult, a certain hope of immortality—not, at first, for the individual but for the succession of generations. This evolution had taken place by the end of the archaic period. Later on, in liberal fifth-century Athens, when the individual felt he was freed from the bonds of family and tradition, he came to desire personal immortality. The Eleusinian Mysteries ended by promising the initiate even this: a life of happiness was reserved for him in the nether world. But this belief was not a natural outgrowth of the rural cult, it was rather a beginning of deviation.

One may note another interesting feature of the Eleusinian Mysteries. They had been a family cult at the outset; the head of the family admitted those whom he pleased to admit. This explains why it was possible for foreigners, women and slaves to attend the celebration of the Mysteries. These, then, offered the most disinherited members of society a compensation for the wretchedness of their lot; and from this point of view—the universal character they possessed, at least in principle—the Mysteries in some measure anticipated the Christian religion.

From the eighth century onwards the Greeks were as much a seafaring as a peasant people. With the *Odyssey*, they went out to discover and colonize the lands of the western Mediterranean, and we know how hard were the conditions and how wretched their boats. Compared to Odysseus tossed about over the empty wastes of the Ionian Sea, Lindbergh crossed the Atlantic in an armchair.

But these wastes were not really empty. Round every headland, in every narrow strait, some 'marvel' born of fright, some prodigy fearsome and yet attractive for the heart of a man intent on treasure and adventure, lay in waiting for the sailor who had no compass. 'The cry of the empty belly launches the ships, which cleave the ocean wave.' Yet it was on the sea and its islands, and beyond the vast spaces of ocean, that one could 'see strange things', and discover the world, and count up its wonders.

The 'marvellous' element in the *Odyssey*, deriving from popular beliefs older than the *Iliad* itself, had refashioned the forces of nature as strange creatures with forms gigantic or grotesque, or as beings immortally fair. Although these beings could not be the objects of a cult, they were none the less significant of the dual feeling that the vast sea inspired in primitive man: the feeling of its immense destructive power, and of the perfidious attraction it exercises. We laugh at the adventure of the Cyclops because, by overcoming it, a very cunning man has made it possible to laugh; but sailors who had lost their way off the shores of Sicily or Naples did not laugh when they heard Vesuvius or Etna growling and rumbling.

Under the cover of their peaceful, pastoral life, the Cyclops are absolutely enigmatic to man. There is no possible prayer that Odysseus can offer to Polyphemus, that man-eating monster, that anti-social atheist. The poet insists on the horror the Cyclops feel for everything connected with civilized life, such as boats, laws and assemblies. Like the other monsters in the poem they illustrate what appeared to the understanding of primitive man as the brutal, irrational and quite incomprehensible character of natural phenomena.

Take Charybdis and Scylla: the one represents the mechanical power of a whirlpool to engulf successive vessels; the other is a monster with six heads, each having three jaws and teeth 'full of black death'. Such creations are a mythical expression of the sailor's horror in face of the terrifying powers of destruction which the sea possesses.

With Circe and the Sirens we are in presence of a more complex symbol. These fair nymphs are the traps laid by nature, that aspect of nature which attracts and 'enchants' us—in the sense in which they are 'enchantresses'. But the smile of the nymphs scarcely conceal the fundamental hostility, towards man, of the natural world, though one must read beyond this too metaphorical language. Circe uses her 'charms' to change men into beasts and shut them in her stables. The voice of the Sirens is divine, but the field where they sing is strewn with human bones. Nature is here represented in the contrast we imagine to exist between her beauty and her mortal aversion for human life. Once the men have been drawn to her by Circe, the witch simply brings them into the realm of nature where she is sovereign; and they, whether they have become lions or pigs, forget that they have a homeland. So that here, as in the other adventures in the *Odyssey*, every time that men make their way into the forbidden zone, which is the blind world of nature, every time they let themselves be won over by one of those double-visaged creatures which the poet took from traditional lore to express his conception of the world, they lose their homeland which is the symbol of their common humanity, they lose 'the return', as the poet also expresses it. They lose their character as men living in the social state.

And if they do not wholly lose it, if they do not let themselves be annihilated by this dehumanizing terror, it is because Odysseus is a man. I will not say a hero. No supernatural fire shines on his head as it does on the head of Diomed and of other warriors in the *Iliad*. His very human face is marked only by the struggles he has waged and the experience he has gained from them. He is a man by all the links that bind him to society: love of his wife and son in the first place, love of his land and love of work which creates things and inspires actions. And he returns to his homeland because, by mobilizing all the resources of his mind, his heart and his hands together, he has overcome the demons of the sea.

But as early as the composition of the *Iliad* and the *Odyssey*, a part of the fear inspired by the 'marvels' of the sea had been overcome. The positive-minded Odysseus, when relating his adventures to his Phaeacian hosts, is capable of smiling momentarily at the fantastic and terrifying world which his seafaring ancestors had created; and there are other signs in the *Odyssey* that this 'marvellous' element was already a thing of the past. The Greeks were incapable of accepting so much that was mysterious and incredible, they could not resign themselves to the incomprehensible; and so in their traditions they soon substituted, for these monstrous gods and cruel nymphs, deities of human shape, deities whom imagination or reason therefore found easier to interpret. On the sea and elsewhere a comforting anthropomorphism began to reign. Thus Poseidon, Prince of the Sea, harnesses his steeds like some noble warrior in the *Iliad*. It is true that these horses fly over the waves. Dolphins, dogfish and whales gambol joyously around him. Lord of the watery plains, he has a palace and a consort—queen Amphitrite—in the ocean depths. He reigns over a numerous people of fishes and monsters, an elusive and perfidious folk. He himself, always as furious as the waves, pursues with his anger not only Odysseus but all the sailors who venture on the waves. But, in short, he has the shape, thoughts and feelings of a man, and hence mariners who are exposed to his sudden fury may seek to discover the reasons for his anger and try to appease him.

This anthropomorphism, this humanizing of the gods, not only affected the sea but extended to the world as a whole. Zeus had at first been a god of the sky and the weather, a god of thunder and tempest, lord of the clouds which pile up and burst in rainstorms more destructive than salutary: 'the god rains' or 'Zeus rains' were almost interchangeable expressions in Greek. Then Zeus became the god of the enclosure. One of his ancient epithets was Herkeios: the Zeus of the hedge or the fence. He became the god of the house, who protected the inmates against inclement weather; then the god of the hearth. As such, Zeus Herkeios had an altar in every home. He was adored as Zeus *pater* (Jupiter), which did not mean that he was the ancestor, but the protector, of the family. As Zeus *Ktesios* (the acquirer), a title he bore in many Greek lands, he protected both the house and its resources. And because he protected the house and watched over the provision of salt and bread, the basic food, and because he offered them to the traveller who entered, he was regarded by those who called on his name as a gracious host, full of humanity towards strangers and homeless wretches. He was therefore human both as to form and feelings, and he was at once the most powerful and the best of the gods.

So it was with the other gods who became gods of Olympus. Take the example of Apollo. He was as fair as the day, his face shone with light. A whole portion of his activity reveals his solar origin. His arrows inflicted sudden death, as a sun-stroke may do. But he also healed the sick, as also do the sunrays. This very human god was often very kind; not only did he purify and heal the body, he also washed away the stains of crime when the guilty man came to pray at his altar or to wash in the spring near the sanctuary of Delphi—although, as an ancient text makes clear, he had to do so with a pure heart. How could one fail to picture in human form a god so near to man?

But in several parts of Greece, and notably among the Arcadians who were a shepherd people, we come across another origin of Apollo, a god whose figure combines many others of very various origins by a process of syncretism. Here he is Apollo Lukeios, which means god of the wolves. He is the slayer of wolves, he protects the flocks and herds, he carries lambs and calves in his arms. Thus he is represented in archaic sculpture as a good shepherd. An image which has traversed centuries and religions. The representation of Apollo or Hermes as a good shep-herd carrying the young of the flock on his shoulders is also that of the beardless Christ which you may see in the catacombs of Rome or the mosaics of Ravenna[1]— the most ancient representation of God incarnate in man.

Apart from that, Apollo god of the day has an eye so piercing that he knows the future and reveals it. In the sanctuary of Delphi, in a valley on the lower slopes of Parnassus, there stood a famous temple of Apollo venerated by the ancient world,

---

[1] 'Les vitraux (?) de Ravenne.' The reference is presumably to the mosaics. There is, for example, in the Mausoleum of Galla Placidia, a mosaic representing the beardless Christ with the sheep reposing beside Him (Translator).

by Greeks and barbarians alike. Here the god inspired his prophetess, and the priests interpreted in oracles the inarticulate words of the Pythoness. Apollo knew what was best for individuals and for cities. Believers thronged his sanctuary in their thousands. They consulted the god concerning every kind of business, much as today one consults the barrister, the solicitor or the vicar. In many cases his advice was excellent. If it was a question of founding a new city overseas, the god indicated the most promising site and mentioned the resources of the distant country to which one was emigrating. Of course the priests who delivered oracles obtained information about these lands, unknown to the people who consulted them, by means scarcely different from those of a modern travel-agency. But they made few efforts to conceal the fact and the faithful were not unaware of it. Delphi was filled with the most splendid treasures from all over the world.

Sometimes, however, the god's oracles were deceptive; sometimes they inevitably misled those who wished to follow them. It was thought that the god intended in this way to show that the divine omnipotence and liberty may always prevail over the good will of mortals. Apollo was then withdrawing to a proper distance.

The god of light was also the god of harmony. He had invented music and poetry for the delight of man. He practised and loved these arts more than anything else. So the best way of winning the favour of this distant but benevolent god was to offer him festivals at which choirs of boys and girls sang and danced round his altars.

For that matter, most of the gods were fond of fine festivals. They were the joyous gods of a merry people which sought to win the divine favour by organizing beautiful performances, sporting competitions, torch-races and ball games. To pray and offer sacrifices to the gods was good; to celebrate festivals in their honour, and even to perform very funny plays where they would be made game of *en vassant*, was still better. The gods loved laughter, even if it just scratched them a little. On Mount Olympus where they assembled in the palace of Zeus, their own laughter, according to Homer, was 'inextinguishable'. So, to execute to the accompaniment of the flute a fine dance in their honour, to dance with one's whole body filled with and responding to the music, was especially pleasing to these gods who were carnal gods, as sensitive as man to the beauty of rhythm and melody.

◎

Such were a few of the gods of Olympus, as their figures took shape after primitive times. Refashioned by Homer, that poet of genius, in the *Iliad*, the Greek gods became impressively human. We are aware, through all our senses, of their physical presence. It is not enough to say they are alive: we can hear their cries and sometimes their howls. Zeus and Poseidon have hair blacker than nature: it is almost blue, it is blue-black. We can see the dazzling whiteness or the deep blue of the goddesses' robes, or again their saffron hue. Their thin veils dazzle us 'like the sunlight'. Hera wears precious stones as large as mulberries. Zeus is not sparing of gold in his accoutrements; his cloak is of gold, and so are his sceptre, his whip and the rest. Hera's shining tresses hang down on both sides of her head, and the perfume she uses is powerful: it fills heaven and earth. Athena's eyes glitter, Aphrodite's shine like marble. Hera sweats. Hephaestus sweats and sponges his face; his chest is hairy, and he limps ostentatiously. One could continue indefinitely. These physical gods deafen and blind us; they come near to offending us.

Corresponding with their physical presence, the gods have a physical life equally powerful. It differs from that of the heroes in being not more complex but more obscure. These gods of flesh and bone may seem to reflect our own image too closely at times, and they are certainly more human and therefore more accessible to our prayers than the primitive gods who were owls, pebbles and so on: yet they have in themselves something ineffable—in fact that something which is what makes them gods. Sometimes a mere detail gives us a glimpse of it. When Aphrodite, who has come down on to the battlefield, is wounded by Diomed, the poet tells us:

> And when, hard on her track through the great crowd,
> He came on her at last, proud Tydeus' son
> Lunged with his sharp spear as he sprang at her
> And pierced the skin of her soft hand; the spear
> Passed quickly through the ambrosial raiment which
> The very Graces wove her, and bored through
> The bone above the palm; and forth there flowed
> The goddess' blood immortal. . . .[1]

From this singular touch, from the tearing of the well-nigh immaterial fabric that veils the divine flesh, we realize that Diomed has wrought an unheard-of deed, and that 'the weakest of the goddesses' is still a great goddess. For truly the humanized gods of the *Iliad* are still very formidable gods. They are Powers. Something about them resists a complete humanization, and indeed the reader would himself reject it. In the midst of the sorrowful world they govern, the amazing exuberance of their joy is a terrible confirmation of their divine character. On the approach of death, men know them as the gods of the living; and in fact they live in such a plenitude of life that the believer cannot but adore them. He is filled with their joy

[1] *Iliad*, Book V, p. 103. Trans. Sir William Marris.

through the image which the seer-poet has drawn. No matter if they use their sovereign liberty in ways impossible to foresee. No matter if a deep gulf separates the human condition from the divine. The only thing that touches us is that the gods dwell in a state of endless bliss, that they live in gaiety and laughter and absolute joy. 'Tears are reserved for men,' says Homer; 'laughter for the gods.'

The religious feeling that such gods may inspire is not without a certain grandeur. It is still connected with the fear of the unknown Power; but this fear is mingled with a sort of disinterested joy in knowing that there is in the world, separate from it and yet very near to it, a race of immortal beings, a race of men exempt from the heavy yoke with which mortals are burdened—in brief, a race of gods who live on the serene and shining Olympus, themselves serene because they have been freed from death, suffering and care. For these gods, morality has no meaning. Morality is a human invention, a kind of science drawn from man's experience and designed to ward off the principal accidents that may befall us. But why should the gods of the *Iliad* need a moral system, if the passions they give way to, in the profusion of enjoyment, do not entail for them the unpleasant consequences they entail for mortals? We know that the wrath of Achilles entails the defeat of the Greeks and the death of many warriors under the walls of Troy. But the wrath of Zeus with Hera, which we read about in the same book of the *Iliad*, simply turns into a domestic scene and ends in a burst of 'inextinguishable' laughter. All the passions of the gods, expressed in a life of care-free adventure, end in laughter.

Such reflections on the nature of the gods were not without cruelty for the Greeks. The greatest poets had these thoughts and expressed them. Nevertheless, the believer contemplated Olympus as a spectacle which 'ravished' him, in the strong sense of that term. The gods of the *Iliad* are very indifferent to the quarrels of mankind, and in fact they exist for themselves, for the pure joy of existing, and not in relation to man or in the capacity of policemen engaged in the service of right or justice. They quite simply exist, like one of the many forms of life, like the sun, the rivers or the trees, whose only apparent reason for existence is to please us by their beauty. They are free, not with the kind of freedom we understand—a liberty wrested from nature after a hard struggle—but with a freedom which is a gift of nature. One can never sufficiently emphasize the heroic character of a conception which entrusted the government of the world, and man's destiny, to great forces which were not immoral but amoral and obscure, forces of which the object was not clearly defined though not perhaps impossible to ascertain, and for which the principle of causality scarcely operated at all.

The Greeks were a courageous people, and their courage was not one of resignation but of struggle. They adored in their gods only what they were quite decided to win one day for themselves, namely, a field of unlimited opportunity for their *joie de vivre*.

This religion of the great *figures* of Olympus was not, as some have maintained, static; it was not a sort of aesthetic consolation for the evil of being born a mortal. The cult of art was a threat to it, and yet, despite the countless masterpieces it owed to this cult, the religion did not founder. This was because, at the time when it appeared and flourished, the Greeks carried within themselves many other creative resources. It must however be added that by displaying to man's mind a humanity more successful than his own, filled with a happiness always active because not threatened, happier in short than himself, Greek religion invited him to vie with this new kind of humanity. It invited man to 'contend with the Angel'. There was certainly peril in so doing, and the Greeks gave the name of 'hubris' to the dangerous combat. The gods are jealous of their happiness and defend it in the manner of a privileged class. 'Hubris' (pride) and 'nemesis' (jealousy) are primitive beliefs. The Greeks were slowly to cast them off. Now in tragic drama one of the main lines of the conflict will be the struggle against the peril of 'hubris' and the threat of 'nemesis'. Tragedy will reply either by accepting the risk of human greatness or by putting men on their guard against an ambition too lofty for mortals. It will, in general, assert both the greatness of the man who has been struck down and the omnipotence of the gods who strike him. But tragedy will still, in one way or another, have to justify their action. It will still be necessary that the gods should be just. We have not yet reached that stage. The gods of the *Iliad* care little about a justice which would limit their sovereign power and freedom.

But what, after all, was to become of this fine religion of 'figures', which, in forms clearly grasped and defined, displayed to the mind of man both his unconfessed desires and the most valuable achievements of his future? This religion was destined quite simply to dissolve into the human. The deities of Olympus, who in the era of the cities were 'poliad' deities, were to become the leaders of the civic communities, or even, in the case of Zeus and Apollo, of the Hellenic community. The gods would now be little more than the city-standards, flapping in the winds of conflict; or else they would be humanized until they were no more than the symbols of those forces that act in our thoughts or in our blood, and that keep us going. But when that happened, Greek religion which had now become blended with the power and glory of the city or with the most compelling motives of our conduct, would be near its end. It would become frozen in poetic images, beautiful perhaps but hollow.

Greek religion, in fact, by becoming human, became secular. The city-state and the gods were henceforth indissolubly united. The temples raised in Athens by

25. Head of Zeus. Archaic bronze (c. 500 B.C.)

Peisistratus, and later by Pericles, celebrate not simply the glory of the gods, but the glory of the community that has built them; in the case of Pericles, the glory of Athens, metropolis of an empire. Religious feeling is now giving place to patriotism, to the pride of offering the deity such splendid monuments, such opportunities for dazzling festivals, such objects for the admiration of mankind. But by identifying itself with civic pride, the religion of humanized gods once again moved away from man's heart and developed it less than it supposed. At that moment, however, the Greeks had taken firm hold of another weapon or rather another tool with which to rebuild the world: namely, science. Would they be able to use it?

We must now speak of the artificer gods. Science, as we shall see, was to be an outcome of manual work and especially of techniques in the use of fire. In archaic times, man attributed his inventions to the gods. Inventions became more frequent in the age when the Greeks had ceased to be simply peasants or sailors and when a new social class, already numerous in the time of Solon in the rapidly growing cities, made a living by the work of its hands. This was the artificer class, comprising workmen, tradesmen, shopkeepers and merchants. They too had their gods, who were worker-gods in their own image.

After Prometheus, Hephaestus was the god of fire, not the fire of the thunderbolt, but the domesticated fire of the kitchen and the forge. He had his workshops inside volcanoes, where you could hear him toiling with his gangs of men. A great number of tools were at his disposal, hammers and fire-tongs, an enormous anvil and twenty pairs of bellows to heat up the furnaces. All day long he toiled, stripped to the waist, with a workman's cap on his head, while he hammered out the metal on his anvil. In fifth-century Athens, where he was simply called the Workman, he had a very fine temple in the lower town which was the principal working-class district. It is still almost intact. On the esplanade of his sanctuary, the people celebrated his festivals with dancing and noisy rejoicings; these festivals have remained popular and are celebrated even at the present day. The ancient festival, reserved for the working-class, was called 'Chalceia'. Strictly speaking, it was the Tinkers' Festival; but the other artisans, notably the potters, took part in it. It was presided over by Athena in her capacity as Worker-goddess ('Ergané').

The goddess who had given her name to Athens was the most perfect image of the industrious city of the archaic and classical ages. Herself a good worker, she was the patroness of all her hard-working people. To her carpenter and mason owed their T-square. She also protected the metallurgical arts and particularly the multitude of potters who gave their name to the great suburb of the Cerameicus.

K

26. *Murder of Aegisthus (Bas-relief in old-fashioned style, to illustrate 'The Choephoroe')*

It was Athena who had invented the potter's lathe and made the first vases in terra cotta. She was on the watch to prevent accidents in laying on the colours and also in the firing. She drove off the devils who broke pots or cracked the varnish—the demons Syntrips, Sabaktes and Smaragus who lay in ambush in the oven or in the clay itself. The whole team of potters—masters, modellers, composers, draughts-men, painters who laid on the black, leaving the red clay bare for the figures, and who touched up the design with a wine-coloured stroke or a white stroke, some-times using a brush with one bristle; the craftsmen who saw to the firing; the workers who kneaded the clay—all of them invoked Athena. We possess a very touching popular song composed by one of them. It begins with a prayer to Athena that she will extend her hand over the oven, so that the vases may be baked to the right point, that the black varnish may preserve its gloss, and that the sale may leave a good profit. On one of the vases we see Athena herself, escorted by little Victories, appearing in the midst of a potters' workshop and placing crowns on the craftsmen's heads.

The Worker-goddess also watched over women's handiwork. Spindle and distaff were in her eyes more precious attributes than the spear. It was 'with Athena's fingers', people said, that the girls and women of Athens wove and adorned with embroidery the fabrics that were sometimes soft and transparent, so that they sprayed out at the waist, sometimes heavy so that they fell in noble vertical folds. Four little girls, from seven to eleven years of age, were confined for nine months in the opisthodomos of the sanctuary on the Acropolis, where they wove, and embroidered with mythological scenes, the new dress that was presented every year to the goddess for her birthday. The Worker-goddess mingled in the daily life of her people and was their perfect representative. Tall and grand as she stood on the Acropolis, wearing her helmet and grasping her spear, she defended them. In the streets of the lower town and in the suburbs, she offered the humble folk, without mysteries or mysticism, a religion that was honest and, for the times, very reasonable.

The following appeal occurs in a chorus of Sophocles: 'Come down into the street, all ye folk who work with your hands, ye who worship the daughter of Zeus, Ergané of the piercing eyes; come down with your baskets of sacrifice and stand beside the anvils.' The passage is a fragment and therefore requires great care in the interpretation; but no doubt, this 'come down into the street' is not to be taken as a summons to a revolutionary mob. One may suppose that it is simply a sum-mons to some festival common to the two deities who protected workmen. The festival was in any event a popular one and the whole population of manual workers celebrated it.

Very near to Hephaestus and Athena, and very popular all over Greece, was the old deity of the pile of stones. Hermes had now become the sly and artful god of travellers, traffickers, shopkeepers, tradesmen and merchants. His statues could be seen in market-places and beside the paths and roads taken by travellers with their merchandise. These statues served as landmarks and protected one against thieves. It is an error to describe Hermes as the god of thieves; he protected merchants against them. He also protected the customer against the merchant. It was he who had invented scales, and weights and measures, to safeguard the interests of both parties. He took pleasure in the bargaining between them; he sharpened the tongue of both buyer and seller, inspiring each to make the most honest and profitable offers until final agreement was reached between them.

Hermes favours conciliation in all circumstances. When there is a conflict between cities, he puts diplomatic formulae into the minds of the ambassadors. He loathes above all else the violence of war because in war both commerce and humanity perish. The only profits that this commercial god does not favour are war profits. He consigns to the tender mercy of bandits those makers of spears and bucklers who hope there will be a good war to increase their business turnover. Astute as he is, the god detests the lies of war propaganda which peoples feed on, to their ruin. Aristophanes in one of his comedies puts into the mouth of Hermes a spirited invective against those evil politicians who drive away peace from the nations by their bawling. The poet also says that Hermes prefers the breath of the goddess of Festivals to the smell of the soldier's knapsack.

It was in this way that the Greeks 'humanized' the hard necessities of their toil. Many other examples might have been cited. The last named gods were, more than the others, the outcome of necessity; they were born of the struggle of the lower classes against the obstacles they encountered in the social structure. It was in the working-class and in the merchant-class that these gods were born and changed and assumed the forms I have indicated. They expressed the people's desire to enlist the gods themselves in the workers' camp and to use them in their conflict with the ruling class.

The ancient fear inspired by unknown gods was now giving place to friendship —a very profitable friendship which enlisted the gods in the service of men and in some sort tamed and domesticated them.

◎

Not all the gods, however, were completely humanized. Owing to the oppression exercised by the ruling classes and owing to men's ignorance of the true laws that govern the world and society, certain of the gods remained incomprehensible forces, resolutely hostile to the life and progress of communities. The oracles, which powerful individuals did not scruple to use in their private interests, allowed themselves rather readily to be manoeuvred, and Zeus and Apollo were often 'humanized' in most undesirable ways.

But there was a deity who seemed absolutely resistant to any kind of humanization, namely Destiny or, as one said in Greek, 'Moira'. Moira was never invested with any human form. She was a kind of law of the universe, an unknown law which, however, assured its stability. She intervened in the course of events to restore things to their place when they had been thrown into disorder by the relative liberty of men and the almost absolute liberty of the gods.

Among the Greeks the notion of liberty was by no means that of a fatalism which refuses any liberty to the beings inhabiting the world. Moira was a principle placed above the liberty both of men and of gods; a principle which, inexplicably, causes the world to be truly an Order, a thing in order. For the purpose of a rough comparison, she was something like what the law of gravitation, or the laws governing the movement of constellations, would be. A conception of this kind was the conception of a people who could not yet understand the play of causality but who, nevertheless, knew that the world is an organic whole with its own laws, and who guessed that man's task was, one day, to penetrate the secret of this order.

If then the observation of Moira's existence has not been explained, it none the less depends on a fundamental rationalism, because it supposes an order which is stable and ultimately knowable. From this angle, at any rate, the non-human law has been brought within the measure of man. The very word for the Universe in Greek is highly significant, because 'cosmos' means at one and the same time 'Universe', 'Order' and 'Beauty'.

Greek religion, even in the centuries of piety, was only one form of Greek humanism. But we must go further than this. After the Homeric and archaic ages the principal effort of this religion, in the classical period, was to consist in trying to connect the divine world and the mind of man even more closely than before. Originally, as we have seen, these gods were hardly moral beings; and in the services and benefits they conferred they still remained very capricious. Now the religious conscience of the Greeks absolutely required to know whether they were just; conscience rebelled against the thought that these beings, who were more powerful than man, might not be obedient to Justice.

A peasant-poet, the small country landowner Hesiod, who did not live much later than the author of the *Odyssey*, put a question which had also been formulated, though less firmly, in the *Odyssey* itself. Hesiod said:

. . . upon the bounteous earth Zeus has thrice ten thousand spirits, watchers of mortal men, and these keep watch on judgments and deeds of wrong as they roam. . . . And

there is virgin Justice, the daughter of Zeus, who is honoured and reverenced among the gods who dwell on Olympus, and whenever anyone hurts her with lying slander, she sits beside her father, Zeus . . . and tells him of men's wicked heart. . . .

The eye of Zeus, seeing all and understanding all, beholds these things too, if so he will, and fails not to mark what sort of justice is this that the city keeps within it. Now, therefore, may neither I myself be righteous among men, nor my son—for then it is a bad thing to be righteous—if indeed the unrighteous shall have the greater right. But I think that all-wise Zeus will not yet bring that to pass.[1]

Following the age of Hesiod, during the seventh and sixth centuries which were the era of the struggle for written law and political equality, similar declarations arise from the whole of Greek lyrical poetry. It is as though a multitude were begging for divine Justice as well as human. Poets associated with public life state that Zeus is just and must be, or they insult him (which comes to the same thing) if they observe that the supreme god does not go to the assistance of Justice. We know this from Solon. But there is a passage from Theognis, the exiled poet of Megara:

Dear Zeus! I marvel at thee, Thou art lord of all, alone having honour and great power; well knowest Thou the heart and mind of every man alive; and Thy might, O King, is above all things. How then is it, son of Cronus, that Thy mind can bear to hold the wicked and the righteous in the same esteem, whether a man's mind be turned to temperateness, or, unrighteous works persuading, to wanton outrage.[2]

Such cries of rebellion mean that the religious conscience of the Greeks required that the gods be just, contrary to the feeling of such earlier poetry as that of the *Iliad* in which they were simply very powerful and free.

In the fifth century, with Aeschylean tragedy, a just and good god begins to reign over the world and over men's souls. This is, indeed, the great problem for Aeschylus, the problem that causes his tragedies to be tragic. The author of *Prometheus Bound* and the *Oresteia* sees the world as having passed through thousands of years in which brute force had reigned supreme among gods as among men, but as now entering on an era in which, at the command of the universe, new gods are slowly taking their place in heaven, gods who have themselves acceded to justice and who by their just action support the progress of society.

This, then, is one line of evolution followed by Greek religion. By being humanized, becoming first anthropomorphic and then moral, the gods become symbols of a universe which is on its way to realize Justice.

[1] *Hesiod, The Homeric Hymns and Homerica.* With an English translation by Hugh G. Evelyn-White. Cambridge, Mass. and London, 1943. 'Works and Days', pp. 21–23.

[2] *Elegy and Iambus* . . . edited and translated by J. M. Edmonds. London and New York, 1931, Vol. I, p. 275.

CHAPTER NINE

TRAGEDY: AESCHYLUS AND THE
PROBLEM OF DESTINY AND JUSTICE

Of all the achievements of the Greeks, tragedy was perhaps the loftiest and boldest. The action of tragedy is, after all, rooted in our most instinctive fears and yet it flowers in our dearest hopes. Greek tragedy produced a few unrivalled masterpieces of a beauty perfect and convincing.

The birth of tragedy which arose towards the middle of the sixth century, on the threshold of the classical period, was connected with historical conditions that we must now recall if we are to grasp the meaning and direction of the new genre. On the one hand Greek tragedy took up and pursued the efforts of earlier poets to bring the divine world and human society into harmony, by a further process of humanizing the gods. In spite of the contradictions offered by every day reality, in spite also of the mythical tradition, Greek tragedy urgently demanded that the gods should be just and should cause justice to triumph here below. On the other hand, it was also in the name of justice that the Athenian people continued to wage a very hard fight, both in the political field and in the social, against the possessing class which was also the ruling class, to wrest from it full equality of civic rights—in short, what was to be called the democratic régime. It was during the final period of these struggles that tragedy appeared. Peisistratus, who had been raised to power by the multitude of poor peasants and who helped the people in their struggle for land, founded contests in tragic drama at the festivals in honour of Dionysus. These competitions were designed for the pleasure and education of the citizen-body.

The primitive 'tragedy', which existed a generation before Aeschylus, seems to have been still rather undramatic, wavering as it was between the lascivious laughter of satyrs and the pleasure of weeping. But now, suddenly, an unforeseen event decided in favour of 'gravity', and 'tragedy' bravely accepted the burden of this gravity which was henceforth to be its characteristic. Tragedy chose as its proper subject the encounter of the hero with destiny, together with the risks and the instruction this encounter implies. Now the event that imparted to tragedy the 'grave' tone, which was not the tone of Attic poetry in the immediately preceding era, was the Persian War, the war of independence that the Athenians waged twice against the Persian invader. Aeschylus, who fought at Marathon and Salamis, now succeeded Anacreon, the wit and court-poet.

Aeschylus, who was a fighter, refounded the old tragedy in the form we now know, perfectly in command of its means of expression. But he founded it as a combat.

Every tragic spectacle is the spectacle of a conflict—what the Greeks called a 'drama' or action. This conflict is interspersed with songs of anguish, or hope, or wisdom, sometimes songs of triumph; but always, even in the lyric songs, there is an action that keeps us breathless because we, the spectators, share in it, hovering as we do between fear and hope, as if it were a question of our own lot. Now the action involves the collision of a man four cubits high, says Aristophanes—of a hero—with an obstacle which is taken to be insurmountable and is in fact insurmountable. It is, in other words, the struggle of a champion, who appears to be our champion, against a power shrouded in mystery, a power which, with or without reason, usually crushes the fighter.

The men who wage this struggle are not 'saints', although they place their hope in a just god. They commit faults, they are led astray by passion, they are hasty and violent. But all of them have some great human virtues. All of them have courage, many have patriotism or love of their fellow men; many love justice and have the will to make justice triumph. All are enamoured of greatness.

They are neither saints nor even righteous men, but heroes, that is, they are in the vanguard of humanity and illustrate by their struggle, in action, man's incredible power to resist adversity and overcome misfortune in human greatness and in joy, on behalf of other men and, in the first instance, on behalf of their own people.

There is something in them that exalts in each of the spectators the poet addresses, and even in ourselves, the sense of pride in being a man, the desire and hope of being more and more a man, by widening the breach which these bold champions of our species have opened in the enclosing wall of our servitudes.

'The tragic atmosphere', writes a critic, 'always exists as soon as I identify myself with the personage, as soon as the action of the play becomes my action, that is to say, as soon as I feel myself involved in the adventure that is being enacted. . . . If I say "I", my whole being, my whole destiny, is then at stake.'

What then does the tragic hero fight against? He fights against various obstacles that men come into collision with in the course of their activity, the obstacles that impede the free development of their person. He fights so that an injustice may not be done, so that a death may not take place, so that crime may be punished, so that regular law may overrule lynch law, so that enemies who have been vanquished may inspire a feeling of brotherhood, so that the mystery of the gods may cease to be mystery and become justice, or, at any rate, so that if the liberty of the gods has to remain incomprehensible, it should not offend our liberty. To put it simply: the tragic hero fights in order that the world may become a better place or that, if it must remain as it is, men may have more courage and serenity to live in it.

The tragic hero also fights with the paradoxical feeling that the obstacles he encounters are both insurmountable and necessary to surmount, at least if he wishes to realize himself to the full and fulfil that dangerous vocation of greatness that he carries within himself, without however offending what remains in the divine world of jealousy or 'nemesis', and without committing the fault of being overweening, the fault of 'hubris'.

The tragic conflict is therefore a struggle undertaken against the fatality in question. For the hero who undertakes this, it is a struggle to affirm and display in action a belief that the thing is not fatal or will not always remain so. The obstacle to be vanquished has been placed in his path by an unknown power over which he has no hold and which he hence calls divine. The most fearsome name he gives to this power is Destiny.

The tragic hero's struggle is hard. But, however hard it be and however much his efforts appear condemned in advance, he undertakes the struggle; and we, whether Athenian public or modern spectators, are with him. It is a striking fact that this hero who has been condemned by the gods is not humanly condemned, I mean condemned by the crowd of men who witness the spectacle. The greatness of the tragic hero is a stricken greatness: most frequently he dies. But then this death, far from making us despair, as we were expecting, inspires us with horror, it is true, but, beyond this horror, fills us with joy. This is the effect of the deaths of Antigone, Alcestis, Hippolytus and many others. And, all through the tragic conflict, we have shared in the hero's struggle with a feeling of admiration and, I will add, of close friendship. The sense of participation and the feeling of joy can mean only one thing, since after all we are men: namely, that the hero's struggle contains, even in his death—itself a witness—a promise, the promise that his action will contribute to free us from Destiny. Otherwise the tragic pleasure and the spectacle of our misfortune would remain incomprehensible.

Tragedy, then, employs the language of myth and this language is not symbolical. The whole era of the first two tragic poets, Aeschylus and Sophocles, was deeply religious. Men believed in the truth of the myths. They believed that, in the divine world which tragedy presented to the spectators, there subsisted oppressive powers who seemed to be dooming human life to annihilation: Destiny, for example, was one of them. But in other legends Zeus himself was represented as a brutal tyrant, a despot who was hostile to mankind and would have liked to destroy the human species.

These and many other myths considerably older than the birth of tragedy, it was the poet's duty to interpret, and to interpret in terms of human morality. This was the social function of the poet speaking to the Athenian people at the great Dionysia. Aristophanes confirms the fact in his own way, through the mouths of two great tragedians, Euripides and Aeschylus, when he puts them on the stage. However much they may be opposed to each other in his comedy, they at least agree on the definition of the tragic poet and the aim he should set before himself. 'Why should a poet be admired? For this reason, that we make men, in the cities, better men.' The word 'better' means stronger, better fitted for the struggle of life. Tragedy here asserts its educational mission.

In the age of Aeschylus the tragic poet did not judge that he had a right to correct the myths, still less to reinvent them in his own way. But there were many different variants of these myths; and among the variants current in the sanctuaries or in popular tradition, Aeschylus selected. He had to make this choice and he made it in the sense of justice. That was also why the poet who wished to educate the people chose the legends that were hardest to interpret, those that appeared to offer the most striking contradiction to the notion of divine Justice. It was in fact those legends that disturbed him most as they also disturbed the conscience of his public. They were the *tragic* ones, which would make a man despair of living, if indeed the tragic could not in the last resort be resolved in a just harmony.

But why this demand for divine Justice, a demand always difficult to satisfy? Because the Athenian people bore in their own flesh the wounds of the struggle they had waged, and were still waging, for *human* justice.

If, as many people think today, poetical creation and literature itself are purely and simply a reflection of social realities (the poet may be unaware of this, but it does not matter), then the tragic hero's struggle against Destiny is simply—expressed in the language of myth—the struggle waged by the people, from the seventh to the fifth centuries, to free themselves from the social constraints that still oppressed them at the moment when tragedy first appeared; and also at the moment when Aeschylus became its second and authentic founder.

It was in the course of this age-long struggle of the Athenians for political equality and social justice that the representation of that other struggle of the hero against Destiny—which is what makes tragic drama—was established in the most popular festival of the city.

In the first of these struggles, you had, on one side, the power of a class that was noble or rich, pitiless in any case, a class that possessed both the land and the money, was dooming to poverty the population of small peasants, artisans and labourers, and in the end threatening to disintegrate the community itself. On the other side you had the powerful vitality of a people which willed to live, which was demanding that justice should be equal for all men and that law should be the new bond insuring the life of the individual and the continuance of the city.

The second struggle which was an image of the first, was the struggle between a Destiny brutal, arbitrary and murderous, and a hero greater than ourselves, stronger and more courageous, who fights so that there may be more justice and human kindness among men, and glory for himself.

Now there was a point in space and time when these two struggles converged and reinforced each other. The time was the occasion of the two spring festivals of Dionysus; the place was the theatre of the god on the flanks of the Acropolis. There the whole people assembled to listen to the voice of the poets; and the poets, by explaining to them the myths of their past, which were regarded as history, helped them in their effort to continue making their history the long struggle for emancipation. The people knew that the poets were speaking the truth; it was their proper function to instruct the people in truth.

At the beginning of the fifth century, that is of the classical era, tragedy appeared in the light of an art conservative of the social order, and at the same time as a revolutionary art. It was conservative of the social order in the sense that it allowed all the citizens to solve harmoniously, in the fictional world to which it introduced them, the sufferings and struggles that each of them went through in his daily life. Tragedy was conservative but not mystifying.

But this imaginary world was an image of the real world. Tragic drama bestowed harmony only by awakening the sufferings and rebellions it appeased. It did more than confer harmony, by means of pleasure, on the spectator, as long as the performance lasted; it also promised harmony to the future development of the community by reinforcing in every man a refusal to accept injustice and the will to fight against it. In the hearts of the people who listened with unanimous sympathy, it mustered all the energies for struggle that that people carried within itself. In this sense the action of tragedy was no longer conservative but revolutionary.

Let us now take some concrete examples, and begin by examining the harsh struggle in *Prometheus Bound,* a tragedy of unknown date but probably composed between about 460 and 450 B.C. Aeschylus believes in the divine Justice, he believes in a Zeus who is just, though in a way that often remains obscure to him. In a tragedy earlier than the *Prometheus* he had written:

> *O would that Zeus might show to men*
> *His counsel as he planned it;*
> *But ah! he darkly weaves the scheme,*
> *No mortal eye hath scanned it.*
> *It burns through darkness brightly clear*
> *To whom the god shall show it;*
> *But mortal man, through cloudy fear,*
> *Shall search in vain to know it.*[1]

Now Aeschylus must explain to his people how the justice of Zeus 'burns brightly clear' through the obscurity of the myth.

Prometheus was a god full of goodness toward mankind. He was very popular in Attica where, together with Hephaestus, he remained the patron of small artisans and, notably, of those potters of the Cerameicus who were partly responsible for the wealth of the city. Not only had he given men fire but he had invented for them the arts and crafts. In honour of this god held in high esteem, the city celebrated a festival including a relay-race, with rival teams competing, in which a torch was handed on from runner to runner.

Now it is this 'benefactor of mankind', this 'Friend of man' whom Zeus punishes for the benefit he has bestowed. Zeus has him bound by Hephaestus who, because he feels over-sympathetic for Prometheus, is supervised by Zeus's servants, Might and Violence. Their cynical language corresponds to their hideous countenance. So the Titan is nailed to a wall of rock in the Scythian wilderness, far from all inhabited lands, until such time as he has become resigned to recognizing the 'tyranny' of Zeus. Such is the striking scene with which the tragedy opens. Prometheus utters no word in presence of his tormentors.

How was all this possible? Aeschylus was no doubt aware that by 'stealing fire', a privilege of the gods, Prometheus had been guilty of a grave fault. But from this fault arose relief for the misery of mankind. Such a myth filled Aeschylus with tragic anguish. He felt that his faith in a just Zeus, the master and maintainer of order in the world, was threatened. But he did not evade any of the difficulties in the subject which he had decided to look in the face. He wrote the whole of his tragedy against Zeus.

The 'Friend of man' (the 'Philanthrope' as Aeschylus says, inventing here a word which in its novelty expresses Prometheus's love for mankind) is therefore

---

[1] *The Suppliants,* First Stasimon, strophe 4. Trans. J. S. Blackie.

left in solitude in a wilderness where he will hear no 'human voice' nor see the 'face of man' henceforth.

Ye is he alone? Rejected of the gods, inaccessible to men, he is now in the bosom of that Nature whose son he is. His mother is named Earth and Justice. It is this Nature, in which the Greeks always sensed the presence of a powerful life, that Prometheus now addresses in a lyric song so exquisite as almost to defy translation:

> *O divine Sky, and swiftly-winging Breezes,*
> *O River-springs, and multitudinous gleam*
> *Of smiling Ocean—to thee, All-Mother Earth,*
> *And to the Sun's all-seeing orb I cry:*
> *See what I suffer from the gods, a god!*[1]

A little further on he tells us the reason for his punishment:

> *The gifts I gave to man*
> *Have harnessed me beneath this harsh duress.*
> *I hunted down the stealthy fount of fire*
> *In fennel stored, which schooled the race of men*
> *In every art and taught them great resource.*[2]

At this moment there is a sound of music: Nature is replying to the appeal of Prometheus. It seems as if the sky itself were beginning to sing, for the Titan sees the twelve daughters of Ocean, the chorus of the play, coming towards him through the air. In the ocean depths they have heard his plaint and are coming to sympathize with him in his wretched plight. A dialogue now opens, the dialogue of pity and rage. The Oceanids offer their tears, with timid counsels of submission to the law of the stronger. Prometheus refuses to submit to injustice. He reveals other iniquities committed by the master of the world. Zeus, whom the Titan had assisted in his struggle to win the throne of heaven, has shown only ingratitude to Prometheus. As for the race of mortals, he has been meditating their extermination:

> *resolving to destroy*
> *All human kind and sow new seed on earth.*[3]

But the Friend of man has frustrated this design. It is the love he shows for the human race that has now brought this punishment upon him. Prometheus was aware of this; he has chosen to commit the fault, he knew what its consequences would be, and accepted the penalty in advance.

[1] *Aeschylus: The Prometheus Bound*, edited with an Introduction, Commentary and Translation by George Thomson. Cambridge, at the University Press, 1932, p. 55.
[2] *Ibid.*, p. 57.   [3] *Ibid.*, p. 67.

Meanwhile, however, Aeschylus has found the means of introducing action, a dramatic element, into this tragedy which, owing to the nature of its theme and the situation of its hero, nailed to the rock, seemed as though it should be devoted simply to the pathetic. He does this by giving Prometheus a weapon against Zeus. This weapon is a secret he has learned from his mother, a secret that involves the security of the tyrant. Prometheus will only reveal this secret in return for the promise of release. Will he reveal it or not? Will Zeus force him to do so or not? This is the crux of the drama. As, moreover, Zeus cannot appear on the stage, an act that would diminish his greatness, the struggle between him and Prometheus goes on across space. From his seat in heaven, Zeus hears Prometheus's threats against his power, and begins to tremble. The threats grow more definite with the few words that Prometheus deliberately lets drop about his secret. Will Zeus brandish the thunderbolt? We are aware of his presence from beginning to end; and then, too, there pass by the rock of Prometheus various persons who are on terms of friendship, hatred or servility towards Zeus and who, following Might and Violence whom we saw at the beginning, inform us more fully of his treachery and cruelty.

At the heart of the tragedy, in an important scene with which the reader is already familiar (see pp. 17-18) and which clarifies and widens the bearing of the conflict, Prometheus enumerates the inventions of which he has conferred the benefit on mankind. Here he is not simply, as he had been in the primitive myth that Aeschylus inherited, the god who has stolen fire, but the creative genius of early civilization. He is confused with the creative genius of man himself, inventing the arts and sciences and extending his power over the world. Thus the conflict between Zeus and Prometheus acquires a new meaning; it signifies man's struggle against the natural forces that were threatening to crush him. Now we know what were the achievements of early civilization: the building of houses, the domestication of animals, metal-work, astronomy, mathematics, the art of writing, and medicine.

Prometheus has in short revealed to man his own genius.

Here the play is still being written against Zeus. Men—and I still mean the spectators, of whom the poet has the mission of being the instructor—cannot deny their benefactor and side with Zeus without at the same time denying their own humanity. The poet's sympathy for the Titan never weakens. Prometheus's pride in having raised man from ignorance of the laws of the world to a knowledge of them and to reason, Aeschylus shares. He is proud of belonging to the human race and he communicates this feeling to us by the power of poetry.

Among the figures who pass by the rock of Prometheus I will speak only of the unhappy Io, a touching and pathetic figure. Capriciously seduced by the lord of heaven and then basely abandoned and delivered up to the most horrible torments, Io in her delirium is, so to speak, the type-victim of Zeus's amours, as Prometheus is the victim of his hatred. So far from inducing Prometheus to dread the wrath of Zeus, the sight of Io's undeserved suffering only exasperates his rage.

So now, brandishing more openly, as a weapon, the secret he possesses, he takes Zeus to task and hurls his defiance across space:

> *And yet shall Zeus, so obstinate of spirit,*
> *Be humbled, such a marriage will he make*
> *Which shall o'erthrow him from his tyranny's*
> *Celestial seat for ever; and then the curse*
> *His father Cronos uttered as he fell*
> *From his ancestral throne shall be fulfilled.*
> *Such is his fate, which to avert can none*
> *Of all the gods instruct him, only I—*
> *I know the manner of it. So let him sit*
> *Proudly exultant in his airy thunders*
> *And brandishing his bolt of lightning-fire;*
> *For nothing can avail to save him from*
> *Downfall disastrous and dishonourable.*
> *Such is the wrestler he now trains against*
> *Himself, a prodigy unconquerable,*
> *Whose strength shall battle down the lightning blast*
> *And master the mighty roar of heaven's thunder;*
> *And then that brandished spear which plagues the Earth,*
> *The trident of Poseidon, shall be shattered,*
> *And, stumbling upon disaster, Zeus shall learn*
> *How far from sovranty is servitude.*[1]

But Prometheus has only shown part of his hand. The name of the woman it will be dangerous for Zeus to seduce (and he is not in the habit of refraining from seducing mortal women), he keeps to himself.

Prometheus's move produces its effect. Zeus is afraid and delivers a counter-thrust. He sends his messenger Hermes to summon Prometheus to divulge the name; failing which, worse chastisements await him. The Titan now only mocks at Hermes, treats him as an ape and lackey and refuses to reveal his secret. Hermes then announces the judgment of Zeus; but Prometheus haughtily awaits the catastrophe which must engulf him in the ruin of the whole world.

And now the earth begins to reel, and Prometheus answers:

[1] Trans. George Thomson, *op. cit.,* pp. 117, 119.

O mark, no longer in word but in deed,
Earth has been shaken;
The reverberant thunder is heard from the deep,
And the forked flame flares of the lightning, the coiled
Dust flieth upward, the four winds are at play
Frolicking wildly in ruin and riot,
And the sky and the sea in confusion are one:
Such is the storm Zeus gathers against me,
Ever nearer approaching with terrible tread.
O majestical Mother, O heavenly Sky,
In whose region revolveth the Light of the World,
Thou seest the wrongs that I suffer![1]

Prometheus is overthrown but not vanquished. We love him to the end, not only because of the love he shows us, but because of his resistance to Zeus.

The religion of Aeschylus is not a kind of piety made up of passively accepted habits, nor is it naturally submissive. The wretched plight of mankind causes the poet, who is a believer, to rebel against the injustice of the gods. The woes of primitive man render it plausible that Zeus, who permitted them, did formerly conceive the notion of destroying the human species. Feelings of rebellion and even hatred as regards the laws of life exist in all strong personalities; and here, in the person of Prometheus, Aeschylus liberates these feelings magnificently, in brilliant poetry.

But rebellion was only one phase of his thought. There existed in him another exigency, quite as imperious: the need for order and harmony. Aeschylus felt the world not as a play of anarchical forces but as an order of which the changing system was something that it was for man, assisted by the gods, to understand and regulate.

Hence, after the drama of rebellion, Aeschylus wrote for the same stage the drama of reconciliation, *Prometheus Unbound*. The *Prometheus Unbound* was in fact a part of what the Greeks called a connected trilogy, that is, a group of three tragedies associated by unity of thought and composition. The two other plays in the trilogy have been lost; we only know that the *Prometheus Bound* was immediately followed by the *Prometheus Unbound*. Of the third play, which may have opened or may have completed the trilogy, we have no certain knowledge. But, regarding the *Prometheus Unbound*, we possess some indirect information and we also have a few isolated fragments.

We have just enough to show that in this play Zeus agreed to give up his whim

[1] Trans. cited, p. 131.

for the woman whose name had been Prometheus's secret. He performed this act of renunciation so as not to throw the world into fresh disorder; and thereby he showed himself worthy of remaining lord and guardian of the universe.

This first victory gained over himself entailed a second. By laying aside his anger against Prometheus, Zeus gave satisfaction to Justice. Prometheus for his part, by submitting and no doubt by regretting what element of pride and error there had been in his rebellion, bowed down to the lord of the gods who was now worthy of his position. Thus the two adversaries, by these acts of self-conquest, agreed to a limitation of their anarchical passions with a view to serving a supreme object—order in the world.

The period of thirty centuries which separated the action of the two tragedies lent verisimilitude to this transformation in the divine.

In other words, the mysterious forces which Aeschylus regards as presiding over the destiny and evolution of the world, forces which at the outset had been purely arbitrary and fatal, are slowly moving on to the moral plane. The supreme god as the poet conceives him to have been, during the aeons of time that have elapsed, is a god in process of becoming. His transformation, exactly like that of the human societies from which this image of deity proceeds, is into Justice.

The *Oresteia*, a regular trilogy which has been preserved intact, was performed at the Dionysia of 458 B.C.. It is the poet's final attempt to harmonize Destiny and Divine Justice, in his own and in the public conscience.

The first of the three tragedies of the *Oresteia* is the *Agamemnon,* the subject of which is the murder of Agamemnon, on his victorious return from Troy, by his wife Clytemnestra. The second is entitled *The Choephoroi* which means the Oblation-Bearers. This shows how Orestes, the son of Agamemnon, avenges his father's murder upon Clytemnestra, his own mother, whom he slays, thus exposing himself in turn to divine punishment. In the *Eumenides,* the third play, we see Orestes being pursued by the Furies, who are the deities of vengeance. He is arraigned before a court of Athenian judges, a court founded on this occasion and presided over by Athena herself; and here he is in the end acquitted and reconciled with gods and men. The Furies themselves become benevolent deities, and this is the meaning of their new name, Eumenides.

The first tragedy is that of the murder; the second that of the vengeance; the third, of the judgment and pardon. The trilogy as a whole displays the divine action operating in the midst of a guilty line of kings, the Atreidae, of whom Agamemnon and Orestes are but the last links in a fatal chain. This action of the

27. *Head of Athena, found on Aegina. Parian marble (mid 5th Century)*
28. (Overleaf, left) *Bust of Pericles. Copy of a work by his contemporary, the sculptor Cresilas*
29. (Overleaf, right) *The Parthenon rising above the limestone wall built upon the rock of the Acropolis by Cimon*

gods is represented as a grim destiny, bent on the ruin of the House of Atreus. Yet this destiny is no more nor less than the work of men; it would never exist, it would have no force, if men were not feeding it, so to speak, with their own faults and crimes, each of which gives birth to the next. This destiny is severe in its working, but it is finally appeased in the trial of Orestes, in the reconciliation of the last of the Atreidae with the divine Justice and Goodness.

Such are the general meaning of the work, its beauty also and its promise. Terrible as divine Justice may be, it yet leaves man a way out, a portion of liberty which allows him, under the guidance of those benevolent deities, Apollo and Athena, to find a way of salvation. This is what happens to Orestes throughout the course of his grim ordeal, the murder of his mother and the terrifying ordeal of the madness that for a time overwhelms him. He is saved in the end. Thus the *Oresteia* is an act of faith in the goodness of a severe deity. This goodness is hard to win, but is indubitable.

Let us read the work more closely and try to grasp the power of this destiny which was first thought of as inhuman and then changed into Justice—so that we may also try to perceive its extraordinary beauty.

The plot of the *Oresteia* is woven and develops on the plane of human passion and on the divine plane simultaneously. It even seems at moments (but this is only in appearance) that the story of Agamemnon and Clytemnestra could be related simply as the story of any wife and husband who have serious reasons for hating each other, so serious in Clytemnestra's case that they impel her to murder. This human but brutal aspect of the drama is indicated with unsparing realism.

Clytemnestra, the only personage common to all three tragedies, is here drawn as a terrible figure of conjugal hatred. This woman has never forgotten, and it is natural that, during the ten years of her husband's absence, she should not have forgotten. When setting out for Troy, and to insure the success of this absurd war of which the only object was to restore his adulterous wife to Menelaus, Agamemnon had not feared to slay his daughter, Iphigeneia, on the strength of an oracle. For ten years Clytemnestra has nursed her rancour, awaiting with relish the hour of vengeance:

> *It abides yet,*
> *Terrible wrath that departs not,*
> *Treachery keeping the house, long-memoried,*
> *   children-avenging!*[1]

In these terms the Chorus describes her at the beginning of the *Agamemnon*.

[1] *The Oresteia of Aeschylus,* edited with Introduction, Translation, and a Commentary ... by George Thomson. Cambridge, at the University Press, 1938, p. 109 (First Stasimon).

L

30. *Drum of a column. This figure shows the square hole in which was inserted a metal bolt to insure the connection of the drums*

But Clytemnestra has other reasons for hating and slaying, reasons sprung from her own misdeeds. During her husband's absence she has installed in the royal bed a lion, but 'the faint-hearted lion', who has remained at home while the soldiers are fighting—

> *stretched in the bed,*
> *Who keeps house for my master.*[1]

Clytemnestra has in fact taken a lover, Aegisthus, a brutal dastard who with her lies in ambush, awaiting the victor's return. Thus there will be two to strike the blow. The queen is deeply in love with this insolent coward whom she sways to her will; after the murder she will proclaim as much, insolently and proudly, in face of the Chorus. Aegisthus is her means of revenge.

> *Low lies the man that shamed his wedded wife,*
> *Sweet solace of the Trojan Chryseids.*[2]

And now Agamemnon has insulted her by bringing back to his home and recommending to her care the fair captive whom he prefers to her, Priam's daughter, the prophetess Cassandra—an insult which further exacerbates the old hatred and carries her will to slay the king to the point of frenzy. Cassandra murdered

> *brings to me the spice that crowns my joy,*

cries the queen.[3]

Clytemnestra is a woman of character, 'a woman with a man's will,' says the poet. She has prepared a cunning trap and the game she plays is infernal. In order to obtain swift warning of her husband's return she has established between Troy and Mycenae, across the Aegean islands and on the coast of Greece, a line of beacons which in a single night will flash news of the taking of Ilium. Thus, in front of the city's notables, she stands adorned for the event in the attitude of a faithful, loving wife, full of joy at seeing her husband's return. On Agamemnon's disembarking, she acts the same hypocritical part before king and people, and then invites him to enter his palace, where the bath of hospitality awaits him. Later, as he gets out of the bath, defenceless and with his arms hampered by the robe she holds out to him, she kills him with blows of her axe.

> *He falls into the bath,*
> *Treacherous bowl of blood.*[4]

---

[1] *Ibid.*, p. 177 (Cassandra speaking).   [2] *Ibid.*, p. 191 (Clytemnestra speaking).
[3] *Ibid.*   [4] *Ibid.*, p. 169 (Cassandra to the Chorus).

This is the human, the conjugal aspect of the drama of Agamemnon—an atrocious drama which reveals, behind a mask worn with some difficulty, horrible depths of wickedness in the soul of Clytemnestra. Her soul is corroded with hatred. Once the murder has been accomplished, the mask is off. The queen without a blush defends her action, justifies it, glories in it with triumphant obstinacy.

But in the person of Agamemnon, who is the tragic hero, this drama of low human passions is rooted in another of far wider scope, a drama in which the gods themselves are present. If Clytemnestra's hatred is dangerous to Agamemnon, this is only because, for long years past, there has been accumulating in the divine world a menace against the king's greatness, against his very life, a menace heavy with doom. There exists in short among the gods a *destiny* for Agamemnon, and this because the gods are what they are, just gods. How did this threat arise? What is this weight of fatality that will end by crushing a king so enamoured of greatness for himself and his people? It is not easy at first glance to understand the justice of Aeschylus's gods. However, this destiny is simply the sum total of transgressions committed by the family of the Atreidae of whom Agamemnon is the descendant, ancestral transgressions to which are now added the ones he has committed himself. His destiny is the aggregate of these offences that demand reparation and that now turn against him to strike him down.

Agamemnon belongs to a race of adulterers and fratricides. He is the son of that Atreus who, after inviting his brother to a feast of reconciliation, had caused to be served up to his brother the limbs of the man's own children whom Atreus had murdered. Now Agamemnon carries the burden of these awful crimes, and of others. Why? Because in the mind of Aeschylus one of the hardest but most indubitable laws of life is that none of us is alone in the world, responsible only for himself; that there exist offences for which we are responsible because we belong to a certain family or community. That we are accomplices in the transgressions of others, because we have not vigorously rejected them in our hearts—of this Aeschylus has a deep intuition, though he expresses it differently. He has the courage to look this old belief—this old law of life—in the face: the law which requires that the sins of the fathers should be visited upon the children, and should be for them a destiny.

At the same time the whole play shows that this inherited destiny could not of itself strike Agamemnon, and in fact only strikes him because he himself has committed the gravest offences. In the last resort, his own life of crimes and errors has opened the way for the divine vengeance which was lying in wait for the descendant of the Atreidae.

The choruses in the first part of the *Agamemnon* remind us in splendid songs how, in more than one circumstance, the gods had, by subjecting Agamemnon to a temptation, left him free to escape the clutch of destiny and save his life and soul by refusing to do evil. But Agamemnon had succumbed to temptation; and after each of his transgressions his freedom in respect of destiny has been impaired.

His worst fault has been the sacrifice of Iphigeneia. The oracle that prescribed it was an ordeal in which the king's paternal love ought to have triumphed over his ambition or duty as a general; the more so as this duty was not a real one. He had been wrong to involve his people in an unjust war, a war in which men would be sent to die—for what? for an adulteress. Thus, in Agamemnon's arduous life, errors beget errors. When the gods refuse to allow his fleet to sail for Troy, they involve him in a painful debate with himself. It is necessary that Agamemnon should choose; that in his inmost heart, now darkened by previous transgressions, he should definitely choose the right. By choosing to sacrifice Iphigeneia, Agamemnon delivers himself over to destiny.

This is how Aeschylus describes the inner debate:

ANTISTROPHE 3

Even so the elder prince,
Marshal of the ships of Greece,
Never thought to doubt a priest;
Nay, his heart with swaying fortune swayed.
Harbour-locked, hunger-pinched, hard-oppressed,
Still the host of Hellas lay
Facing Chalcis, where the never-tiring
Tides of Aulis ebb and flow.

STROPHE 4

And still the storm blew from out the cold north,
With moorings wind-swept and hungry crews pent
In idle ships,
With tackling unspared and rotting timbers,
Till Time's insistent, slow erosion
Had all but stripped bare the bloom of Greek manhood.
And then was found but one
Charm to allay the tempest—never a blast so bitter—
Cried in a loud voice by the priest, 'Artemis!' whereat
the Atreidae were afraid, each with his staff
smiting the earth and weeping.

ANTISTROPHE 4

And then the King spake, the elder, saying:
'A bitter thing surely not to hearken,
And bitter too
To slay my own child, my royal jewel,
With unclean hands before the altar
Myself, her father, to spill a girl's pure blood.
Whate'er the choice, 'tis ill.
How shall I fail my thousand ships and desert my comrades!
So shall the storm cease, and the host eager for war
    crieth for that virginal blood righteously!
        So pray for a happy issue!'

STROPHE 5

And when he bowed down beneath the harness
Of dire compulsion, his spirit veering
With sudden sacrilegious change,
Regardless, reckless, he turned to foul sin.
For man is made bold with base contriving
Impetuous madness, prime seed of much grief.
And so then he slew his own child
For a war to win a woman
And to speed the storm-bound ships from the shore to battle.[1]

The blood of Iphigeneia was, besides, only the first blood to be shed in the course of a greater crime. Agamemnon had chosen to shed his people's blood in an unjust war; for this too he will pay, and justly so. Throughout the course of this seemingly endless war, the anger of the people has been growing against the day of the king's return. The grief and mourning of the people, bereaved in the loss of their young men, unite with the wrath of the gods and together deliver him up to Destiny.

Here again Aeschylus's poetry expresses the crime of an unjust war in brilliant imagery. I cite only the conclusion of this chorus:

ANTISTROPHE 3

A people's wrath voiced abroad bringeth grave
Danger, no less than public curse pronounced.
It still abideth for me, a hidden fear wrapped in night.
Watchful are the Gods of all

[1] Trans. George Thomson, *op. cit.*, pp. 111, 113 (*Agamemnon*, First Stasimon).

Hands with slaughter stained. The black
Furies wait, and when a man
Has grown by luck, not justice, great,
With sudden overturn of chance
They wear him to a shade, and, cast
Down to perdition, who shall save him?
In excess of fame is danger.
With a jealous eye the Lord Zeus in a flash shall smite him.[1]

And now for the last time the gods offer Agamemnon the possibility of regaining his freedom by doing homage to their power. This is in the scene of the purple carpet. Here we see uniting the drama of human passion and the drama of divine action. It is the terrifying Clytemnestra who has thought of this last pitfall. She believes in the gods and in their power, but she makes a sacrilegious calculation respecting them, by trying to involve them in her plot. For the pride of the conqueror of Troy she prepares a temptation, which the gods permit. But what is in her eyes a trap is for the gods an ordeal, the last chance of salvation. When the king's chariot halts before the palace gates, Clytemnestra orders her servants to spread a purple carpet over the ground so that the victor's feet may not touch the earth. Now this honour was reserved for the gods, when their images were carried in solemn procession. If Agamemnon makes himself equal to the gods, he will once more be delivering himself to the destiny that lies in wait. We see him first resist the temptation, and then yield to it. He walks along the purple carpet. Clytemnestra triumphs. She now thinks she can strike with impunity, because her arm will be simply the instrument that the gods use in striking. She is mistaken. The gods may choose her arm, but she is none the less criminal. The gods alone have the right to strike, they alone are pure and just.

The palace gates close behind the couple; the axe is ready.

Agamemnon is going to die. We no longer judge him. We know his greatness, we know too that he was a man capable of erring.

In order to make us throb to the pitiful death of the conqueror of Troy, Aeschylus invents a scene of extraordinary pathos and dramatic power. Instead of describing the king's death after the event through the mouth of a servant from the palace, he shows it almost happening before our eyes a few moments before it actually happens—he pictures it through the ravings of Cassandra, the prophetess who is bound to Agamemnon by a fleshly bond. Mute hitherto in her chariot and insensitive to the presence of those around her, Cassandra is suddenly seized with a frenzied transport.

[1] *Ibid.*, p. 129 (Second Stasimon).

Apollo, the god of prophecy, is inspiring her; he shows her the murder of Agamemnon that is being prepared and also her own death which will follow his. But it is in successive fragments that the future—and also the bloody past of the House of Atreus—take shape on the screen of her mind's eye. This is enacted in the presence of the chorus who either mock her or give up trying to understand. But the spectator knows and understands. Thus, in the following stanzas where Cassandra is speaking:

> *Alas, O wicked! Is thy purpose that?*
> *He who hath shared thy bed,*
> *To bathe his limbs, to smile—how speak the end?*
> *The end comes, and quickly:*
> *A hand reaching out, followed by a hand again!*
>
> .   .   .   .   .
>
> *Ah, ah! O horrible!*
> *What is appearing now? Some net of mesh infernal.*
> *Mate of his bed and board, she is a snare*
> *Of slaughter! Oh, murderous ministers,*
> *Cry alleluia, cry,*
> *Fat with blood, dance and sing!*
>
> .   .   .   .   .
>
> *Ah, ah! Beware, beware!*
> *Let not the cow come near! see how the bull is captured!*
> *She wraps him in the robe, the hornèd trap,*
> *Then strikes. He falls into the bath, the foul*
> *Treacherous bowl of blood. . . .*[1]

Cassandra, not without mortal fear, enters the palace where she has foreseen the death that awaits her on the block.

Finally the palace doors open. The bodies of Agamemnon and Cassandra are shown to the people of Mycenae. Clytemnestra, with the axe in her hand and her foot on her victim, triumphs 'like a raven of death'. Aegisthus is at her side. Will the criminal hatred of the adulterous pair have the last word? The elders who form the chorus stand out, as best they can, against the queen's exultation and throw in her face the only name that can disquiet her—the name of her exiled son, Orestes, the son who, according to the law and religion of the time, is the appointed avenger of his father.

The *Choephoroi* is the drama of a vengeance that is difficult and perilous. In the

[1] *Ibid.*, p. 169.

centre of the drama we see Orestes, the son who must kill his mother, because the gods order it; he has in fact been given the order by Apollo. And yet what a horrible crime to plunge the sword into one's mother's breast, a crime which beyond all others is an offence against gods and men. Now while this crime has been commanded by a god in the name of justice—because the son must avenge the father and there is no law but this family law which allows for the punishment of Clytemnestra—the same crime will, also in the name of justice, be prosecuted by the deities of vengeance, the Furies, who will demand the death of Orestes. Thus the chain of crime and vengeance seems as though it may be endless.

Orestes then, the tragic hero, is caught between two exigencies of the divine: to kill and to be punished for having killed. He knows this in advance. For an upright conscience there appears to be no way out of the snare, because the world of the gods, who must be obeyed, seems to be divided against itself.

And yet, in this terrible conjuncture, Orestes is not alone. At the beginning of the *Choephoroi* he and Pylades arrive in Mycenae, a city from which he has long been absent. Before his father's tomb, a mound rising in the centre of the stage, he encounters his elder sister Electra who has been living for long years in expectation of his return, passionately loyal to the memory of her murdered father, hating her mother, and treated by her mother and Aegisthus as a servant. Hers is a solitary soul, with no confidants but the palace-servants, the Choephoroi; but a living soul because it is inspired by an immense hope, the hope that her dear brother Orestes will return and strike down the abominable mother and her accomplice and restore the honour of the house.

The recognition scene between brother and sister, beside their father's tomb, has a marvellous freshness. After the atrocious scenes of the *Agamemnon,* in which the world was slowly being intoxicated with low passions, with the queen's hypocrisy, the baseness of the king, and the atmosphere of spreading hatred, and which ended cynically in an outburst of jubilation—after that tragedy which almost stifled us, we at last have a breath of fresh air in the joy the two young people experience on meeting. Yet we know that a terrible task awaits them. Agamemnon's tomb is there, and so is Agamemnon himself blind and voiceless in the tomb, and unavenged. It is a question now of awakening Agamemnon's anger so that Orestes, who cannot yet hate his mother as he does not know her, may be filled with his father's fury and feel his father living again in himself until he has drawn from this close bond between father and son, from the continuity of blood in his veins, the strength to strike his mother.

The principal and, poetically speaking, the most beautiful scene in the drama is the long incantation in which the chorus, Electra and Orestes are facing the king's tomb. All in turn seek to meet him in the silence of the grave, that shadowy world of the dead; all try to recall him, to make him speak for them and to awaken him in themselves.

Further on comes the scene of the murder. First of all Orestes has killed Aegisthus. There has been no difficulty about this; a trap to be laid, an unclean beast to be struck down. But now he is faced with the task of striking his mother. Hitherto he has represented himself as a stranger who has been commissioned to bring her a message—news of the death of Orestes. After Clytemnestra's first shudder of maternal tenderness, we have seen the frightful joy she felt at the death of her son, the avenger she has always feared, the only avenger to be feared. Yet she is still distrustful. She has not forgotten a fearsome dream she had had the previous night: she had been feeding a serpent with her milk; the serpent bit her and from her breast blood as well as milk poured out.

After the killing of Aegisthus, a servant comes to knock on the door of the women's quarters to announce the news to Clytemnestra. The queen coming out encounters her son, with the bloodstained sword in his hand, and his friend Pylades. She understands at once, while still uttering a cry of love for Aegisthus. She begs and implores Orestes, baring to his eyes the breast from which he had drawn in 'the milk of life'. Orestes has only a moment of weakness when he seems to waver before the horror of an impossible deed, and turns to his friend:

Orestes. *Pylades, what shall I do? Shall I have mercy?*
Pylades. *What then hereafter of the oracles*
         And solemn covenants of Loxias?
         Let all men hate thee rather than the Gods.[1]

Orestes drags his mother into the palace and kills her.

And once again, as at the end of the *Agamemnon*, the palace doors open and in the place where Agamemnon and Cassandra had been lying, now lie Clytemnestra and Aegisthus. Orestes shows the bodies to the people and justifies the murder.

Orestes is innocent since he has obeyed the orders of a god. But can one murder one's mother and remain innocent? Behind the words he utters in self-justification we are aware of a mounting terror. He proclaims his right and the justice of his cause. The chorus tries to reassure him: 'Thou hast done well.' But anguish continues to rise up in his soul and now his reason begins to waver. Suddenly they rise before him: he sees them—the terrible goddesses, the Furies. We cannot see them as yet; for us they are only the spectres of Orestes' delirium. Yet they are terrifyingly real. What will they do to Orestes? We do not know. This drama which had opened with a breath of young life and in a movement of liberation, a brave attack upon the sinister destiny of the House of Atreus—an attack led by the only

[1] *Oresteia*, p. 269.

innocent son of the family—this drama which had begun in hope ends at a point deeper than despair: in madness.

The *Choephoroi* shows the failure of man's effort in the struggle against Destiny. It is the failure of a man who nevertheless was obeying a god's command, in his attempt to put an end to the sequence of crimes and vengeances, each of which begets the next, in the accursed house of the Atreidae. But the reason for the failure is clear. If man cannot regain a liberty that has been impaired by ancestral crimes; if, even with Apollo's authority behind him, he cannot raise his arms to heaven and be received in the arms of the gods; it is because the divine world seems, in human eyes, to be tragically divided against itself.

Yet Aeschylus believes with his whole heart in the order and unity of the divine world. What he shows in the *Eumenides,* which is the third drama of the *Oresteia,* is how a man of good will and good faith, whose intentions are as innocent as a man's can be, may, through a judgment which he has submitted to in advance, be absolved from the crime that fate has imposed on him, gain a new liberty and be at last reconciled with the divine world. But, in order that this may take place, it has been necessary for the divine world to effect a reconciliation with itself and for it to appear henceforth to man as an harmonious order, pervaded through and through with justice and goodness.

Into the details of the play we will not enter. The principal scene shows us the trial of Orestes which, by a piece of daring uncommon in the history of tragedy, takes place a few yards from the theatre—actually on the Acropolis, in front of an old temple of Athena. Here, pursued by the Furies who are eager to drink his blood, Orestes has taken refuge. He is on his knees with his arms clasping that old wooden statue of Athena, the image that had fallen from heaven and that was so familiar to the Athenians. At first he prays in silence, then supplicates the goddess aloud. But the Furies have followed his trail and now, in an infernal ring, they hem him round. As the poet makes them say:

> *I feel*
> *My senses wooed with smell of human blood.*[1]

However, before long, Athena, the young goddess who is just and reasonable, appears beside her statue. In order to decide the fate of Orestes, she establishes a tribunal composed of human judges—citizens of Athens. Here we see the divine world drawing near to the world of men, the goddess becoming incarnate in the most necessary of all human institutions, the lawcourt. Before this court the Furies maintain their accusation; they declare that for the shedding of blood, the shedding of blood must of necessity answer; this is the law of retaliation. Apollo is advocate

---

[1] Trans. George Thomson, *Oresteia, op. cit.,* p. 301.

for the defence. He reminds the court of the atrocious circumstances surrounding the death of Agamemnon, and he asks for the acquittal of Orestes. Exactly half the jury vote for condemnation and half for acquittal; but Athena gives her casting vote on the side of those who are for absolving Orestes, and so he is saved.

It is furthermore decided that, from now on, crimes like those which had been committed by the family of the Atreidae shall no longer rest with private vengeance but come under the jurisdiction of the court founded by the goddess, a court whose members will decide the fate of the innocent and the guilty according to the dictates of their conscience.

Thus Destiny has become Justice in the strictest sense of the word.

The last part of the play confers on the Furies, who have been frustrated of the victim they were awaiting, a kind of compensation, simply by a modifying of their inner nature. Henceforth the Furies who have now become Eumenides, or Kindly Ones, will no longer be blind and greedy seekers after vengeance: their formidable power has suddenly, in the words of a critic, been 'polarized towards good', thanks to Athena's action. They will be a source of blessings, for those who deserve them, promoting respect for the marriage-laws and working to maintain harmony among the citizens. It is they who will preserve the young men from a premature death and who will give the maiden the husband whom she loves.

It seems, at the end of the *Oresteia,* that the fatal and vengeful aspect of the divine is being pervaded with benevolence and that Destiny is not satisfied with being assimilated to divine Justice but is inclining towards goodness and changing into Providence.

◎

Aeschylus shows his courage in making dramatic art treat, again and again, of the most formidable conflicts between man and the world in which he lives. We have seen how he renews this courage by drawing on his profound faith in an harmonious order in which men and gods are at last working together.

At this moment in history when Athens was initiating a first form of popular sovereignty—the form of social life that was in time to deserve the name of democracy—the poet Aeschylus was attempting to show justice as firmly established in the divine world. By so doing he vigorously expressed the Athenian people's love of justice, and respect for right, and faith in progress.

◎

At the end of the *Oresteia,* Athena composes a prayer for her city:

Chorus. *What song then shall I chant over the land?*
Athena. *A song of faultless victory: from earth and sea*
From skies above may gentle breezes blow,
And, breathing sunshine, float from shore to shore;
That corn and cattle may continually
Increase and multiply, and that no harm
Befall the offspring of humanity;
And prosper too the fruit of righteous hearts;
For I, as one who tends flowers in a garden,
Delight in those, the seeds that bring no sorrow.[1]

[1] Trans. George Thomson, *op. cit.*, p. 343.

CHAPTER TEN

PERICLES THE OLYMPIAN

Pericles gave his name to his century, the fifth before the Christian era. This was a great honour if it was deserved.

Let us however lay down the inside limits of this 'century'. After a short political struggle with his Athenian enemies, both inside and outside his own party, Pericles came into power in 461 B.C. Apart from a period of eclipse lasting only a few months, he remained from this date until his death in 429 the one and only leader of the city. His 'century', then, was scarcely a third of a century: it lasted thirty-two years.

It is true that political events followed one on the heels of another in increasing tempo. Masterpieces of art crowded one after another. During the period in question there were few years which did not see the appearance of one or even several of the most dazzling works that man has produced, whether works in marble or bronze, or works of poetry or scientific thought.

But what share had Pericles himself in this sudden flowering of Athenian genius in every domain of art and especially in the plastic arts? And what was the price paid by the citizens and allies of Athens, and indeed by the whole of Greece, for this period of marvellous production? This we must try to ascertain.

Pericles completed the formation of Athenian democracy. He at the same time directed it and was its leader—should we also say its 'tyrant' (the Athenians said so), a tyrant long unchallenged. Thucydides calls him the 'first of Athenians'. He possessed four virtues which, when united in one person, produce the great statesman. He had intelligence, that is, the power of analyzing a political situation, of foreseeing exactly what will happen, and of replying with an action. He had eloquence: he could win the whole people over to his opinion and get them to participate in his actions. Every time he spoke before the popular Assembly, it was as though he laid his diadem at his feet and only replaced it on his head after everyone had consented. It was because, as people said, he had the lightning on his tongue.[1]

[1] Plutarch records this.

His third virtue was the purest patriotism; he put nothing before the interests of the community or the honour of Athens. And, last of all, he was absolutely disinterested. What use indeed would the first two gifts have been—the power of discerning the public interest and of convincing the people of it—if he had not been wholly devoted to his country and completely incorruptible? In this portrait of Pericles at the opening of his great history, Thucydides has drawn a picture of the statesman towering above the other statesmen he compares with Pericles, each of whom lacks one of the essential gifts that characterize every great leader. Not only does Pericles, in Thucydides' history, dominate all the other statesmen, however intelligent, eloquent, patriotic or honest they may be, but he had so perfect an understanding of Athens and her greatness, and of the power which it was for the Athenians to seize at this decisive moment if ever, that he was able to unite this people which was always internally divided by setting before its eyes a goal that transcended it, a goal common to all the strife-torn cities of Greece.

In the pages of Thucydides, indeed, Pericles does sometimes speak in Pan-Hellenic terms, like a man who has planned at long last to unite all the Greek peoples under the leadership of the city which is in every respect worthiest to command. For thirty years Pericles moulded Athens so as to make her 'the school of Greece', by which, the context shows, we are to understand the political school. He wanted to make his city the brilliant, active centre of the Hellenic world, persuaded as he was that the mastery in the plastic arts which she was going to assert under his direction would express the love of life that burned in the heart of every Greek. But especially did he wish to make Athens the heart of Greek political life as a whole, a heart that beats never more strongly than in response to the love of liberty in action. Thucydides reports him as uttering words that carry a magnificent echo of this love dear to every Greek: 'Convinced as you are that happiness lies in liberty and liberty in courage, look the dangers of war in the face.' Now in spite of appearances these words were not addressed merely to the Athenians; they reached all the Greeks and all their cities by virtue of the deep feeling which, by comparison with other peoples, characterized them all on the level of a supreme sacrifice to happiness—the love of liberty. His words did more than express a feeling, they demanded an act founded on the most Greek of all the virtues, an act of courage.

If Pericles conceived the plan of uniting the Greeks scattered among other cities within the bosom of the mother-city of Athens, and if he failed in this plan, it was partly because, before he was able to realize it, he was struck down at the height of his powers and in the midst of his career by the plague—the death which could be least of all foreseen by a mind so adept in foresight; and it was also because the other Greeks called the Athenian patriotism of Pericles, which claimed that it could unite them, by a different name—they called it Athenian imperialism.

Such, according to Thucydides, was Pericles and such his destiny.

◎

But was all this true? Or rather, how much truth was there in it? A host of questions present themselves at this point. The splendid figure of Pericles as the historian offers it is painted in colours too shining not to disquiet us, much as a Sphinx disquiets. It contains contradictions which can be explained by the age in which he lived but which none the less restrict its value. It also appears too perfect not to have been idealized; and yet too precious for us not to attempt to rescue those elements of truth that went to its making before they evaporate like some fair dream of the past. Let us try to penetrate the complex secret of the man.

Pericles was distinguished physically by little more than the oblong shape of his cranium—a head 'which never comes to an end', a contemporary said. For this reason and on account of his haughty manners, the comic poets nicknamed him 'The squill-head Olympian'.[1] His bust which was made by a contemporary, the sculptor Cresilas, and of which three copies have been preserved, conceals the singular shape of his skull by means of a helmet. The expression of the face is neither haughty nor arrogant but simply proud, with the hint of a cunning smile.

Through his father Xanthippus, Pericles descended from an old family of Athenian nobles; but his father, before he was exiled by ostracism, had been leader of the democratic party. On his mother's side he descended from the very noble family of the Alcmaeonidae, a family extremely powerful and wealthy but which had also been banished from Athens in consequence of being accused of sacrilege and treason. Among his maternal ancestors Pericles could count a great-great-grandfather who had been tyrant of Sicyon (and in the ancient world tyrants were nearly always raised to power by the masses); and also a great uncle, the legislator Cleisthenes. Now in 508 B.C., Cleisthenes had taken up the unfinished work of Solon, renewing and completing the reforms associated with the ancestor of Athenian democracy. Pericles was born a little after this event, probably about 492 B.C.

Aristocratic birth and democratic traditions, these latter being both of the dictatorial kind and the more specifically democratic—such was his family heritage.

---

[1] Plutarch quotes Cratinus in *The Thracian Women* as writing:

> The squill-head Zeus! lo! here he comes, our Pericles,
> The Odeum like a cap upon his cranium,
> Now that for good and all the ostracism is o'er.

Plutarch's Cimon and Pericles, trans. Bernadotte Perrin, New York, 1910, p. 123 (Translator's Note).

Which party would he choose when he came to devote himself to the public life to which his temperament seemed to call him? 'In his youth', Plutarch tells us, 'he felt great repugnance for the people.' Always grave and distant himself, he hated the easy-going, familiar manners of his senior, Cimon, leader of the aristocratic party and victor in the last Persian war. In spite of the inborn disdain which he perhaps felt for the populace, a feeling which he denied and which he tried to offset with abrupt acts of generosity, his political instinct and impeccable logic did not mislead him. It was not the handful of aristocrats in the orbit of that frivolous coxcomb Cimon[1] who could carry Athens to the pinnacle of greatness, which was the aim that Pericles had set before his eyes from youth upward. Only the masses of the people whose rights he felt it necessary to extend while remaining in a position to dispose of them and guide them toward the end in view—only these masses, heirs of the future, were capable of winning for Athens the immense material power that seemed feasible and the primacy in art and culture that could follow from it. Pericles decided to serve the democratic party, and at the age of thirty he became its sole leader.

By education Pericles was a rationalist; but he was not without a certain keen sensibility, both ardent and refined; and he also had a sort of religious feeling intermingled with his love of the city. This religious respect for, and deep love of, his country prevented his rationalism from falling—as so often happens—into vulgar individualism.

The thinkers who had formed his mind were not men who lived in an ivory tower. Damon, who was perhaps his principal master, a composer and also a theorist of music, took his art seriously enough to declare that 'one cannot touch the rules of music without at the same time overthrowing the fundamental laws of the State. . . . Music should be made the citadel of the Commonwealth.' When Zeno of Elea and Anaxagoras settled in Athens, they became Pericles' principal masters in philosophy. It was Zeno who established in Athens the monotheistic doctrine of the Eleatic School. 'There is only one God,' he said. 'By the mere force of his mind, without difficulty, he sets all things in motion.' Now was not this precisely what Pericles was striving to do, in public life?—to govern by the power of thought. Anaxagoras, whom we shall meet with in the second volume of this work, was, we know, closely associated with Pericles. He taught that the Principle

---

[1] 'Cimon avantageux et léger.' This may refer to the tradition that Cimon was rather much of a ladies' man. But Thesimbrotus, a contemporary chronicler who knew Cimon, and Plutarch who drew from Thesimbrotus, Ion of Chios (also a contemporary) and many other sources, give an extremely favourable account of him. He is described as open-handed, and generous, excellent in a national crisis, a brave and sagacious general. His policy was one of war with Persia and a balance of power in Greece, involving peace with Sparta. It is difficult to escape the conclusion that this was a more far-sighted policy than Pericles's (Translator's Note).

31. *Horseman's head. Ionic frieze of the Parthenon*

which has drawn the world out of primitive chaos, has organized it and continues to rule it, is pure Intelligence. From the teachings of Anaxagoras, Pericles derived the whole of his scientific education which was as extensive as the age permitted; a confirmation of the rationalistic form of his thought; and a principle and model for the government of the city. All the speeches that Thucydides attributes to him are examples of deductive eloquence, but they are also deeply imbued with the lively passions of the Athenian nation. The speeches he made and the narratives of his conduct, in Thucydides, display the active and sovereign intelligence of this 'tyrant' in the government of the city. Nietzsche says: 'When Pericles appeared in public to harangue the people, he seemed to be the image of *Nous* (Intelligence), the human incarnation of constructive, motive, analytical, marshalling, far-sighted and artistic power.'

Anaxagoras did not escape condemnation for atheism; but Pericles extricated him.

Pericles' religion embraced as it were in a single aspiration both the cult of the ancient Powers who had formerly presided alone over human action, and the cult of that action itself in which they were henceforth incarnate; that is, the action of men striving within the framework of the city to obtain well-being, progress, social justice and glory, these men being drawn on by the suddenly increasing power of the community. This religion was inscribed in the temples he built, in the statues of gods and Athenian heroes and in fact in all the monuments he raised to the common glory of gods and men. It was to this communion between citizens and tutelary gods that he raised toward heaven so many columns and so much sculpture. Yet it is a striking fact that the gods never once appear in the speeches Thucydides puts in his mouth. Even their names are absent from the splendid eulogy of Athens and of the good things which it was hers to safeguard by the sacrifice of her young men—the eulogy pronounced by Pericles over those who had died in the first year of the Peloponnesian War. How could the names of the gods be missing on such an occasion? Because the brilliant name of Athens is everywhere present—as if Athens were the visible deity of Pericles.

Let us see now what actions his love of Athens inspired. Pericles began by completing the democratic system, that is, by completing the laws and customs that had existed since the times of Solon, Peisistratus and Cleisthenes who had preceded him in this work. He had no desire to see a class-government or party-government; there was no question in his mind of organizing for the benefit of the poorer classes a social and political monopoly which the richer classes would be called on to pay for. Athenian democracy was, in Pericles' mind, the whole city at

M

32. Temple of Athena Niké, on the Acropolis

work, for he honoured work. 'It is not poverty', he once told the Assembly, 'that we regard as shameful, but the fact of doing nothing to escape from it.'

To make Athens, by which of course is meant the Athens of the *citizens*, fully democratic, he had to widen the field from which the magistrates were recruited. This field had remained limited to the two more well-to-do classes. Pericles knew, on the other hand, that any participation of the poorer classes in the magistrature would be quite theoretical as long as the citizens who were candidates for the posts to which they were eligible were not paid; as long as they had not the leisure to be Archons or to sit in the Court of the Heliasts without anxiety regarding the loss of working days. Pericles therefore extended eligibility to the Archonship to citizens of the third category, the smaller bourgeois and artisans with modest incomes, leaving outside the members of the fourth and last class, namely the workmen and labourers. As to payment of expenses, he created such payments for members of the Council of the Five Hundred, for the Archons, for the judges in the Court of the Heliasts (six thousand members), for soldiers, and also to enable all the citizens to take part in the very numerous festivals of the Republic. On the other hand, he never allowed any payment for attendance at the popular Assembly where he considered the presence of all the citizens as a duty.

The extension of the Archonship and payment of citizens in the exercise of public functions, except at the Assembly, were the two measures which Pericles regarded as completing the democratization of Athens. One should add to this the suppression of the right of veto of the Areopagus, a right which had in many cases limited the scope of popular sovereignty. This change had been effected in 462–461 B.C. by Ephialtes, an upright citizen who had indicted the Areopagites guilty of peculation and had soon afterwards been mysteriously assassinated. From this time onwards, the Areopagus was little more than a name, its functions being inherited by the popular Assembly and the popular Tribunal.

In the political life of Athens laws counted for less than customs. The Archons did not govern the city, they administered it, they executed decisions taken elsewhere. All important decisions were taken by the popular Assembly which was composed of all the citizens and from which the absentees were peasants who were somewhat averse to leaving their farms, rather than the city workmen and the sailors from the Piraeus. It was the working population of the city that made up the majorities, and there was no need to pay it to take part in such fascinating shows as the contests in oratory.

It was here that Pericles conducted his campaign for the goal he had fixed for Athens, namely power; conducted it without the support of any title or office save the triumphant primacy of intelligent discourse and honest, uncorrupt patriotism. He was simply the 'prostates tou demou', which meant both that he was leader of the democratic party and head of the democratic community as a whole. He was also a 'strategos', that is, a general elected annually by popular vote to the board of ten generals. We have positive proof, except for a year or two, that he was re-elected over the whole period from 460 to 429 not only by his own tribe, an administrative unit which had the right to appoint one of its members to the board of generals, but for the greater part of the time by the whole civic community. This rare unanimity, which is unique even in Athenian history, no doubt means that Pericles had persuaded the people to march on the path he had prescribed but that it belonged to the people alone, as sovereign, to choose. Truly, therefore, the popular sovereignty of Athenian citizens was no matter of mere words.

The Assembly exercised a direct and permanent control over the officials, or Archons in the broad sense of the term. Now in order that everyone's chances should be equal on the one hand and that, on the other, competence should be insured, these officials were appointed by a combination of drawing by lot and election, or sometimes by one system exclusive'y. With the exception of the strategoi, no one could possibly be elected two years running or hold two offices simultaneously. Thus power was made dependent on the people; but it was also controlled in another way. On entering office, an official had to undergo an examination either before the Council of the Five Hundred, which was composed of former Archons, or before a section of the popular Tribunal, the Heliaea. On laying down his office, he rendered account of his period of tenure and as long as this report did not entirely satisfy the people, the official could not dispose of his fortune. Furthermore, even when he had obtained discharge, he could still be accused by any citizen, he could be the object of a prosecution called 'graphé alogiou', or accusation of illegal procedure. This was not all. During his year of office, an official remained under the direct and permanent control of the people who, by means of the 'confirmatory' vote, could always suspend him and refer him for judgment to the popular tribunal.

The people also exercised full sovereignty in judicial matters. A large portion of the citizen body sat annually in the Court of Heliasts, which judged most cases, public or private, without appeal. In certain cases, such as attempts against the democracy, membership of a secret society, treason, political corruption, etc., the popular Assembly sat as a court of justice or referred the indictment to a section composed of at least a thousand members of the popular Tribunal.

By virtue of these and other arrangements Athenian democracy was a wholly democratic régime, a government by the people and for the people, and it was the most complete realization of democracy known to the ancient world.

But it was very strongly counterbalanced by the great authority that his wide intelligence and vigorous oratory conferred on Pericles. This democracy of the

Periclean age was a *managed* democracy. Thucydides makes a decisive remark about Athens at that time: 'It was', he says, 'a democracy in name, but in fact it was a government exercised by the first among the citizens.' This enables us to see how Sophocles, who was well acquainted with Pericles and liked him, was nevertheless able to borrow from him certain features for the character of Creon in the *Antigone*.

But there is more and worse to be said. At the same time as Pericles was completing democracy and also counterbalancing and putting a brake on its exercise by his personal influence, it may also be said that he was closing it.

Aristotle tells us that in 451–450 B.C., it was decided, on Pericles motion, that no one should enjoy political rights unless both his mother and father were Athenian. Now according to Solon's legislation, which was authoritative in this matter, sons born of a marriage between a citizen and a foreign woman enjoyed full civic rights. This had been the case with Themistocles, Cimon, the historian Thucydides, the legislator Cleisthenes and others, all of them great Athenians. Many foreigners even had obtained the citizenship in consideration of having rendered exceptional services to Athens. Many people also had got their names entered on the civic rolls by fraud, thanks to the connivance of corrupt officials. Now from the time of the new law, the lists were frequently and strictly verified. Thus in 445–444 when, on the occasion of a serious famine, Psamettichus, a little king of the Delta, had sent thirty thousand bushels of wheat to be distributed among the citizens of Athens, several thousand names were struck off the civic rolls; and of those whose titles were recognized as valid, 14,240 citizens applied for the allocation. How many did not apply? About ten thousand, no doubt. In any event the number of citizens at this date did not exceed 30,000.

However that may be, after the date when Pericles so to speak closed and tied up the democracy, this city, which was the most democratic in Greece, numbered only 14,240 citizens exercising their civic rights out of a total population of 400,000.

When an institution has reached its flowering season, it is on the verge of decline.

◎

When Pericles came into power, Athens had, for some fifteen years past, been at the head of an important confederation of cities, the League of Delos. At the time of its formation in 479, during the latter part of the Persian war, the League had been assigned a purely military object. Its purpose was to continue naval hostilities against Persia, to free those Greek cities that were still subject to the Great King, and to remove the possibility of any new invasion of Greece by the

Persians. A war of liberation and also of revenge, a war both defensive and pre-ventive, such were the objects proposed by the League and successfully achieved under the direction of Themistocles, Aristides and Cimon.

The capital of the Confederacy, which was at once a sanctuary, the meeting-place of the Federal Council and the depository for the treasure, was the sacred isle of Delos, in the middle of the Aegean.

Now in this Confederacy Athens had enjoyed peculiar privileges from the outset. She owed these to the unique power of her fleet. She had command over military operations and, as a consequence of this, free control of the finances. The allies were under obligation to furnish the league with vessels armed and equipped for war against Persia. But it was also agreed at a quite early date that certain of the allied cities whose vessels were no longer of up-to-date pattern might replace the ships they were expected to supply with a monetary contribution. In 454 B.C. there were, apart from Athens, only three members of the Confederacy who were con-tributing ships and not money: these were Samos, Chios and Lesbos. Athens on the other hand counted about one hundred and fifty tributary cities and the annual financial contribution at this time was equivalent to nearly three million gold francs.[1]

It was also in 454, under Pericles' régime, that it was decided to transfer the treasury of the League from Delos to Athens.

In theory all the allies were autonomous cities with equal rights. In fact there was a serious disparity between the power of Athens, who controlled military operations as well as the budget, and the relative weakness of the allied cities. This disparity gave rise to disputes inside the Confederacy and very quickly also to attempts at withdrawal that were brutally repressed by Athens. Naxos was the first to rise in revolt, in 470; then Thasos, in 465. Both were vanquished, and from being allies now became simply subjects. Athens alone fixed the amount of their annual tribute. These first defections and repressions were beginning when the aristo-cratic party was still in power, and it was Cimon, its leader, who reduced the rebels to obedience with fire and sword.

When Pericles came into power, the movement was simply hastened. Three great cities of Ionia, including Miletus, rebelled; then in 446 the cities of Euboea: Chalcis, Eretria and others. Owing to the fact that Sparta intervened in support of the insurgents, the Euboean rebellion was a mortal threat to the Republic's existence. While Pericles was engaged in harshly subduing Euboea, Megara took the opportunity of betraying the League by opening the way into Attica for a Spartan army. Attica was now invaded, and Pericles was obliged to abandon the

---

[1] In present day Swiss currency. Rather less than £250,000 sterling (Translator).

operations he was conducting in Euboea in order to fly to the help of Athens in peril. His lightning return compelled the Spartans to withdraw. He then went back to Euboea and subdued the whole island. Garrisons were placed in some of the cities; others saw their oligarchs expelled and their governments 'democratized'.

After every new rebellion Athens concluded a treaty of subjugation with the city she had subdued by arms. Sometimes she demanded hostages. In various places she installed governments devoted to her cause. She also, in certain important towns which it was a question of keeping well in hand, established governors who controlled the whole political activity of the subject city. Lastly she made a more general use of the system of 'cleruchies', which were colonies of armed Athenians. These men received a grant of lands near the cities that were suspect—lands confiscated from the 'rebels' who had been driven out or liquidated. They also had the duty of seeing that henceforth 'order' should reign in that region.

The Federal Council had long ceased to meet. It was now the Athenian people who fixed the tribute every three years. Any disputes that arose between Athens and her subjects, or her few allies, were judged before Athenian courts. The Confederation of Delos had become the Athenian Empire.

It was an empire continually threatened from within. At the height of Pericles' régime, in 441, a new defection, this time of Samos, brought a repetition of the same story. Pericles was involved in two years of barren but bloody warfare. Samos capitulated in the end; she ceded part of her territory to Athens and paid for the cost of the war, which was enormous; and then, as if by a miracle, once her government was 'democratized', everything became orderly.

This empire was not a simple matter of governing the cities that Athens had subdued; it was according to Pericles neither more nor less than a 'tyranny' of which Athens was herself a prisoner. He says this, in so many words, in one of the speeches in Thucydides. He told the people, on one occasion, that they were not struggling only

'to escape one evil . . . but to avoid loss of dominion also, and danger from the animosities' they had aroused in their 'exercise of that dominion. And from this it is no longer possible for you to retire; if through fear at the present time any one is for so playing the honest man in quiet. For you now hold it as a tyranny, which it seems wrong to have assumed, but dangerous to give up.'[1]

Here is the monster of 'imperialist democracy'. And we should never forget that this democracy is reigning over a population of slaves and now growing rich on the blood, toil and resources of numerous subject peoples.

[1] Thucydides, *The History of the Peloponnesian War*, Book II, Trans. Henry Dale. London, 1912, Vol. I, p. 128.

As long as it lasted, however, this imperialist policy procured Pericles enormous sums. Year after year money flowed in to the annual value of millions of gold francs. It was enough to maintain, on wages fairly modest in themselves, a swarm of officials; and to undertake costly works of art which for twenty years would provide a livelihood for the whole working population and, for the city of Athens, 'imperishable glory'.

The brutal transformation of the League of Delos into an Athenian Empire had not been effected without arousing strong protest in Athens itself. According to Plutarch, Pericles' enemies in the Assembly cried out:

The people has lost its fair name and is in ill repute because it has removed the public moneys of the Hellenes from Delos into its own keeping. . . . And surely Hellas is insulted with a dire insult and manifestly subjected to tyranny when she sees that, with her own enforced contributions for the war, we are gilding and bedizening our city, which, for all the world like a wanton woman, adds to her wardrobe precious stones and costly statues and temples worth their millions.[1]

Pericles had a reply. Appearing one day before the popular Assembly, he declared in substance that the Athenians were the guardians of the Aegean Sea against the Persians, that they had paid and would still pay, if necessary, their own contribution in blood, and that the cities allied to Athens were furnishing for the common defence of Hellas,

not a ship, not a hoplite, but money simply; and this belongs not to those who give it, but to those who take it, if only they furnish that for which they take it in pay.

An unanswerable argument! He added with pride or, if you like, with a frankness not unmixed with cynicism:

And it is but meet that the city, when once she is sufficiently equipped with all that is necessary for prosecuting the war, should apply her abundance to such works as, by their completion, will bring her everlasting glory. . . .[2]

Plutarch goes on to say that Pericles' expeditions supplied those who took part in them

with abundant resources from the common funds . . . and . . . he boldly suggested to the people prospects for great constructions . . . in order that the house-and-home

[1] *Plutarch's Cimon and Pericles*, newly translated, with Introduction and Notes by Bernadotte Perrin. New York, 1910, pp. 119–20.

[2] *Ibid.*, p. 120.

contingent, no whit less than the sailors and sentinels and soldiers, might have a pretext for getting a beneficial share of the public wealth. The materials to be used were stone, bronze, ivory, gold, ebony, and cypress-wood; the arts which should elaborate and work up these materials were those of carpenter, moulder, bronze-smith, stone-cutter, dyer, veneerer in gold and ivory, painter, embroiderer, embosser, to say nothing of the for-warders and furnishers of the material, such as factors, sailors and pilots by sea, and, by land, waggon-makers, trainers of yoked beasts, and drivers. There were also rope-makers, weavers, cobblers, road-builders and miners. And . . . it came to pass that for every age almost, and every capacity there was distributed and scattered abroad by such demands the city's great abundance.[1]

One could not more clearly explain how the great public works undertaken by Pericles on the Acropolis and elsewhere were designed to procure the means of a comfortable livelihood for all the citizens, especially the working-class, at the expense of the tributary peoples.

A democratic policy, a 'tyrant's' policy, if ever there was one. The Parthenon illustrated the everlasting glory of Athens and at the same time furnished bread for the citizens. But the subjects of the Empire were doubtless to have neither bread nor glory.

◎

It was on the strength of the decree voted in 450–449 on Pericles' motion, a decree authorizing Athens to draw from the funds of the League in order to re-build the temples that had been destroyed in the second Persian War—it was on the strength of this decree that Pericles undertook these public works, among others the reconstruction of the sanctuaries on the Acropolis. Apart from the statues set up in the open or in the temples, four great projects date from this period which marks the zenith of Athenian architecture and sculpture: a zenith dominated by Pericles in person, enamoured as he was 'of beauty in simplicity', to quote the phrase that Thucydides puts in his mouth, though he also applies it to the Athenians as a whole. These four exemplary works were, as is known, the Parthenon, the Propylaea, the Erechtheion and the temple of Athena-Niké. I shall limit myself to the Parthenon.

It is not proposed to describe the history or evolution of Greek temple-architecture but simply, in connection with this sketch of Pericles' personality, to make a few marginal observations on that 'love of beauty in simplicity' which is manifest in the great monument to Athena and her people.

When the Persians departed in 479 B.C., the Acropolis was no more than a vast

[1] *Ibid.*, p. 121.

cemetery of heaped up stones and broken statues. Themistocles and Cimon applied themselves to what was most urgent—military necessity: they rebuilt the two walls which rise from the rocky hill, the former building on the north side, the latter on the south. These walls which completely encircled and protected the hill-top were constructed so as to extend the summit-plateau of the Acropolis and allow of its surface being more or less levelled. In the space between the upper edge of the wall and the plateau, the authorities carefully buried the statues of the maidens painted in red and blue which the preceding generation had set up in the days of its prosperity. These statues have only been excavated in our own days; their colouring was still fresh.

Now Pericles saw in art a means of asserting the pre-eminence of Athens over the whole Hellenic world. The Parthenon was to dominate Greece as it has, in its calculated perfection, dominated land and sea and reigned through the centuries.

Pericles kept an eye on everything. He discussed the architect's plans as well as the choice of materials; supervised the execution, visited the work-yards and controlled the expenditure. In the year 450 Pheidias was appointed general overseer of the work on the Acropolis. This Athenian sculptor, who was now forty-two years of age, was already known for several pieces of work executed in different parts of Greece. It was in the same year, 450, that he erected the statue of Athena on the Acropolis. With her curls confined by a plain ribbon, her aegis held loose and the helmet in her hand, she appeared as the embodiment of youthful splendour. The spear had been transferred to her left hand, serving now not as a weapon but as a support for the arm. This was not the Warrior Maid but the bright image of Peace restored. In later years Pheidias erected two other Athenas on the Acropolis, one of them a colossal and warlike figure that bespoke the artist's mastery of bronze. It also bespoke Athenian imperialism, suggesting that peace was an unstable thing, hardly restored before war once again loomed on the horizon. Lastly there was the Athena Parthenos, idol and guardian of the city and the city's treasures, shining in gold and ivory amid the gloom of her sanctuary. One can imagine this tall and ornate ivory statue, clad in gold and framed at the end of the double colonnade of the cella. Her tranquil countenance, which seemed to come alive in the deep shadows, towered above piles of precious offerings, rich fabrics spread over marble tables, and shields suspended from the columns. She was the proud and splendid image of Athenian supremacy.

In addition to all this, Pheidias carved with his own hands a large part of the decorations of the Parthenon. He carved or at any rate inspired the continuous Ionic frieze, in which his chisel created the procession celebrating the Festival of Athena with a simplicity so near to the ideal that one's heart almost stops beating as one gazes at it. Here we see the cavalcade of young horsemen, the slow march of the elders whom age has scarcely touched, the metics and the subject-peoples with their offerings, and the maidens who, clad in their long dresses as in the very adornment of modesty, have for this rare occasion emerged from the gynaeceum. There is no expression on these faces, not even a smile; it is as though, on approaching the gods who await them at the end of the frieze, men acquire the gods' impassivity. But this was the first time that plain citizens, and not gods or heroes, were represented on the frieze of a temple. Both Pericles and Pheidias had so desired it.

Pheidias also personally carved the sculpture in the two pediments which are too much damaged for one to describe them; we can only say that here divine power is expressed not in the violence of some bold gesture but in the nonchalance of godlike muscles in repose. Caught motionless, as it were, in the midst of some act, the strength of the gods would appear limited; yet in this calm repose their strength, though unexercised, seems indeed limitless and divine.

Pheidias let his pupils carve the greater part of the metopes in the Doric frieze.

This artist lived in the closest intellectual sympathy with Pericles, and the latter remained faithful to him when Pheidias was in disgrace, in 432 B.C., and even until he died in prison shortly after his condemnation.

For eighteen years he had been director-general of the works on the Acropolis. Nothing had escaped his severe yet always constructive criticism. He had taken as much interest in the general planning of the various monuments as in the smallest technical detail of their construction. No doubt the architecture of the Parthenon owes him a good deal more than its sculptural decoration.

Pheidias may doubtless be reckoned with Sophocles and Pericles as one of the three men of genius produced by this historic era. They collaborated in the Parthenon, a monument created by collective effort. We may recall in this connection that, at the very moment when he was composing the *Antigone*, Sophocles was chairman of the financial commission—the College of Hellenotamiae[1]—which administered the public treasure levied from the allies. These three men were engaged, if not in the same political direction, at least in the service of an enterprise by which, through the building of the new Acropolis as through the flowering of Sophoclean drama, the greatness of the people governed by Pericles found splendid expression. Sophocles, for his part, did not think that the *Antigone* and the *Oedipus* dispensed him from the duty of presiding over an important commission with the intelligence and loyalty of a good citizen.

The beauty of the Parthenon is of the simple kind; but this simplicity, like the simplicity of all great works of art, is the outcome of something rare and complex, something that escapes our first impression.

[1] That is Keepers of the Greek Storehouse.

At first glance, indeed, the Parthenon looks like a purely geometrical construction: the solution of a problem in geometry in which the material is assembled in perpendiculars, circles, straight lines and triangles in such a way as to stand up in successful equilibrium. It seems to have been built of dimensions. This was because it represented the culmination of generations of study on the part of Greek temple-architects who had been seeking out the right proportions between the length and breadth and the height of the building; the ratio between the diameter and the height of the column, the ratio between the breadth of the column and the space between the columns, the ratio between the diameter of the column at its base and the diameter at the top of the shaft—and many others.

Yet this quest of mathematical perfection would, if it could be fully accomplished, only satisfy our reason. It would please us in the manner of a theorem correctly solved. But the Parthenon does not please us in this way, or rather not merely in this way. It satisfies and prolongs our organic sensation, our joy in the consciousness of life. It touches us as if it were, not an Absolute, but a living thing. It is an order, but an order as mobile as that of natural orders and species.

How, we may ask, has this come about? Because the straight lines that compose it are only approximately straight, like those in life. The circles and even the ratios are only approximate. The mathematics of the Parthenon are never more than a tendency to exactitude; their rigour is only the rigour we find in the laws of the real world, thought out anew by man, expressed in art, and always relative and mobile. It is this relativity and mobility that give life to the Parthenon.

Let us take some examples. The four courses in the base of the temple are of unequal height. The first, which is the regulating course set on the rock, is the lowest; the last is the highest. The difference is of the slightest, felt more by the foot than by the eye. But as seen from a distance the three steps look equal and the upper step does not give the impression—which it would give if they were really equal—of sinking under the weight of the edifice.

Furthermore, the surface of each step is not exactly horizontal but slightly convex. A level surface, when seen from one end, tends to appear hollow in the middle. This is why a slight swelling was calculated so as to prevent this optical illusion.

Hence, owing to these and other features, the base on which the monument stands is constructed in false straight lines and planes falsely horizontal, which, however, the eye sees as the straight lines and planes of real life. The base therefore, as someone has observed, 'can henceforth optically resist the weight of the monument' it supports.

What are we to say about the diversity of the columns, which appear all alike and all perpendicular? And what of the illusory equality of the spaces between the columns? In this poem written in marble none of the dimensions is the same in corresponding positions; in this work that seems to offer a pledge of eternal stability, everything is mobile and unstable. We are indeed touching eternity, yet this is the eternity of life, not of the Absolute.

I will give only a few details regarding the columns. No one of them is perpendicular and no one is exactly parallel with its neighbours.

Were it strictly vertical, the column would only fulfil an individual purpose, that of supporting a limited portion of the building. But, when inclining toward the interior of the building, as each of them does, the columns enter into a kind of community that collectively supports the weight of the edifice. This inclination of the column varies according to the place it occupies in the colonnade, and according to the colonnade itself. It is a very slight inclination, varying from 6.5 to 8.3 centimetres, but it is concentric, and its effect on the eye is to extend the supporting function of each column and to make the whole colonnade appear as if engaged in a single 'effort of converging co-operation'.

Perhaps there was a technical necessity behind all this. It may be that, had the columns not been so devised, the weight of the entablature, the pediments and the whole upper part of the temple would have caused the building to split open and collapse. But this technical necessity, if it existed, was also an aesthetic requirement. The eye seems to prolong the axes of the columns into the sky until they all unite at a point very high above the temple. Thus the Parthenon does not offer itself to our gaze as a mere house surrounded with columns. It appears, on the contrary, as an edifice whose mobile stability, subdued to the human eye, rises toward heaven as an imaginary pyramid, by a coherent effort that we have imposed on it.

This planned inclination of the columns produces still other effects. 'It throws the balance of the cornices inwards, thus bringing the projecting portions of the building back towards the main mass.' But the columns at the angles do not participate in the same inclination. As these four columns constitute an independent group and are set less aslant, they appear more outside and apart from the main cluster; and they more evidently support the summit of the monument at its four angles. Their major function being thus brought into evidence, they reassure us regarding the solidity and durability of the temple. The shafts of these same angle-columns are also slightly strengthened so as better to resist the glitter of the light of which they have to bear the impact more than do their neighbours. For the same reason these four columns are also sensibly nearer to their immediate neighbours. If the space between them were identical with the spaces between the others, this would create a luminous void that would make them appear more slender. Now, of all the columns, these four must be, and look, the strongest, because they have to support the total mass above.

It is because this temple was conceived according to the laws of a geometry which is the geometry of life, that it seems a living thing, a tree as it were heavy with fruit and growing out of the soil of the Acropolis. To the eyes of one climbing the hill, it looks, when seen from below, a small insignificant thing; or at most perhaps a half-hidden face that throws a disquieting glance at us. We continue to climb the road (a difficult ascent in ancient times); we lose sight of the Parthenon, but we reach the Propylaea and enter. They have been set there only that they may conceal the Parthenon as long as possible from our eyes. Suddenly it stands up before us, not insignificant now or disquieting, but immense and utterly fulfilling our expectation. Not that it is immense arithmetically, but in its appeal to our hearts. Its dimensions are not huge. Thus the Cathedral at Lausanne measures 100 × 42 × 75 metres; the Parthenon, 70 × 31 × 17.5 metres. But writers have said and repeated that 'a Greek temple has no dimensions, it has proportions'; and again: 'Whether great or small, one never thinks of its size.' What does one think of, in face of the Parthenon? We must not pretend or invent. We think only of being happy, and we have more strength to be happy. This is because we love it as we love a living creature.

Living creatures, alas, are able to reproduce themselves. The Parthenon and other monuments of Greek architecture have, in the course of centuries, been abundantly reproduced in banks and churches, from Paris to Munich and from Washington to Moscow. They have given birth, generally speaking, to monstrous creatures like the Madeleine. The Parthenon is the child of one soil, it dwells in the mood of one landscape, it was the fruit of one moment in history. If you uprooted it from the Acropolis, it would lose its beauty and its very life-blood. Forming, as it does, a part of the limestone hill-top and of the walls built by Themistocles and Cimon which seem to complete it with their stones of the same colour, the Parthenon is the crown on a landscape. Despite all its dilapidation, we can still feel, in its ivory-like marble, in the contrasting interplay of angles and hollows, in the alternations of light and shadow that fill the hollows of the flutings with darkness and sharpen their ridges with sunlight until the columns themselves seem to dance in a motionless rhythm full of majesty—in all these things we still feel, we have the sensation of, the life that genius enclosed in marble. A marble ever sensitive to light. There are days and hours when the ruined monument may appear quite dark brown, or grey, or nearly black; it may be pink in the dusty air of evening or mauve with patches of yellow. It is never white as people say marble is white; or, if white, then in the manner of an old man's skin, with brown streaks showing on the limbs.

It may indeed seem very old and greatly ruined, but, in its ruined old age, it is impossible not to hear it repeating that love of wisdom and beauty which had given birth to it in the days when its people were young.

◎

The end of Pericles' reign was difficult.

Towards the middle of his ascendancy he appears in that oblong head of his to have conceived a plan for uniting all the Greeks. Regarding this attempt we have but little information, and that little comes only from Plutarch. By a decree voted on his motion, about 446 B.C., all the Greek cities in Asia as in Europe, except those in Sicily and Italy, were invited to send deputies to Athens to deliberate on matters of general interest; such as the rebuilding of temples burned by the Persians and the sacrifices to be offered in national sanctuaries to render thanks to the gods for the victory won by the united peoples. Other questions were the policing of the seas and the means of establishing peace among all the Greeks. Twenty Athenian citizens were appointed to proceed, in groups of five, through the various regions of the Hellenic territory to open peaceful negotiations in the name of Athens. The preliminary steps were taken. But, says Plutarch, these proposals encountered the decided opposition of the Spartans who rejected the principle of a Pan-Hellenic Congress convened by Athens and implying, *ipso facto,* the supremacy of the great city. So the congress never met.

It is difficult as always in such circumstances to throw the blame for the failure of negotiations on one of the two parties concerned. For more than ten years past, the imperialist policy that Pericles had pursued as regards the allies had been contradicting in hard fact the policy of 'appeasement' that he was now proposing to the Greeks as a whole. In this same year 446 when he sent his peace emissaries to the confines of the Hellenic world, he was crushing the insurrection of the Euboean cities, who were near neighbours of Athens, just as previously he had suppressed the separatist movement in Ionia. And it was also prior to this date, namely in 451–450, that Pericles caused the Assembly to vote the decree on civic rights which, so far from extending the civic community of Athens to all the defenders of her Empire, restricted it to what was no more than a selfish category of privileged citizens—to such as were doubly Athenian by birth. And lastly it was again in 446 that, by laying the first stone of the Parthenon, Pericles indissolubly connected the policy of great public works which had previously been announced, with the necessity for exploiting the Greeks of the Empire to meet the expenses.

And since he was, so to speak, shackled by the blood he was shedding, by the money he was extorting and the liberties he was destroying, since he was becoming every day more and more a prisoner of this policy deeply imbued with imperialism, how could he hope to persuade anyone, by these proposals for a general pacification of Greece, that the Pan-Hellenic Congress of Athens could be anything but a confirmation of Athenian omnipotence, a consecration of the exclusive supremacy of Athens over the whole of Greece? Plutarch seems rather naïve when he says, in this connection: 'I have cited this incident . . . to show forth the man's disposition and the greatness of his thoughts.'[1]

Pericles could now scarcely avoid hastening his country's progress toward war. This is not the place to recall the circumstances that provoked the Peloponnesian War, that mortal and irreparable strife between the Greeks. The enemies of Athens, and Athens herself, had their measure of responsibility. But by getting the Athenians to enact against Megara the decree that closed the markets of Attica and the ports of the Athenian Empire to the ships and products of that city, Pericles bears the heaviest share in it. Was it a measure of retaliation, of reprisals for the events of 446? Explanations of this sort are always ready to hand. But by this time Pericles was already caught, so to speak, in the cogs of a machinery that he had himself created. For long years now, the die had been cast. He could no longer escape the necessity of a war which his whole policy had provoked and which he now tried to represent as defensive while at the same time he extolled it as a means of glory. He really counted on winning the war, by dint, as he said, 'of intelligence and money'. And by winning the war he meant also to win the peace.

Yet in one very clear direction this acute intelligence of his was limited by an obstacle he could not see. His patriotism failed to transcend the limits of the city he wished to aggrandize. He thought of the unity of Greece only as an extension of Athenian greatness. As to the other cities, he would subjugate them. The cities are 'slaves', laughed Aristophanes when a young man of nineteen; and his laughter bared the truth.

But can we detect the real obstacle which it was not given to Pericles to surmount? The society to which he belonged was more deeply impregnated with slavery than it realized. The slavery of the cities was only an extension of an ineradicable sense of racial superiority. Slavery created the patch of oil in which Greek civilization was to perish. We have not yet presented the noblest fruits of that civilization, but we already know there is a canker in them.

The incomparable beauty of the Parthenon does not console us for the knowledge that it was not bought merely with money but with the blood of men enslaved.

There lies the inexpiable offence. It was not even the offence of Pericles in particular, but was written in the earlier and contemporary history of his people. A slave-owning society could produce no true democracy but only a tyranny reigning over a people who were slaves in name or in fact.

However brilliant was the age of Pericles, the failure of his conceptions—their

[1] *Life of Pericles.* Trans. cited, p. 131.

ultimate issue in war—very clearly shows us that a civilization can only endure if it is able to reach all living men. Therein lies the most important teaching that the history of Greek civilization offers. While its most splendid fruits fill us with joy and hope and courage, they yet leave in our mouths a certain bitter taste, which perhaps—if we know how to read aright even in the shadowy past the lessons of Greek history—the fruits of coming ages will not leave.

Civilization is like a green apple which it will have taken long, very long, for time to turn red. The sun does not shine every day in the history of mankind. You were young, O civilization of the Greeks, but your acid and refreshing savour promises us that taste of a fruit 'warmed by the sun', as the poet of the *Odyssey* puts it—that taste of a fruit that is ripe.

BIBLIOGRAPHICAL NOTE

THIS work is designed for the general reader and does not pretend to give a complete history of Greek civilization. The subject is presented in perspective and illustrated by a number of cases which seem typical examples. The author simply wishes to throw light on the rise of Greek civilization; and, in the second volume, on its full flowering and rapid decline; he has also attempted to explain the causes of these phenomena.

It goes without saying that he cannot indicate all his sources; and of course that the most important of these—the sources from which he has constantly drawn—are the Greek authors themselves.

For the general confirmation of facts and events, the author has had recourse to

G. Glotz, *Histoire Grecque*. 2 vols. Paris, Presses Universitaires de France, 1925 and 1930.

The following is a summary of the sources used in successive chapters, sometimes very closely, but without references, so that this work might be easier to read:

CHAPTER I
A. Jardé, *La Formation du peuple grec*. Paris, Renaissance du Livre, 1923.
G. Glotz, *La Civilisation égéenne*. Paris, Renaissance du Livre, 1923.
George Thomson, *Studies in Ancient Greek Society*. London, Lawrence and Wishart, 1949.

CHAPTER II
C. M. Bowra, *Tradition and Design in the Iliad*. Oxford, 1930.

CHAPTER III
Emile Mireaux, *Les Poèmes homériques et l'histoire grecque*. 2 vols., Paris, Albin Michel, 1948, 1949.
J. A. K. Thomson, *Studies in the Odyssey*. Oxford, 1914.

CHAPTER IV
François Lasserre, *Les Epodes d'Archiloque*. Dijon, Imprimerie Darantière, 1950.
François Lasserre and André Bonnard, *Archiloque* (texte, traduction et commentaire). To be published by the Société d'éditions 'Les Belles Lettres', Paris.

CHAPTER V
C. M. Bowra, *Greek Lyric Poetry, from Alcman to Simonides*. Oxford, 1936.
André Bonnard, *La Poésie de Sapho, étude et traduction*. Lausanne, Mermod, 1948.

CHAPTER VI
C. M. Bowra, *Early Greek Elegists*. Oxford, 1938.
G. Glotz, *La Cité grecque*. Paris, Renaissance du Livre, 1928.

CHAPTER VII
G. Glotz, *Le Travail dans la Grèce ancienne*. Paris, Alcan, 1920.

CHAPTER VIII

Martin P. Nilsson, *La Religion populaire dans la Grèce antique*. Paris, Plon, 1954.

Mircea Eliade, *Traité d'Histoire des Religions*. Paris, Payot, 1953.

R. Pettazzoni, *La Religion dans la Grèce antique*. Paris, Payot, 1953.

G. Van der Leeuw, *La Religion dans son Essence et ses Manifestations*. Paris, Payot, 1948.

CHAPTER IX

Max Pohlenz, *Die griechische Tragödie*. Leipzig and Berlin, Teubner, 1930.

Pierre-Aimé Touchard, *Dionysos: Apologie pour le Théâtre*. Paris, Editions Montaigne, 1938.

George Thomson, *Aeschylus and Athens: A Study in the social origins of drama*. London, Lawrence and Wishart, 1950.

CHAPTER X

Léon Homo, *Périclès*. Paris, Robert Laffont, 1954.

Henry Caro-Delvaille, *Phidias ou le Génie grec*. Paris, Alcan, 1922.

Victor Ehrenberg, *Sophocles and Pericles*. Oxford, Blackwell, 1954.

INDEX

GEORGE ALLEN & UNWIN LTD
London: 40 Museum Street, W.C.1

Auckland: 24 Wyndham Street
Bombay: 15 Graham Road, Ballard Estate, Bombay 1
Calcutta: 17 Chittaranjan Avenue, Calcutta 13
Cape Town: 109 Long Street
Karachi: Methersons Estate, Wood Street, Karachi: 2
New Delhi: 13–14 Ajmeri Gate Extension, New Delhi 1
São Paulo: Avenida 9 de Julho 1138–Ap. 51
Sydney, N.S.W.: Bradbury House, 55 York Street
Toronto: 91 Wellington Street West